WE

MARCH

AT

MIDNIGHT

WE
MARCH
AT
MIDNIGHT

A WAR MEMOIR

RAY
McPADDEN

BLACK

Printed in the United States of America

First edition: 2021
ISBN 978-1-9826-9101-1
Biography & Autobiography / Military

1 3 5 7 9 10 8 6 4 2

CIP data for this book is available
from the Library of Congress

Blackstone Publishing
31 Mistletoe Rd.
Ashland, OR 97520

www.BlackstonePublishing.com

To my son, Audie. You'll get it someday.

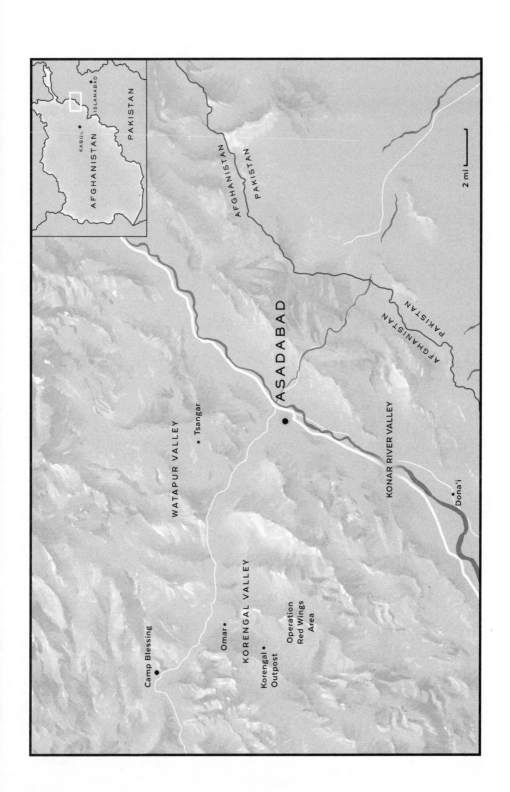

THIRD PLATOON
ALPHA COMPANY

HEADQUARTERS

Platoon Leader	RTO	FO	Platoon Sergeant	Medic
McPadden	Cigrand		Siercks	Vaccaro

FIRST SQUAD

Squad Leader

Haff

ALPHA TEAM

BRAVO TEAM

SECOND SQUAD

Squad Leader

Patterson

ALPHA TEAM

Correll   Berben

BRAVO TEAM

Robinson

THIRD SQUAD

Squad Leader

Dole

ALPHA TEAM

BRAVO TEAM

MACHINE GUN SQUAD

Squad Leader

Gallegos

GUN 1

GUN 2

PROLOGUE

HINDU KUSH RANGE, AFGHANISTAN
SPRING 2006

We can't find the bodies.

The crater beside me keeps smoking. The stench of diesel fuel hangs. Fifty of us are gathered in darkness along a road carved into a mountain. The names of our dead are whispers. One is Vince Bell, my Ranger buddy. He was the type who always stood up for a handshake. Only in death can we call him Vince. A good infantryman has to die to get his first name back. I'm still Attack 3-6, and I'm pissed at Vince for getting killed.

I wear night vision and an assault rifle. I chew on what could have happened. A tank mine struck an unarmored ATV. The blast could have vaporized our missing men or daubed them all over the road. More likely they've been launched from the vehicle, perhaps landing in the stone village below, where all lanterns and fires were put out quickly after the explosion. No one will be left behind. This is our vow to each other. We'll rally the cooks and mechanics if we have to. We'll torch this whole country to find our men.

Crows scream before winging out of an orchard beside the village. A sergeant emerges from the trees. He leads one of the search teams from Charlie Company. Looking totaled, he walks up to me and says, "Went all the way down. The canal is clear. So is the village." He gulps from a canteen then stalks into shadows, where he slams his buttstock against a tree, hissing, "They *have* to be here."

The search area must be expanded. Farming terraces loom over the bomb site. Starting at the bottom, we divide into twos and fours and wade into chest-high beanstalks. The terrace levels are all somehow connected, the retaining walls between standing six feet high. No surprise, navigating upward is a goat rope. We swim and tumble, the stalks *swishing* against us as we forge little paths from level to level. To avoid friendly fire, each search team turns on an infrared strobe. Blinking lights fill the terraces.

I stall and manufacture ways to get stuck. I want to find Vince, but I do not want to be the one. The search goes on. And on. High above the road, a thirsty ravine slashes through the terraces. Lying among stones at the bottom is Vince. He is broken, flash-cooked. At twenty-five years old, Vince has died in the open air below a beautiful summit in what had once been a beautiful war.

The search team radios for a litter. Up comes the medic. He slides his arms under Vince's shoulders and lifts him onto the litter. In full battle rattle, Vince weighs two hundred twenty pounds, so even with a litter, this is going to be sweaty work.

First, the team straps down the body. A corporal calls, "One, two, three, lift." With rocks flipping underfoot, the litter team hauls the load up from the ravine and onto the terraces. They shuffle to a terrace lip and set down the litter. They are careful not to abuse the load. It doesn't matter in a practical sense; just the right thing to do. Two men jump down to the lower level and shoulder the litter, scooting it past the ledge, grunting with the weight on their shoulders.

The others jump down and take the back half. They shuffle ten feet and do it again. All said, it takes a full squad to get the body down from the terraces. Then, we must find Vince's rifle. When we are done, the bean crop is ruined.

This is how we clean up the mess the enemy has made of us. We are infantry. A good unit is tidy. And when Boys get killed, you don't go to base for a week and cry it out.

You punch back.

PART 1
CRAWL

1

WHERE A FOOT SOLDIER BELONGS

FORT DRUM, NEW YORK

FALL 2005

I am an infantry officer right out of school, which makes me dangerous. I can make a mess with two-thousand-pound bombs. My first assignment is to report for duty in a battalion just returned from Iraq. They may not fight again for two years. For now, peace and good health are assured.

But I feel gutshot.

My whole identity is wrapped up in this job. That's not saying I wear combat boots to the mall on Saturday or sit for the barber and order the high-and-tight with skunk stripe. And for God's sake, dinner is at seven, not 1900. What I am saying is there are people in this world who burn to do something noble, who must prove everything to everyone. That's me. Joining the military didn't take much thought, was easy in fact. My dad had been a career naval officer. Marine and navy bases were the backdrop of my youth, though I never took to water. When airplanes hit the towers in New York, I could not turn away. Soon after, the first images of the war in Afghanistan jumped right out of the TV. Machine gun–toting soldiers were fighting on a mountain shaped like a fang. One look and I was taken. The infantry called to me. The marines, I was told, had night-vision goggles from Vietnam, so I joined the army.

Five years of training got me to Fort Drum, New York, home of the 10th Mountain Division. I am expensive, having graduated from a handful of the army's elite schools and Texas A&M University. I have practiced a lot, in woods and swamp and stinging snow. I've rappelled from roaring helicopters. I've killed a thousand make-believe bad guys. I am the terror of plastic targets.

Practice has me weary. I want to be tested. What better way than hunting al-Qaeda? They are easy to demonize, with their werewolf faces and medieval ways. Their god is an angry god. Their beliefs are shit. I want to destroy them.

I am in division headquarters today, asking to see the colonel in charge of personnel assignments. A cherry lieutenant has probably never tried what I am about to. This is way outside the chain of command.

I march into the colonel's office, finding her seated behind a wooden desk. A mountain of paper is stacked in front of her. She glares at me for a moment before scratching her pen across a form. "What?" she snaps.

"Ma'am, it's about my orders."

She keeps writing, never looking up. "What about your orders? Let me guess, you've injured your back. You can't deploy."

"No, it's the opposite. I belong in Afghanistan. The sooner the better." I stand with my left shoulder pointed toward her, showcasing the Ranger tab on my woodland camo. I name off the schools I've graduated from, five-mile run time is thirty minutes, and so on.

Every little win in life pours out. I'm ready to spew high school football stats when she puts her pen down and studies me. Drawing a breath, I puff up and hold it at length. She turns to her computer, works the keys, then slides in her chair to the printer before flicking a sheet of paper into my hand, telling me, "Go away." I read orders saying report to 1-32 Infantry. They will deploy to Afghanistan in four months.

I speed home, piloting an old Toyota Corolla through the dour facade of Watertown, the community beyond the base. Neon signs flash in the windows of rub-and-tugs run by Korean ladies. I'm drumming the steering wheel while the radio blares. I'm about to break this news to my wife, Elizabeth Vasquez. Our marriage is one month old. We met in high school, both of us fourteen. She was a track star who rolled with the stoner crowd. In her eyes I saw evidence that her Aztec ancestors built skull towers and ripped out human hearts. From the beginning she had me by magnetism. I asked, "Hey, pretty, you wanna go around with me?"

Now we are twenty-two. We have come here to start our lives together. The housing supply in Watertown is tight, so we live in the upstairs level of a two-story Victorian. The house has flaking lead paint and pink carpeting. The landlord's mom lives downstairs. Her voice is like doom, from a lifetime of smoking.

I park on the curb outside the house and ascend the stairs in threes. In the living room, Elizabeth is hammering a nail into the wall, hanging pictures. I wave my sheet of paper banner-like, saying, "Guess what? I'm going to Afghanistan."

Elizabeth turns to me. A strained silence passes, during which it appears I will be murdered with a hammer. She turns back to the wall and smashes a nail in. At last she says, "That's great."

"We talked about this."

She busies herself with another picture. She knows I want to be in the fight. This is the plan: first a combat tour with big army, then I join the Ranger Regiment to become a parachuting superman. The details of this plan are vague. Largely it is a desire to *be* something, with little thought given to what might be accomplished as such. This, I suppose, is a common aspiration of youth.

She levels a picture, turns to me, and grins. "Can I come?"

"Shit, girl."

"I mean . . . I, I don't know anyone here."

"Let's get a dog."

"Really," she says. "What am I supposed to do?" She pauses and thinks on this. "What am I supposed to do?"

I say, "When I leave, you don't have to stay here. Go back home to Texas."

"I will," she says. "How long will you be gone?"

"A year, more or less. Hey now. Don't give me that look. What's a year?"

I reach for her, but she spins away, saying, "We are off to a great start."

She is right to be mad.

Whatever.

* * *

Next week I report to 1-32 Infantry. The battalion is conducting twenty-five-mile foot marches, nighttime machine-gun ranges, and land navigation. All the platoons already have lieutenants. I am excess. Someone must get wounded, dead, or fired before I become a platoon leader; we deploy on March 1, so it shouldn't take long. With little else to do, the battalion sends me to more training. In Nevada I attend a tracking course, where I learn to hunt men by the prints they leave. Next it's Wyoming, where I lash supplies to donkeys and mules and lead them through the mountains.

I return to Fort Drum just in time for the deployment briefing. Platoon by platoon, eight hundred infantrymen file into a cold theater on base. Our battalion commander, Lieutenant Colonel Cavoli, takes the stage. He has this Napoleonic look about him, and he is God to this pissant lieutenant. I can see Cavoli loves this moment in front of his men. His voice is complete authority.

"We will fight in the Hindu Kush Range, against the Pashtuns." Our destiny is Kunar Province, right beside the Pakistan border, where big mountains have no names. The Pech River Valley will be the fulcrum of our combat operations. We are replacing a marine unit that has spilled a lot of blood establishing a presence on the Pech. Every week or so, the marines drive upriver to meet a tribal elder. They share a meal with some old craggy face and talk about building a girls' school. On their return to base, the marines get blown up and ambushed. Enemy bombs are shaking the whole province. Dinner parties with the locals aren't fun when it means driving home on Afghanistan's deadliest road.

As the enemy wakes from winter and the mountain passes shed their snow, our battalion will take ownership of this patch of the Kush. The larger strategic objective is to secure population centers, big cities. Our unit will push deep into enemy territory, take the war into the enemy's backyard. By moving the fight to the mountains, we'll help the new Afghan government solidify its control of cities and major infrastructure. At the tactical level, this strategy means platoons and companies must build outposts deep in the mountains. Each small unit will be isolated. We must be capable of fending for ourselves.

The mood in the theater is somber. The jaws of war are bloody. We are counting down.

* * *

Weekends with Elizabeth are precious. We pretend there is no war, no bloody jaws yet. Watertown is besieged by a blinding winter, just like last winter and the one before and, come to think of it, all winters here for as long as anyone can remember. On the fringe of town is a park with a steep hill where the local kids sled. Elizabeth and I buy a toboggan and head for the hill. At the base we build a ramp. An eight-year-old boy with a dirty smile coaches me on angles. Then Elizabeth and I ascend the hill, mount the toboggan, and bomb down. The ramp sends us airborne. Our crash is a plume of snow and limbs. We repeat. The local kids keep yelling, "Yard sale!" I throw snowballs at them. Soon we are at war. A child army coalesces from the neighborhood beside the park, little groups yelling to each other as they maneuver into position.

On Monday at work, the battalion commander sees my face and asks, "Who kicked your ass?"

In late January our medics put on the combat lifesaver course. Everyone who will deploy learns basic medical and surgical tasks. In a darkened barracks room, we practice starting IVs, something I dread, as needles are my secret terror. With an eighteen-gauge needle in my shaking hand, I lance my partner, missing the vein repeatedly then punching through it until the crook of his arm is black and blue. Now his turn. I go into a cold sweat and look elsewhere while he makes carnage of my arm. When we are done, the tile beneath us is slippery with blood.

The first weekend in February, Elizabeth and I head to a bar in Sackett's Harbor, a town on the shore of Lake Ontario where infantry go to pretend they aren't infantry. Booths with vinyl seats line the wall. Old Glory hangs above the liquor bottles. It is like any other bar, except all the customers are military, everyone coming from and going to war. It is easy to distinguish the vets from the newbies. The noobs are easy laughs. They shotgun beers and thump their chests. The vets have a dark look about them, like devils have infected their brains. In this bar veterans and newbies stick to their respective gangs.

Elizabeth still has the track-star figure, so I rush her past the gangs to an open booth in back. We slide in. Wasting no time, Elizabeth orders three shots. She winces after gulping each one. The countdown is eating at her, I figure, as drink after drink go down her throat. After five shots— or ten—she stops wincing. At midnight she digs in her purse, fishes out black lipstick, and applies liberally. Some is smudged on her teeth. She slurs, "I'm Simone Ragoo."

Her booze-induced alter ego has arrived, as expected. Not good.

She scoots out of the booth and teeters onto her feet. "I need another drink." She staggers toward the bar and plows into a bevy of vets. She spins off a tall guy wearing red flannel, stumbles, and makes a wobbly recovery, then screams at him to, "Fucking watch out." She waves her drink around, spilling alcohol on her boots, telling him, "My husband will kick your ass." Now the flanneled hero is yelling at me to watch my bitch.

One trait you should know about me is that I am not quick with words. When someone casts a sharp line at me, my typical response is to blush, and only much later do I think up something smart to say. So for lack of a quip, I spring to my feet and attack this man, gathering his flannel in my hands and slinging him sideways. The vet windmills his arms but manages to keep his feet. He grabs hold of my shoulders and tries for a headlock. We jostle into the crowd, knocking down barstools, while onlookers rush in to break us up. It occurs to me I'm in a bar fight and that everyone is watching. I let go of him and raise my palms, saying, "Let's not." I grab Elizabeth's hand. "We're leaving *now*." Elizabeth downs the rest of her drink and slams the glass on a table, then turns to my opponent, now restrained by the coolheaded among us, to say, "Eat shit and die," which would have taken me two weeks to think of.

Outside, a blizzard is sweeping in. A streetlamp casts a yellow hoop of light, making the blowing snow look like sawdust. In the parking lot mush, two guys with cropped hair are fighting over someone's wife. The husband, I gather, is deployed. The two Romeos throw sloppy punches as they roll between parked cars.

On the way home Elizabeth and I scream at each other like we've lost our wits. The screaming goes on until I can't remember how it started. She escalates to, "I hate you," which she's been slinging in fights since we were teens. She wants out of the car. We are doing fifty miles per hour, and she's fumbling at the door handle, yelling. Another mile and she passes out.

Arriving home, I clomp up the stairs with her in my arms. I deposit her on the couch and wipe the skift of snow from her hair. "I'm sorry," I say. She's out cold with all her clothes on. I pull off her alcohol-wet boots and lie on the pink carpet beneath her. Her gentle snoring is heavenly. In the middle of the night, she wakes up sobbing about me leaving for the war. Afghanistan is a big hiking trip, I tell her. It's in the bag.

We do this many nights in February. Mostly we fight for fun. We are learning how to be married. On Valentine's Day, I buy her a black Labrador. We name him Bruno Valentine. Right away Elizabeth loves this dog with all her heart. Bruno is running interference. He will make the leaving easier. We both know it.

The countdown ends. We wake to a gilded sunrise. Elizabeth and I get in the Corolla. Bruno hops into the back seat. I am going to drive us to the base because Elizabeth always wants me to drive, and because I like chauffeuring her around. Our plan for today is to say goodbye in the car. Elizabeth won't come into battalion headquarters. We can't risk an ugly cry in front of soldiers. I key the ignition. Elizabeth says, "Let's go the long way."

I say, "Of course."

We pass dairy farms buried in snow. I am holding her hand. In silence we ride, wondering what today might mean a decade from now. We pull up in front of battalion headquarters and sit quietly. Bruno is whining in the back seat, his breath steaming the window. He knows something's up.

Elizabeth says, "You know what you're doing, right?"

"Of course I know what I'm doing. Big hiking trip." I pause as a pack of soldiers walk by our car. "Let's not make a production of this."

She says, "No, I'm good. Are you good?"

"Yeah. I'm good. We are super calm, right?"

Her voice trembles when she tells me, "Don't be a hero."

"I won't."

From the back seat, Bruno licks my ear. I say, "Bruno, you look out for your mom."

I kiss Elizabeth, and then I'm gone.

2

WAR IS FREEDOM

PECH RIVER VALLEY, AFGHANISTAN

WINTER 2006

We arrive in the dark, a vast formation with glowing eyes, driving Humvees along the border flats, past sand people with their camels, and up into the mountains. Our engines growl at the grade as we snake through a dun valley, then another and another. We snatch ground from the enemy, platoon by platoon, in the floodplains along the muddy river.

At last I get the job I want. My radio call sign is Attack 3-6. *Attack* is A Company, *3* is third platoon, and *6* means platoon leader. From day one I aim to be perfect. I strive for "the moment"—a chance to prove to myself that I'm a true combat leader.

My forty-three-man platoon holds a position along the Pech River that consists of nine Humvees arranged in a triangle in a knot of trees. The landscape has a heroic beauty. We are nestled against the toe of a mountain. Canyons pinch our flanks, and a battery of metallic summits frames the sky. Below us the swollen Pech River has piled boughs against the piers of a swinging bridge. Upstream, the river boils past a hamlet shadowed by cliffs.

It is everything I have hoped for.

The Boys in my platoon have bronzed faces and sun-dried bodies. Their uniforms are torn at the crotches. It is a scorpion existence along the river, laid up in boulders, hunting after dark. I'm learning their names as we climb shingles and slither through ruins on night ambush. During five years of training, someone was always looking over my shoulder, telling me what I did wrong. Now, no one is telling me anything. I have total responsibility for planning and executing missions. I love every minute. I'm thinking, *War is freedom.* And for a few weeks, the heralded enemy bombs and attacks stop. We have a few dustups but nothing major. Quiet means winning in our war.

Sleep is elusive. I am hyperkinetic, joining all the patrols. We climb and balance across steeps overlooking the Pech. Thunderheads boom. My thighs twitch. My stomach cramps. Red invades my eyes. Flies won't stop fucking my face. I've got the burning squirts. I must pace myself. Between two patrols is the first window for rest. It'll be a four-hour nap in the dirt of our lean perimeter. Around midnight I troop for the sandbags where I keep my pack. Trees overhead filter moonlight so it appears like broken glass covering the ground. I flop down in my nook and peel off my armor. Changing socks, I pause to savor the joy of bare feet. Then I yank a sleeping bag over my head and wink out.

Automatic weapons tear me from sleep.

Prickling blood surges into my cheeks. I look up to the enemy guns ripping across the northern rise, about six hundred meters uphill. A sandbag beside me explodes. Stinging grains blind me in one eye. I jump into armor and boots, then run for my Humvee, pumping the assault rifle in my arms, bullets slashing the air. Rockets etch the night sky. One sizzles downward to detonate against a tree; the flash reveals my Boys scrambling into positions along the perimeter. They need no instruction. I fling open the Humvee door and jump in the shotgun seat. The radio on the dash *hisses*. Enemy bullets spider the windshield, jolting me down in the seat. I grab the hand mike, calling, "Combat Main, this is Attack Three-Six. We're in contact. Fire target reference point twelve."

The fight is at six hundred meters, so I am ordering mortars onto a preset target. This distance and elevation make our light weapons useless, and there's no chance to assault the enemy. The timing and location are no coincidence. We face a seasoned opponent. Mortars are my best weapon right now, and I have one chance. Once shells start falling, the enemy will break off the attack.

Awaiting the first mortar, I direct the .50-caliber machine gun mounted on my Humvee. The gunner, Specialist Fernando Robinson, is shooting low, struggling with bullet trajectory against the forty-five-degree incline above us. I yell to him, "Left . . . up . . . up . . . up, right there, right there." He locks onto a stone brow coruscating with enemy guns. I yell, "Traversing fire."

With two hands, Robinson rocks the .50 cal. back and forth. The bolt *chugs* while three-inch bullets rake the stone brow. A Mk 19 automatic grenade launcher is mounted on the Humvee to my right. The gunner, Private Jaime Locastro, is working another enemy position. His stream of grenades *crump, crump, crump* across the mountainside. In comes the first mortar to sail past the enemy and land in the deep canyon west of us, missing by a half mile. I radio adjustments to the mortar team. Another shell dives in, landing low on the rise, only 150 meters from me. I adjust again. The third shell lands halfway up the ridge but too far east. Steep terrain compounds tiny errors with mortars. I'm learning the hard way.

Meanwhile, enemy gunfire stops. Their attack ends as quickly as it began. I drop more shells, guessing at escape routes. The mortar crews want to conserve ammo, so they call it off. Silence returns. Here comes the sound of the river again.

I yell, "Sitrep."

Squad leaders give their situation reports. "First is up." "Second is up." "Third, up." "Weapons, up." Everyone is good. No casualties.

Beside the Humvee I stand on trembling legs and blink sand from my eye. Bullet-riddled sandbags leak. Enemy fire has left divots on my Humvee door and cracks in the windshield. I am buzzing. This wasn't "the moment," but it was in the neighborhood.

My platoon sergeant, Billy Siercks, marches up to me. He is a magnificent physical specimen, built like a chimney, and very easy to spot in the dark. I flex my legs so that Siercks doesn't see them trembling. I grin at him, expecting a high five.

Instead Siercks reports, "We're fifty percent on Mk 19 ammo. There's an unexploded RPG near second squad. We'll remove it come daylight."

To which I reply, "Good work."

Siercks leans in close, so that only I can hear, and hisses, "Your mortar adjustments were dog shit, sir."

* * *

In the following days, the enemy finds gaps on the Pech. The bombs start again. The ambushes ratchet up. Rockets fly. Bullets zing. The valley gets loud. One evening an enemy mine strikes a vehicle and blows two of our men into the sky. One is Lieutenant Vince Bell, my Ranger buddy, who stopped me from quitting during a sub-zero night in Ranger School. The other is Dave Santos, the driver.

Bell and Santos are my battalion's first dead. War, I learn, has no regard for the ambitions of warriors. The black mass is now with me. The dead are also a signal that the enemy is adapting. He will contest this ground. We must counter enemy moves. We must kill him in the side valleys, in the headwaters of the muddy river. That is how we'll win control of the Pech.

Feeding the Pech near the Pakistan border is a valley called Watapur. Intelligence holds the Watapur as a major enemy nest and supply center. Its dense forest and scarce roads provide ideal conditions for an all-star team of bad guys from around the globe, many of whom are battle-hardened, career jihadists. Mines and rockets bound for the Pech pass through the Watapur, tied to donkeys following ancient foot trails. In 2002 a commando raid deep into the valley narrowly missed killing Osama bin Laden.

Before our first fallen have reached the States, my platoon is put on alert. Lieutenant Colonel Cavoli delivers the orders via radio. "Lead your platoon into the Watapur. Search and destroy. Avenge our fallen." I am flattered Cavoli has handpicked us. A battalion commander at war is a king, and I'd jump on a grenade to impress him. I say, "Roger, sir. Count on us."

Storms pommel the high country. Our target area soars at an elevation of ten thousand feet. We need good weather and a ride up top. Division predicts a high-pressure system will arrive in three days, bringing clear skies and low wind. This is our window. Battalion finds helicopters to insert us. I thank the war gods we don't have to walk; the climb is seven thousand feet.

To prepare for the mission, we move to Camp Asadabad. Everyone calls it "A-bad." After six weeks in the field, we install ourselves in three tents and let someone else pull guard duty. Happy is the grunt who can slide two-ply shitpaper up his crack. Cleaning weapons is the first order of business. Washing uniforms is the second. We must wash some uniforms twice, others three times. Some uniforms we just burn.

My Boys plunge hands in their pockets and stride to a little shop on the camp perimeter. They buy DVDs and lethal Pakistani cigarettes called Pines. In a big gang outside our tent, the Boys chain-smoke Pines, hacking and choking on the foreign tobacco. Surely, Pines are a Taliban scheme to kill us in middle age. Siercks watches over the smoking gang, with them but apart. Now on his third combat tour, Siercks has the irritating habit of waking up, no matter how much sleep, and springing to his feet. Sitting beside him is Sergeant Correll, Mr. Bombs-and-Bullets, and admirer of all tough things. Correll is going on about Megalodon sharks. He swears they still roam the ocean.

Siercks does not know what a Megalodon shark is.

No one does.

Correll explains, "They are the most badass shark ever, a dinosaur shark."

Siercks asks, "How come no one has ever heard of them?"

"They live below the thermocline."

"What?"

"The thermocline, Sergeant. It's, well, never mind. These things are so big they can eat whales. Even submarines."

Siercks says, "Submarines? What are you, six?"

"They could."

"You're high."

"I'm telling you, Sergeant. Look it up. Shit is real."

The new mission has me feeling like a big-timer. Battalion has issued a broad task. The details of execution are up to me. On the morning of day two, the platoon gathers in our tent for the briefing. Forty-three men are serried on cots before me. Their uniforms already look too big for them. Ramrod straight, I stand beside a map taped to the wall and say, "There's a large enemy force in the Watapur. We're not sure exactly where, so this is a hunting mission. It's a Black Hawk infil. We'll post up on high ground, here." I aim a red laser pointer at a knob on the ridgeline. "We'll launch movement-to-contact and ambush patrols down the crest of the ridge. Search and destroy, gentlemen. Fix them with machine guns. Kill them with artillery. We'll kick the enemy's ass in their backyard, and in turn, take pressure off the Pech River."

The Boys look switched on. There are no questions.

Helicopters will insert us in the Watapur. Midmorning I meet the pilots in the tactical operations center, a concrete room adorned with maps, a bank of radios, and secure computers. The place hums with the sounds of control. From here two sergeants, a radioman, an intelligence specialist, and a battle captain track war on the Pech.

In the center of the room stands the head pilot. He has a gut that I envy, has it pressed against a table where a map is spread.

I say, "Hey, chief. You're my ride."

Dragging fingers over the map, we discuss landing zones.

I point to a saddle on the ridgeline. "Drop us here."

The pilot answers, "Too much forest. Can't land." Then he flicks a satellite photo onto the desk. "This spot looks good."

The image shows terraces two thousand feet below the ridge crest. The spot is shit, nowhere close to the top.

"We could just start at the bottom," I say.

"Sorry, Lieutenant. We just lost a bird. Got new safety protocols."

I know the story. A few weeks prior, one of our infantry platoons wanted a helicopter to do some sexy shit: night landing on a steep slope. The helicopter's rotor hit the mountainside, and that great big machine burst into flames and cartwheeled down the mountain, all fire and bodies.

And besides, we are legs. No one is fast-roping into the woods.

We settle on a spot about fifteen hundred feet below the ridgeline. We will insert tomorrow evening.

Before launching, we have to fetch our personal gear from Camp Jalalabad, which we call "J-bad," our original base. Mountains are the future. First the Watapur, and then I don't know where. A supply helicopter whisks away my first squad and their leader, Sergeant Haff, to retrieve our gear.

In the ops center, I pore over maps and intelligence reports about the Watapur. The Afghan Army refuses to go in on their own. "Too hot," they say. "All Taliban." The enemy runs a training camp somewhere in the woods near Gambir village. A cave complex somewhere at the head of the valley was Osama bin Laden's command bunker in the Soviet War. The more I learn, the more reluctant I become. On the upside, we've been in Asadabad long enough to get bored, and one thing is true of all infantry units: if you get them sufficiently bored, they'll attack anything.

About midday, Sergeant Haff sends me a message using mIRC chat, a secure computer feed used to communicate between posts, so as not to tie up radio frequencies. Haff types to me, "Gear is secure. Squad will catch return flight after chow. It's surf and turf tonight."

Only Haff and I can see what is typed. I peck out, "Slacker. Get your ass back here with our gear. Bring Copenhagen and Marlboros. Pines are decimating the platoon."

In the course of our exchange, Haff calls me *dude*, not *sir*.

I don't think much of it. Haff is solid. He has an easy attitude. And I believe he is loyal, no small thing to a new platoon leader. Besides, we're about to charge into the Watapur. Why get balled up over military courtesy? I exit the chat program and head to lunch.

At chow I savor my food in a manner known only to the destitute and those in combat infantry. My thoughts are of the platoon riding in choppers with doors open, boots in the wind, the Watapur sprawling before us. With guns ablaze, we'll leap from the choppers.

Before starting into a pork chop, I'm summoned back to the ops center for reasons unknown. I guess weather or a broken helicopter. Entering, I find the small room crowded. The regulars look deadly serious, glaring holes into their computer screens. Lieutenant Colonel Cavoli and a taller guy are examining the computer where I'd been typing. I notice that the tall one is Sergeant Major Carabello. I fight the urge to bolt from the room.

The two scroll through my digital conversation with Haff, then they bring up the feed on the big screen, where all can see. They enlarge the text, make it huge.

Cavoli reads aloud, "Slacker. Bring Copenhagen and Marlboros. Pines are decimating the platoon." Cavoli looks at Carabello. They frown and shake their heads at one another. Cavoli reads some more. He is getting hot, and I know what is coming. *Shit.* Cavoli happens across my sergeant calling me *dude*.

Cavoli goes psychotic, screaming, "Fucking *dude!*"

He gets in my face, screaming, and somehow he grows taller. Now the Infantry King is towering over me. He screams and screams and jabs a finger in my chest, saying, "You are *they*. When soldiers bitch, it's about you, the things you're making them do. *They* are making us do this. *They* are making us do that."

By now I'm feeling like I might pass out.

Cavoli is spitting while he yells, "They must follow you uphill against machine guns. This you must remember: *You* are the army. You are apart from them. You must always be apart. You will never, ever let them call you *dude*."

I'm dissolving.

Cavoli keeps on nuking me. The others in the room are pretending to be absorbed in their blue screens to avoid ricochets. Cavoli keeps screaming. Over in the corner, Sergeant Major is giving Haff the good news, except Haff is only getting it through the phone. I'm sure Haff is standing crisply at attention.

Cavoli reaches a pitch I did not think possible. He foresees the collapse of the army. I have caused it. Cavoli goes on to say, "How did you get a Ranger tab? Here you are, twenty-four hours from leading a helicopter assault into the Watapur. I have to think on this. I don't know if you're fit to lead it."

After a most spectacular show, Cavoli becomes hoarse and dismisses me. His last words are, "I'm thinking of replacing you."

His blows have me staggering around camp like a car-crash victim. I am not mad at Cavoli. This is no injustice. I'm fucked up, too eager to be accepted by the men with stripes. And I have a habit of letting little things slip, and little things lead to big things, and soon the machine is gummed up and we're all dead in an ambush and the enemy is coming over the camp walls. *That type of shit.*

I rehearse giving Haff a profound ass chewing, a boss-worker, military-bearing tirade. By the wall on the north side of camp, I practice aloud where no one can hear. I practice until I sound like fire. Resolve comes over me. I am going to light him the fuck up. I will call out Haff in front of everyone, but I won't unload until we're alone.

Back in the tents, the Boys are packing extra magazines, Claymore mines, batteries, fragmentation grenades, and more magazines. Two 40-power spotting scopes and three PAS-13 thermal optics are coming with, plus Oreos and little boxes of Lucky Charms. The Boys are mindful of the voodoo in all precombat, the order of packing, what to bring, what to leave behind. Watching them pack, I realize I'll be destroyed if ripped from the platoon. I am just getting started. I'd rather be an amputee than an assistant battle captain at headquarters.

Haff returns after dinner. His squad barges into the tent with our bags. The Boys are running for their shit, pulling out iPods and titty mags and clean undies. I glare at Haff. He avoids eye contact. "Outside, now," I order.

Away from the tent, I square up.

Haff is wine-faced when he says, "I know. I know. I'm so sorry, sir."

I do not doubt his sincerity. This whole thing is on me.

I say, "It's *sir* or Three-six," and that is that.

We go back in the tent. I smoke a pack and sit on my cot with knees bouncing like I'm operating a sewing machine. I do not sleep. In the morning a grim-looking captain from Cavoli's entourage throws aside the tent fly and marches up to my cot. I prefer that he just draw his pistol and shoot me. He says, "Three-six, you're a go for the Watapur. That's straight from the colonel."

Never has someone been so delighted to get inserted deep in enemy territory.

* * *

In the afternoon we shoulder rucksacks. The magazine in my rifle is filled with green tracer rounds, which glow when fired. I'll use the tracers to mark targets and direct the fire of my squads. Between armor, ammo, batteries, food, and water, I am carrying over 120 pounds into battle, which is an exaggeration somewhere between 25 and 35 percent, customary in war stories. By any count I'm running light. The machine-gun teams have to be pulled to their feet.

We trudge to the helicopter pad by the howitzers. The artillery pieces are banging, supporting a battle somewhere north. We'll have our own big slice of the shit soon enough. I drop my rucksack in the dirt, creating a mushroom cloud, and look south for our ride. Soon black dots appear between the hills. The dots take shape, four Black Hawks flying in a V. They land.

Stooped, the forty-three of us hustle for the open doors. I hop in the lead Black Hawk, resolved to be first on the ground. The crew chief counts us and begins sliding the cabin door closed. I grab the door and stop him. "We'll ride with them open," I yell. "Need a quick exit."

"Sorry, sir," he replies. "Safety."

"We are doing a helicopter assault. What the fuck is safe about this?"

The rotor noise is incredible. I can see he doesn't understand me.

"Sorry, sir. Safety."

So we ride with doors closed. I'm thinking, *Lame*, as we go up and over the river and crumpled foothills. In the distance a subrange is still locked in snow and ice, the summits standing like arrowheads toward the sun. At the mouth of the Watapur, the chopper banks hard right. In the cabin, we are sardined against one another. We climb and climb, the rotors struggling to bite thin air while cliffs and scree fields zoom by.

Up come the verdant green terraces. I recognize the landing zone. Just beyond, the forest thickens. In the trees an Afghan woodsman stands in wonder, axe in hand and a bundle of firewood on his back. Our rotor wash pins his flowing garb to his body. Presently, he makes for the shadows and disappears, wanting no part of today's events. In the distance is the village of Tsangar, flat roofs splayed across steep mountainside.

Our helicopters reach the shoulder of the eastern ridge. Just before landing, I rip open the door and alight from the cabin. My feet sting when I hit the earth with a heavy pack. I shuffle uphill, heading for a terrace wall, with Specialist Schnep, my radioman, tailing. The squads make for different corners of the clearing and take positions. Now the choppers are throttling away. Thunderous engine noise gives way to the caws of a crow picking at a dead varmint.

Lingering is not to our advantage. We gather in squad order for movement and begin the hunting trip. I am amped to be on the ground, away from the flagpole. A chance to fight the enemy at the same elevation must not be squandered. I am certain we are about to kill a bunch of mujahideen. Perhaps the crow senses it as well, for he now circles in the uphill thermals.

Spread at ten-yard intervals, we execute the first phase of our mission: march uphill carrying a ton. The weight of my pack cuts blood supply to my hands, and I'm busy shaking out pins and needles. Specialist Kilpatrick, a machine gunner from weapons squad, is traveling with me. Right away, Kilpatrick and his assistant gunner are puffing. Being a gunner is hard; being an assistant gunner may be the worst job in the infantry. The assistant carries the tripod, the traverse-and-elevation mechanism, and much of the machine-gun ammo, but not the killing hardware. The gunner gets to shoot bad guys. The assistant carries the weight. We make the new guy do it. I can't remember his name.

Up we go, a great river of pain. Everyone wiggles in their armor, getting their loads right. My leg muscles loosen. Pumping blood washes away the aches. I settle into my pack.

Lockstep. Lockstep. Chin up. Breathe.

From time to time the terrain breaks us into fragments. We must stop and reform, get our spacing back. Siercks races up and down the column, kicking stragglers. The forest thickens. The cedars grow taller and fatter, the cavities in the trunks big enough to hide a man. We seem to be moving through an arched cathedral. As we clear nine thousand feet in elevation, some of the Boys have their tongues out. Thin air burns going down the windpipe. I don't let them see me panting. Far below, the Pech River is a jade ribbon running through endless brown hills. I can just make out the road beside the river. At this distance, all the dying over this tiny road seems silly.

The slope above has me saying "Goddamn," and then climbing it, I must stop on occasion to say, "Goddamn." By the time we gain the top, my camo top is dark with sweat beneath my armor. A coldness sweeps over the ridgeline. Bronze columns of sun stab through the treetops. One by one, the columns blur and disappear. *Mount night vision.*

On my walkie-talkie, I catch slivers of enemy radio traffic. They speak Pashto. My Afghan translator tells me, "One says, 'Yes, yes, I saw the helicopters with my own eyes. Come to me.' Another answers, 'I'll bring everyone.'"

3

KING OF THE MOUNTAIN

We are hunting the enemy. They are hunting us. This will be a game of traps. After dark we carve a patrol base into the ridge, deep in conifer forest. Patrol base operations are easy, but easy things are hard in the dark. It takes time to lay into the terrain just right, to use the blocks, divots, and rills to our advantage. Ultimately, we arrange ourselves in a triangle around a small clearing. Machine guns go on tripods. Everyone is alert, listening to the woods. In this silence a sneeze from third squad rings like a gunshot.

We take turns digging shallow foxholes. The enemy can get level with us, but not above us. This is a relief. Seizing high ground is simple enough, the difficulty is staying there. We are going to hang out, hunting indefinitely, so we're carrying everything we need. In rough terrain, the average foot soldier can carry a full combat load and three to five days of food and water. There are hard-asses who can carry much more. You have to plan for the average. Balancing sustenance and firepower makes for hard choices. It is better to lick dew off the grass than to yell, "Bang," at the enemy. We brought extra ammo. We'll need more food and water in about three days. If the weather holds, a chopper will bring it.

The enemy is on walkie-talkie again, hissing in Pashto.

"He said bring everyone."

"What about the ones in Gambir?"

"Yes, yes. Everyone."

I flip off my walkie-talkie and scan the forest through night vision. *Yeah, come get us.*

When he finishes position checks, Siercks slides into my command post. Together we sit with our backs against a boulder. We will launch an ambush patrol. I am feasting on the possibilities as I throw a poncho over us, press on a red headlamp, and point at the map. "I'll take a squad and a gun team to the north, about twelve hundred meters. Gonna set up on this trail. See if the Tsangar gang comes sniffing around."

Siercks asks, "Who you taking?"

I think on it. Not Haff's squad. Those dudes move through the woods like a pack of tyrannosauruses. "I'll take second squad."

Siercks said, "The Boys will be jumpy. Make sure it's real before you shoot. That goes for you too."

"Yep."

"You should paint your faces."

"*What?*"

At 2200 I fall in with the ambush patrol. We leave in a file formation. No face paint; it is ink-black below the canopy. The forest swallows us. We creep north, *feeling* the ground more than *seeing* it. An hour later we are bellying into ambush positions overlooking a trail. Tree sap has pine needles sticking to my knees and elbows. We set a Claymore mine. On the killing side of the mine is imprinted, *Front Toward Enemy.* The army is protecting all the "special" kids in the infantry. I place our machine-gun team so that they aim down the long leg of the trail, while the squad stays parallel to the trail. We call this an L-shaped ambush.

Then we wait. For a long time, there is no whispering, coughing, or cracking branches. Just deafening silence. A conifer forest is mostly devoid of life. The needles blanketing the terra have high acidity, so there is no understory or animals, hence, few sources of sound. The result is that the ears begin to invent it. Clicking. Shuffling. Whispering.

Any minute.

Hours drag by. We remain prone, watching our kill zone, cold from the ground radiating into us. I nearly shiver a molar out. More than once, things appear only to be blinked away. No one comes.

At 0500 we return to the patrol base with nothing to report. I am proud of the Boys, though. It was a textbook ambush. Any jerk-off unit can be disciplined on the ambush line for twenty minutes. We held for hours.

This is a hunting mission. We will stay on this ridge until we kill someone. Any bad guys will do.

After a flaring sunrise, we launch a movement-to-contact patrol. Two squads step off, moving north on opposite flanks of the ridge, parallel to each other. If one squad makes contact, the other will gallop over the ridge and flank the enemy. Camo netting adorns our helmets. Every pouch and pocket is brimming with ammo and grenades. We look like infantry should.

I move with third squad. We go by hand and arm signals. Sergeant Langmesser, team leader in third squad, is walking point with a suppressor on his M4 rifle. He stands six feet five and strikes me as a guy who'd had hair on his chest at eight years old. If I had him beside me at the bar, I'd talk shit to anyone. On this tour, he has said about four words. Langmesser is a man of action. He is a point man. Without a misstep, Langmesser takes us three kilometers north. About noon we come upon large white boulders to the left of the ridge.

Beneath one boulder is a cave. As I study the cave opening, my thoughts are of bin Laden's command bunker. I whisper and point. The Boys ready grenades. Guns at the high ready, the squad clears the cave opening.

Nothing. There is a black passage. Someone has to go in.

I am thinking, *Who do I hose with this mission?*

The cave is tight, so we need a skinny private. Langmesser does not wait for me to decide. He turns on his headlamp, drops to his knees, and elbows forward with a 9 mm Beretta pistol. He has no idea what terrible things are hiding in the passage. And I'm not sure one man with a pistol should clear a cave. But we are clearing caves, and this is a war story.

Soon he comes back into sunlight. He has found food. No munitions. No bin Laden. I radio in the location of the cave, marking it as a target for artillery and aircraft. The mission is a success. As we begin heading south back to the patrol base, I alter the route, taking us through a rocky cleft and into clawing trees.

Among windfall, we find a second trail parallel to the main trail. This path hugs the cool north slope, where the Himalayan Fir are thickest and tallest. In the tread, we find the concentric rings left by high-top sneakers. The mujahideen are fond of this footwear. The prints are fresh, left after the last rains. We count prints on a stretch of trail, accounting for their coming and going. I figure fifty or more bad guys. Here is the enemy trail. Shepherds use the wide trail on the crest of the ridge. Bad guys use this narrow trail in rough terrain. It is what I would do too.

Discovering such obvious signs of the enemy puts my mind in turbo. Doubt seeps in, and I am wondering if we have enough dudes. Not only that, but we have been in the patrol base for two days, which is a break from tactical rules. To avoid being pinpointed and attacked, a patrol base should be moved every twenty-four hours. *But we hold good ground*, I reason, entirely defensible with great fields of fire. The enemy can get level with us, but not above, for the first time in the tour. During the night I check our security often. The Boys are alert. They have night vision down, Claymore triggers at hand. The soldiers not on guard catnap and shiver.

We keep hunting. Next morning we handrail the enemy trail, marching far, far north. It is bright and warm, and the patrol feels like hiking. About five kilometers from the patrol base, we find a stone hut in a copse of ancient trees. In the doorway stands a leather-faced old man. He sells chai, naan, and cookies to Afghans moving on the ridge, much like a gas station for shepherds. The old man says it is all free for us. He urges us to come in and sit.

In the hut a steaming kettle sits over a woodfire. We sit. The old man pours chai into tin cups and sets them at my feet. He says, "For your men." Whipping his black beard to the side, the man says, "You are very far from the road."

I tell him, "We are hiking."

"The night is cold. Where are you sleeping?"

"In the woods." Meaning everywhere.

"Where are you going?"

"Where should we go? Where are the Taliban?"

"Gambir," he says, wagging one finger northward. "Everyone knows that. But you don't have enough men to go there. Get the rest of your army and come back."

We finish the chai and leave.

Heading south on the main trail, we circle back a few times to see if we have a tail. Nothing. We beetle down the ridge, swing left, and crawl into ambush positions near the cave. For hours, there is no movement. Lying on the ambush line, I wiggle to keep my hands and feet from falling asleep. Nothing happens.

Where are they?

* * *

It is July 5. We have been in our patrol base for three full days. Little trails have developed between our fighting positions. Sitting around is wearing on me, but resupply comes tomorrow morning. A helicopter will drop food, water, and batteries at the same spot where we landed. In turn we descend and reascend. This enterprise will take half the day. If I move the patrol base farther north, I will make resupply a slog.

The hard, right thing is best. Good infantrymen should not sit still. I examine the risk and decide to stay put, on account of energy. It dominates infantry operations. Marching, digging, shivering, and bounding all take energy. Energy is precious, and I am tired.

We remain in place and stretch the last dregs of water. In the afternoon, the squads dig foxholes a little deeper. Siercks and I confer. Sitting on my shins, I say, "After resupply, I'm thinking we move three clicks north, get into tough ground on the north slope, set a new patrol base. From there, we recon Gambir village." I smile, rubbing my field beard. "No one's been that deep."

Siercks takes a knee. "Don't get too high on this, Three-six. If you die, you lose."

He looks up through the boughs at the sun wheeling toward Pakistan. Into his bottom lip he packs a horseshoe of Copenhagen. I want to talk to him. I ask, "What's this like compared to your other tours?"

"Harder."

I enjoy hearing that. I ask, "How are you holding up?"

He flashes a scowl. This is not what he wants. I do not care. I've earned it.

Finally, Siercks says, "I've got work to do," and, with that, gets up and glides away.

* * *

At about 1800 I begin checking squad positions. As I hustle through the clearing in our center, a string of tracers flash by. The air snaps. The clatter of machine guns erupts. A bullet ricochets off a rock and *whizzes* between my legs. I drop, caught squarely in the open. Turning north, I glimpse the enemy. Guns flash all through the forest. Bullets stutter the dirt on my right. Heavy fire pours from a granite outcrop two hundred meters north, at the same elevation. I judge they have four PKM machine guns.

Panic surges through me. We're outgunned.

The nearest cover in the clearing is a skinny tree. I crawl for it. A volley of RPGs rips through our line, two going high, the other detonating against a boulder. Molten metal streams everywhere. Someone *yelps*, then repeatedly yells, "Fuck." Right now, the thing that matters is cover. I resume my quest for the skinny tree. Scattered thoughts tumble in my head.

The colonel is watching.

I pull myself forward.

I should have moved the fucking patrol base.

I pull myself forward.

Be a leader.

Dragging my cheek through dirt and sap is humbling. Enemy machine guns hew the forest at seven hundred rounds per minute. Pine needles rain down. Rounds *spang* off rocks. Before I can reach cover, a second enemy position opens up, maybe forty yards northwest. Some are within hand grenade range. The sharp, piercing *bang* of one of our Claymores shakes the forest.

I draw a picture of the contact in my head: one enemy group, wielding PKM machine guns and RPGs, opened up first, allowing another group to maneuver into grenade range. If they seize the boulders protecting our north machine gun, we might be overrun. We will have to fix bayonets.

Helmet first, I bang into the skinny tree.

Now what?

I fire at the granite outcrop. Every round is a green tracer. One hits a tree. The hole in the bark continues glowing green. I lower the reticle in my optic; it's better to shoot low than high. I drain a thirty-round magazine. First squad sees my tracers and concentrates fire on the outcrop. I yell for third squad on the west side, thinking they can use defilade to reinforce our line near the boulder. Machine-gun fire drowns my calls.

Sergeant Langmesser crawls into view. He too has been caught in the open.

This is not a good look for me.

Here I am, lying in the dirt shooting my rifle. I should be calling for mortars and organizing a counterattack. Langmesser squeezes in beside me, saying, "Lucky you." That's six words for him on this tour.

Now we're shoulder to shoulder on our stomachs, half exposed behind the skinny tree, while enemy bullets chop off the crooked branches. Splinters fly. Nose on his M4 charging handle, Langmesser starts banging away. He is all fire and death; no regard for himself. *Courage is beside me.* I sponge off him. Inside the perimeter there are balloons of smoke from RPG detonations. Cordite and high explosives foul the air. Roaring, one of our AT4 rockets arrows forward and ends in a treeburst rearward of the enemy. I fire again, spreading bullets across the outcrop until my bolt locks to the rear. I drop the empty, jam another magazine in the well, and ready for a dash to the radio.

"Langmesser, cover me."

He raises his eyebrows, then nods.

It hits us right then. A white flash and searing heat. The air itself seems to shatter. A shockwave rips through me, and for a microsecond it seems my eyeballs will pop and my guts will squirt out my toes. I am thrown sideways, gun torn away, helmet blown off. I roll to a stop. The smell of burned flesh is everywhere. I do not feel pain, but there's a hollowness in me.

I take stock.

Guts still in.

Legs attached.

Balls are good.

I am dizzy, sick. Blue smoke conceals the world beyond. The blast has deadened my senses, and in the haze, I feel very alone. I have no control of this fight. I cough smoke. A buzz is in my ears. Through staggering awareness, events take shape. An RPG detonated against the skinny tree, turning it to a million splinters. Langmesser and I were inside the fireball.

Right, where's Langmesser?

On the left he crawls laterally, leaving a trail of blood in the flattened grass. His uniform is in tatters. At least he is moving. I have to move. The enemy has this spot dialed in. Bullets streak through the grass around me, ending in puffs of dirt. I rally. *Get up, move. DO IT.* Once I begin crawling, control comes back. I head for the radio, fingernails in the earth. *Oh fuck it.*

I spring up and run headlong. These legs don't belong to me. I charge through the stabbing pain in my calf. At last I dive over a rock and land on my radioman, Schnep.

There is blood on Schnep's uniform where I landed. I figure he isn't seriously injured. I want to be cool for him, to be unflappable. "You good?" I ask.

"Roger."

"Why haven't you killed anyone?"

Schnep gives a sheepish grin, then says, "I've got Battalion on the net," and passes the hand mike.

I press the transmit button, then stop. Our second machine gun is still oriented south. The gunner is not firing. I scan the ridge in that direction. No incoming. "Be right back," I tell Schnep. Bent double, I sprint the short distance to the gun. There is no time for the dull pain in my hip and leg.

Private Rene Berben, a grenadier from third squad, is manning the machine gun, scanning for targets. He has stayed in his sector of fire. Now he looks at me. Ole High-Speed is dying to kill bad guys. His eyes are wild as he says, "I need to get this gun in the fight."

I say, "Redeploy north. Suppress the rock outcrop."

Berben does an explosive push-up that ends with him standing. "Fuckin' A." He looks at me sort of funny, asks if I'm okay.

"Yes. Now go."

Berben rips the gun off the tripod, cradles the ammo belt in his left arm, and zigs forward. Enemy bullets hiss all around him, cracking against rocks. This 130-pound kid charges through the fire, carrying our heaviest weapon like a toy. Reaching a boulder, he dives into the prone position, jamming the bipod legs into the dirt. Soon his barrel spews flame and death. Tracers stitch up the rock outcrop. Now, we have both guns in the fight.

At the north machine gun, third squad tosses grenades at the enemy. They use the baseball-throw technique to be accurate in the tight trees. *Boom! Boom!* Our machine gunner, Specialist Ware, has been firing since the contact began, nearly burying himself in brass.

Between the grenades and Ware's machine gun, we stall the enemy advance. When Berben jumps in with the second machine gun, he tips the balance. Our two guns alternate fire, and 7.62 rounds sweep the woods, creating a cone of death. The enemy is crawling backward. They down-cycle into random pulses of fire. I judge they are trying to stretch ammo and sort out, *What now?*

The enemy still has numbers. To win, I must drop mortars onto their support position, then spread shells across the ridge to block escape routes. The goal is to isolate the enemy and then attack. However, in using mortars, I chance friendly casualties. The shells will be close. Elevation and terrain increase the potential for error.

Battalion radios that our mortars are tied up in action along the Pech. One-five-five howitzers are available. This is heavy artillery, and if I get the coordinates wrong, I'll atomize my own platoon. I double-check coordinates then radio the howitzer crew, ordering airburst shells that will detonate in the treetops. A crewman confirms the target and fuse type.

Forever passes as the artillery crews wheel their barrels and get the angles just right.

The crewman radios, "Shot over."

I answer, "Shot out," acknowledging shells in the air.

The crewman says, "Splash over." Moments later the first shell plunges in, landing somewhere east of the ridge, far off target. I am sure the coordinates are good. I order them to fire again, only better this time. Another shell arcs in, detonating on the ridge just behind the rock outcrop. I order a lavish dose. Shells splash across the ridge and raze the forest. Big trees fall, smashing other trees. Crowns catch fire. Boughs rain down. Enemy fire slackens. I tell the howitzers to drop one hundred and repeat. I am walking in the shells, bringing them a little closer to us. *Boom! Boom! Boom!* Smiting detonations shake the mountain. A tree above me drops its cones. *Too close.* "Hold that fire mission."

The enemy has transitioned to sustained rate-of-fire, sporadic *pops*. We have seized the initiative. Sergeant Dole, third squad leader, moves forward. His two teams take turns getting up, dashing forward, and dropping to the ground, firing as they dart from tree to tree in gun smoke. The enemy abandons their assault position, leaving piles of brass scattered among the trees. They never leave the dead, and if they have casualties, they are hauling them away. Rocky ground makes it difficult to tell.

Our situation is precarious. Typically, the enemy attacks to inflict a few casualties, then withdraws before we can come to grips. But we are isolated and outgunned. An aggressive enemy commander will press the advantage. The propaganda value of overrunning Americans is beyond calculation, so reattack seems likely.

I am going to shell their teeth from their heads.

It would be foolish to get the squads strung out, so I order Dole to halt his advance while I bring in another artillery strike, with coordinates farther north. Close by I find my helmet with a piece of shrapnel embedded. I dump the helmet back on and click the chinstrap, leaving my shrapnel ornament in place. From the boulders on the perimeter comes the call so dreaded: "Medic. Medic."

Our litter team brings casualties into the perimeter. One is Langmesser. He has shrapnel wounds galore and a bullet in the leg. Blanched, he flutters in and out of consciousness. Our medic, Doc Anthony Vaccaro, is kneeling beside him, smacking his cheek. "Langmesser. Langmesser. Stay with me, brother." The other casualty is Private Roberts, the assistant gunner at the north machine gun. A bullet blew off the back of his right ankle, but he continued feeding rounds to the 240B. In doing so, he has lost a lot of blood. His entire boot is crimson.

The next wave of howitzer shells comes in. One sails over the ridge and detonates in Tsangar. *Oops.* I call off the artillery. The angles are shit and the artillerymen can't get the propellant right. I toss the hand mike at Schnep, telling him, "Those dudes are useless."

Schnep looks at me through fogged glasses and says, "Hey, sir, you're hit. Sit down a sec."

I do. He rolls me on my side, checking for wounds. My uniform and face are charred. Shrapnel is deep in my shoulder, hip, and calf. Wood shards are lodged in my face from the skinny tree. Using his thumb and index finger, Schnep pulls a two-inch wood dagger from my cheek. Hot blood runs down my face and follows my chinstrap. Until now, I haven't felt much of anything.

With the shooting over, a terrible ache wells up. There are hot coals inside me. The blast has scrambled my brain. The horizon teeters and rocks. I roll on my side and retch. I have not eaten today, so it is greenish bile. Dragging the back of my hand over my mouth, I struggle to my feet.

Schnep is urging, "Sit down. Sit down."

I say, "I can still do my job."

4

COUNTERATTACK

No amount of training or intellectual preparation can prepare new commanders for their first overwhelming contact with the enemy. The operative word here is *overwhelming*—I'm not talking about a fun little shoot-out. I'm talking about getting a whipping. Many young officers, I suspect, die in those first big gunfights, the result of being overeager and inexperienced, and thus, easily cut down. Surviving the first big fight greatly improves one's opportunity for reproduction and to flourish as a leader. So I've got this going for me.

One thing you don't do after contact is circle up saying, "*Holy fuck.*" You move, communicate, reposition. You act, and that helps choke down the fear, which right now is at high tide in me. I gather the squad leaders and, knowing they will mirror my emotion to their Boys, I steady my countenance and say, "If a second wave comes, it'll be from the north again. Everyone go cyclic right off the top."

We hatch a plan to reinforce the north side of the perimeter.

The Boys belly into the forest to set new Claymores. Siercks runs between squads redistributing ammo. We deepen our rifle pits. In the west, a fleet of clouds sails in from Pakistan, carving around the indomitable summits at the border. The clouds finger into the Kunar River tributaries, then drag over the Watapur ridge before dissolving into vapor.

My Boys look ethereal in this white mist, which heightens my fear of the coming dark.

Mist beads on our barrels. In the platoon command post, Doc Vaccaro spills open his surgical pack, scissors off Roberts's boot, and flings it aside. The boot lays tipped in the dirt, and for a few seconds, blood gulps out. Doc lifts Roberts's half foot onto a rock, stuffs the wound with coagulant gauze to stem the bleeding, and then trusses it with a field dressing. "I won't let you bleed out," says Doc. He turns to Langmesser, who is a gallery of wounds. Doc scissors open a pant leg. The bullet hole in Langmesser's thigh is a red medallion. Blood flows. Doc applies a compress.

We are wounded men in a wounded land, and I have to be brave. That means ignoring my gathering pain and betraying no fear. I keep doing my job, ordering a helicopter medevac and reporting Langmesser and Roberts as, "Two urgent surgicals." I give the radio to Schnep, saying, "Tell me when you get a chopper response time."

Soon a perplexed look comes over Schnep. He tells the radio, "Standby," and turns to me. "Sir, uh, uh. Chosin Main wants to know how many enemy we killed."

"What? What about the medevac?"

"They have it, sir. Battalion wants to know enemy casualties."

"Those fucks don't have anything better to do . . . I mean, uh, tell them we are working on it."

Schnep relays the second half, then reports, "Bird is spinning up at J-bad. Forty minutes."

I have a powerful urge to sit. Doc sees me and comes over for a look. He rolls me sideways and takes scissors to my fatigues. It seems Doc expects us all to fight naked.

"Stop cutting my uniform, Doc."

Examining my hip and leg, Doc says, "Penetration wounds. Shrapnel. Can you put weight on the right one?"

He helps me up, and I gimp a few steps, feeling as if I have been stabbed. "Sort of." I flop back down. "I'll be fine."

"Negative. We need to get you out." Doc puts a hand on my chin and turns my head. "There's blood coming from your ear."

I trace warm blood up my neck and into my ear canal.

Doc smiles. "Could be your brain." He digs in his pack. "Don't worry, I've got a cotton ball." Triumphantly, he holds up a cotton ball.

I shove it in my ear. "All better, Doc."

As combat adrenaline subsides, pain washes over me. My right ear, the same one leaking, isn't working. There are bells in it. My leg hurts more. The throbbing is gruesome. Standing over me, Doc surveys the tall trees rising on all sides then looks down and says, "This will be a hoist job, sir. Order of medevac is Langmesser, Roberts, then you. Everyone goes in one lift. Siercks and Patterson are lightly wounded. They can stay."

"One problem, Doc. I'm the one that called for the bird. You can't call for your own medevac." I have just made up this rule.

"Sir, you've got multiple shrapnel wounds. You can barely walk. You're a liability."

"Negative. I'm not calling in my own medevac."

Doc looks magisterial. "Sir, I am the ranking medical authority in this platoon. You're getting on that bird."

"Negative, Doc." I know I'm being belligerent. Remaining on the battle-field is a symbolic gesture. Good leaders understand symbolism. Even in life-and-death situations, the value of a gesture can far exceed any practical considerations, like my own mobility. Of course, I'll sound like a pompous ass explaining this, so I tell Doc, "We're not done. The enemy will be back." The bigger problem is that I have not earned my "moment." Leaving will get me no closer. Hell, it could undo everything. I cross my arms and insist, "I'm staying."

By now Siercks has heard the commotion. He stands beside Doc and says, "Sir, we supposed to carry you around the rest of this op?"

Good point. I am not sure how far I can push this. The good news is I outrank him too, so for now I keep my arms folded tight, responding, "You need to worry about getting the serious casualties out of here."

Schnep, looking sheepish, is hovering beside us with the radio in hand. I say, "What's up, Schnep?"

"Sir, uh, it's Chosin Main again. They want to know enemy casualties."

"Goddammit, Schnep. We are busy."

The medevac comes after dark, guided by our infrared strobe light. The helicopter, a Black Hawk, corkscrews then flares to a hover. The rotor noise is shattering. At seventy feet, it lingers just above the treetops. In the flaying wind, branches and cones angle down. From the clearing in our center, Siercks waves a red chemical light, showing the pilot where our casualties are waiting. The helicopter lowers a basket and a flight medic, who wears a big black visor on an even bigger helmet, looking much like an astronaut. It takes five minutes to get our casualties aboard, then the chopper noses east and thumps down the ridge for A-bad. A ringing silence returns.

I should have moved the patrol base.

Fear prowls through me. I replay all decisions before the attack. Wanting something else for my mind, I pick an inch-long splinter from my neck, then use the heel of my palm to stop the blood, which streams down and follows my shirt collar. I look at the stars. A billion are up there, winking.

As a combat leader, right now it is my job to create a positive story line for the Boys and to believe in it. I am not "selling" anything, as if the Boys have a choice in participating. Rather, I am assigning meaning to violence and testing my prescience. If my "moment" is the entry level of warrior greatness, then the expert level is predictive power, a kind of combat nirvana that stems from knowing your men, the enemy, and the battlefield so well that you can see what will happen next.

I radio the squad leaders and prop myself against a tree while they kneel in a half circle. I say, "Bad guys came for scalps. We smashed their assault. But now they've heard the helicopter and know we've got casualties. Their commanders are telling them to man up. They are coming back tonight. We are going to get the drop on them this time."

I order Sergeant Dole, my third squad leader, to set up a counterattack position. His squad and a machine-gun team will take ground about five hundred meters north. I say, "Post up where you can see the enemy trail. You pick the spot." I draw in the dirt. "If they reinfiltrate, you'll hit them on the flank."

Dole fixes me with a stare. He says, "You want to split the platoon?"

"Yes. Remember, noise and light discipline. You'll get the drop on 'em."

I can see Dole is not wild about my plan, but he springs up and gathers his men.

Technically this is all the same fight: an attack, consolidation, and counterattack. Maybe the movies planted this idea in me of all these steps taking place in one breathless scene. In reality there is friction on the battlefield. Actions that take seconds in your mind take minutes on the ground, and minutes bleed into hours; there're petulant radios, darkness, the unexpected cliff, and casualties. Such things slow a battle, the actions, and reactions. At last, you shake all this out and are ready for more action, then it's, *Hey, where'd what's-his-nuts go? Shit, I dunno. Find him . . . Anyone seen what's-his-nuts? Anyone? Oh, jackass fell in with the wrong squad. Okay, we're ready.*

Twelve men are gathered beside Sergeant Dole. There are no faces in the dark, just the vague shapes of weapons, which is what the Boys are right now, weapons to be deployed: a grenadier, rifleman, SAW gunner, and machine gunner. From inside the knot of them come frightened whispers. I brace myself against a tree and slap them on their shoulders, saying, "Go git 'em." Their eyes are green coins behind night vision. They file out of the perimeter and pad into towering woods. Traces of terrain are visible. The ridge we occupy sweeps northwest, up and up. A gap in the woods looks to be an open mouth, and beyond it lies a desolation of summits and domes stretching to China.

You should be with them.

I hobble back to position and cloister myself in a rock pile to stare at the vast roof of night. Flies rankle me, dancing on my lips, dive-bombing my good ear. The bells are ringing. Pain from my shrapnel wounds drums up my leg. A moan escapes me. *Shit.*

Close by, Doc raises his head. He motors up. "Sir, you've gotta swallow that."

"Sorry, Doc. It snuck up on me."

"I got something for you." Doc serves up a half dose of morphine, and soon it is hectoring me. Lying in the rock pile, I giggle uncontrollably. With eyes closed, an enemy army on the march appears, coming for us, this time with a hundred RPGs and wheeled artillery. They have my wife, Elizabeth, as prisoner. They have her in a blue burka. I cannot see her figure. *Goddamn them for that.* For the first time in many weeks, I linger on my old lady. Thinking of her is an indulgence, a pleasure to be rationed.

If I make it through this thing, I will keep my wounds a secret from her. Nothing good can come from her knowing.

My career choice seems ill-advised at this moment. The enemy has sullied the adventure. Bleeding in the dirt on a moonless night, shivering from morphine and cold, is not the plan. I toy with calling another medevac.

"Three-six, you good?" asks Siercks.

I open my eyes and stutter, "Yeah, yeah, good to go."

"You're shivering."

"I know."

"Were you saying something?"

"I was giving myself a motivational speech. It was going rather well."

He grins. "You're a good man for staying, but you should go out on the resupply bird. You make it through the night, you can be proud of that."

He is right. Prudence dictates an exit. The longer this goes on, the more my symbolic gesture can hurt the platoon. "Okay," I say. "Can you carry me down?"

"Piss off, sir."

In the command post Doc strings up a poncho, and with a bungee cord, secures the corners to tree trunks, making a shelter to hide the light of his headlamp. Siercks and Doc have light shrapnel wounds, and they have made up their minds to dig metal out of each other with a pocket-knife. Siercks plays surgeon first, tongue to the side as he carves into Doc's chest. Doc protests against the blade. "Aw, aw, aw."

The radio *hisses*. Sergeant Dole is calling in from his position, whispering, "Three-six, this is Three-three. We've got movement. Seventy-five meters."

I radio back, "Shoot them! Don't tell me about it. Shoot them."

Dole's men blast into thick vegetation. The forest smothers their muzzle flashes. Dole leads an advance, clearing past the enemy trail. On the ground a faint light draws them like moths. One of Dole's men creeps up to the light, gun at the high-ready, to find a lit cigarette. The enemy has come back. Again, Dole's men drop to their bellies and fire into the woods.

I radio to him, "Sitrep."

No answer.

My voice rises, "Sitrep."

Siercks reminds me, "Easy, sir. Let him sort it out."

We all wait. No one moves for a long time. Finally, Dole reports, "No friendly or enemy casualties." Dole holds position deep into the night, then radios, "No further movement. We're coming in. Tell first squad to hold fire."

In the command post, Siercks tells me, "You were right."

We keep 100 percent security, rifles at the ready. The cold penetrates my slashed uniform, and I blame Doc for that much. No one sleeps. Dawn finds me limping around the perimeter, boots wet from dew, checking on the squads. It is important that they see me on my feet, and it is important to me to be on my feet. I stagger from tree to tree. Doc sees me, rises, and takes my arm, saying, "I got you, sir," as if I am an old woman. I fling his hand away, lose balance, and fall into a shrub where a sharp branch nearly tears my ballbag.

From inside the shrub, I groan, "I'm fine."

Doc frowns. "Suit yourself, Three-six."

Upon reaching the north machine gun, I find the Boys in rifle pits, eyes dark. Some pour water into the heaters of their rations, unleashing an acidic odor. Breakfast will be beef stew, stroganoff, or hamburger patty. Some unfortunates have drawn sausage fingers, the five fingers of death. To breakfast on them is medal-worthy. Specialist Fox, of third squad, mans the M240B. He has the feed tray up, squeezing oil across the bolt. As he slaps it closed, he notices me.

He says, "You stayed! Fuckin' A, sir."

Nothing hurts when he says it.

"Just a bit longer," I reply.

"It was hairy last night on that ambush," he says. "Hairy as fuck."

"You guys broke up another attack."

"Sheee-it, sir."

About 0800, we gather for movement down to the landing zone, or LZ for short. Hesitant to relinquish control, I point to my map and tell Siercks, "When resupply gets back, move north. Find those thick woods, right in here."

He nods. "Adios, Three-six."

"I'll be back."

He is already walking away when he says, "Right."

We lurch down the eastern slope. It takes an hour and a half for me to crawl, limp, and fall to the resupply LZ. Reaching it, we spread out in the tree line and wait. Just before the helicopter is due, I scan the faces of the squad. Only they can give the credibility I strive for, as my "moment" is a mutual contract, something that I have to believe, and that my platoon must also believe.

Someone please tell me it is okay to leave.

I survey each man: Correll, Berben, Bernal, Ware, and Sergeant Patterson, the second squad leader.

They look like men who must each carry a hundred pounds up a mountain, men with no time for my drama. That same enemy force is still out there. The battle is not over. And here I am, a walking wounded. This thing has me sick. It might be better to have gotten a leg blown off. There is more honor in that. But then again, what legless man would say he came out ahead?

I look up, seeing the top of the wooded ridge against the bleeding yellow of morning. In the east, the sun is backlighting an axis of Himalayan summits. Soon a chopper swoops down, and the crew kicks out boxes of food, water, and ammo. The crew chief pulls me aboard. I lie against my pack on the cabin floor, too smoked to try a seat. As the chopper dives for the Pech River, my squad shrinks in the distance, ferrying ammo crates into the wood line. There are no farewells.

Within ten minutes, we land in Asadabad. Left of the helipad are the 155 howitzers that had fired for us during the fight. We are in lowland, and already the heat is alive. The crews hide from the climbing sun in the shade cast by the barrels. Just past the howitzers is a gap in the stone wall that surrounds camp. Presently my ride bounces toward me, a pickup truck with a red cross on the side. I look back to the eastern ridge of the Watapur. The sun is fully upon it. I whisper, "Sorry, Boys."

A howitzer lets loose with a deafening boom, launching a three-foot-long shell. The report is devastating and unexpected. I dive to the ground beside the truck. The driver, a sergeant from the aide station, dismounts the cab and stares at me balled up in the dirt.

I say, "Fuckin' fuck," as he pulls me to my feet. He lifts me under my armpits and sets me in the back seat.

I say, "Drive slow, will ya?"

5

WIN, LOSE, OR DRAW

ASADABAD, AFGHANISTAN

SUMMER 2006

A female surgeon in scrubs receives me under operating lights. The room smells of latex and alcohol. She, on the other hand, smells wondrous, of lotion and estrogen. She helps me peel off my fighting vest. A surgical table is ready in the center of the room. She helps me get on. I wiggle backward while she dons a mask and gloves. The lights overhead are alien aircraft.

She cuts off the remainder of my smoke-tinged fatigues, casts them aside, and readies gleaming instruments. Above the mask, her eyes are green. She is the first woman I have seen for weeks. I want her to be nurturing. Taking up a needle, she says, "Hold still." I say, "I hate needles," and she stabs into the shrapnel wound at my shoulder. I jump at the first stick. I flinch at the second. Then I am numb.

With a scalpel and forceps, she mines shrapnel from my shoulder and drops it in a metal pan. *Tink.* I ask, "Can you put me out for this?" *Tink.* She does her job with cold precision. *Tink.* She does not talk. *Tink.* I lie there with eyes closed, half conscious, feeling the tug of her tools, the rooting inside me. She moves to my hip. *Tink.* She moves to my leg. *Tink. Tink.*

An X-ray reveals deeper pieces of metal. She reports, "We'll send you to Bagram to get those out. I've got to keep space open for urgent surgicals."

"Okay," I say. "You know, my ear hasn't stopped ringing. Can you look?"

She jams an otoscope in. Her assessment, "Your eardrum is ruptured. You'll have to get that fixed. You may need to go home."

"Home?"

"Yes," she says, her latex gloves slapping as she pulls them off. "We'll send you to Landstuhl first." Landstuhl, Germany, is the location of the army's major triage hospital for the Iraq and Afghan battlefields. "They'll decide."

This is moving faster than I want. The flight will be tomorrow. For now an orderly shows me to a concrete house with an empty room, a bed, and shower. He leans a pair of crutches in the corner. In the other corner is a plastic chair that I take into the shower. I sit in the chair until I have exhausted the hot water. I towel off and sit alone in the dark. Being clean and comfortable ignites self-blame. My mind is acid rain: *You froze. You were too slow. The casualties are on you.* My ear rings. Just uphill the howitzers are smashing out rounds. My platoon is still on the ridge.

I crutch to the medical desk and ask for news on my Boys. The medic on duty calls the ops center. The platoon has seen no further contact. Fortified with this news, I crutch back to the room, where I draw the curtain and swallow three painkillers. Soon the pills have me feeling elevated. The howitzers keep thudding. I fizzle out.

* * *

I wake to Lieutenant Colonel Cavoli standing over my bed. I am struck by the sensation that he has been standing there for a while. I throw aside my blanket and try the position of attention. Pain surges. I cannot stand.

Cavoli smiles. His eyes soften. "How you doing, Three-six?"

"Better, sir. They picked some metal out of me."

"Sit."

I do. He sits beside me, grabs my jaw, and turns my head left and right, examining the wounds on my neck and face. After a long time, he asks, "So what was it, win, lose, or draw?"

"The fight, sir?"

"Yes."

This I have not considered. We overran their assault position, which is nothing to blow a bugle over. I should have pursued the enemy much farther. Most of all, I should have moved the fucking patrol base. The casualties are my fault.

His eyes narrow. "Win, lose, or draw?"

There is an answer he wants, and there is the truth. As a field commander, I have to be in the truth business. I say, "Draw."

He grunts, brow pleated, and gets up and paces with hands clasped behind his back. "Draw," he whispers. His eyes go far away. I am sitting before him, bandaged and giggly from painkillers, terrified I might laugh if this keeps on.

"The first battle means everything," says Cavoli. "It burns all the neurological pathways. If you win, your Boys feel like gods, and they'll fight hard the rest of their lives. If it's a loss, they'll be scared soldiers. Some will hide the next time rounds fly, counting on their buddies to fight back. Some of the men in your platoon, right now, their chemistry is morphing. What they become has everything to do with you. Understood?"

"Roger, sir."

"Good. Now, win, lose, or draw?"

"We held our ground, sir. We are in their backyard, playing king of the mountain. We, I mean, my platoon still has the flag planted."

"Very well." Then he leaves.

Next morning pride tells me to leave the crutches in the corner. I check on the platoon again. There has been no further action. Around lunchtime an orderly helps me into a pickup truck, and we make the short drive to the helipad. Parked beside it, we wait for the chopper that will take me to Bagram. Also waiting is a clutch of Taliban prisoners with sandbags over their heads. Six of them are seated abreast, hands in flex cuffs, army green line rope coupling them to each other.

The executive officer of headquarters company, a grifter named Morris, is guarding the prisoners. Seeing me in the truck, Morris strides up and leans into the window, one hand on the roof of the cab. He says, "These detainees are from the Korengal. Big-time dickheads. Your company caught them. Damn fine job."

I smile and throw up a thumb, "That's awesome. Thanks."

"Can you walk? Looks like maybe you can walk."

"Why?"

To the orderly, Morris says, "He can walk, right?" Then to me, "See the problem is, I ain't got no one to guard them on this flight. Can you do it? Otherwise, I'll have to pull guys from a howitzer crew."

"Yeah, why not."

"Just for the flight. I mean, it's not like they are going to take over the bird."

"Of course, why would prisoners want to escape?"

The Chinook arrives. I struggle up the ramp. Morris follows me, then serries the prisoners on the vibrating floor. He gives me the thumbs-up, yelling, "All yours." The helicopter lifts off and noses west for Bagram. The entire ride, the pain in my calf feels like fire. It climbs into my knee. When we land, I limp off the back ramp with my blindfolded flock. Fighter jets streak down another runway. A-10 Warthogs stand ready, carbon smears on their rocket-pods and chain guns. C-17 cargo planes are hangared in rows. Tarmac stretches as far as the eye can see. Jet fuel hazes the distant buildings. Here is a real base, bejeweled with all the might of the American military, home to silver-haired generals who make war sound like science.

The problem right now is no one has come to pick me up. I have prisoners in one hand, rifle in another, and I do the hurt dance in a circle, scanning for a truck. The radio on my vest still has frequencies, so I switch to battalion net and reach our supply sergeant at Bagram, telling him, "I'm going to let six Taliban loose on this fucking airfield if no one's here in two minutes."

A Toyota Hilux races onto the tarmac and skids to a stop. The supply sergeant, Black, and his underling, "Corporal Muffin Top," shove the prisoners into the truck bed. We leave the runway and drop the prisoners at forever jail, then onto the hospital, where I learn my leg is infected.

* * *

It is sunny and hot when I board a medical C-17 at Bagram Airfield. In the cavernous plane it is cold. A couple dozen casualties will ride with me, some better off than others. The plane lifts off. Scorched plateaus and dusty hills fall away beneath the wings. Turbulence over the border has us passengers groaning. Idle on the flight, my brain seems defective. *Had the fight been a draw as I had told Cavoli?* No, it had been a resounding win, then moments later, a stinging defeat, and before long, a draw again. The turbulence continues.

Across the cabin lies a pallid marine on a stretcher. All types of wire and apparatus are strapped to him: tubes, blinking monitors, a bag half full of piss. A nurse flutters beside him. The marine was shot in the stomach, I gather, just below the armor plate. His liver failed. This marine has earned his Purple Heart. *Must find something else to look at.*

We land in Germany. Coming off the ramp, bucolic grass hills greet me, the splendor of green. A bus whisks us to Landstuhl Medical Facility. A nurse takes me to a room in a quiet wing. I lie on a simple bed and listen to the ringing in my ear. A half hour of this inspires a trip to the bookshelf down the hall. I scan from top to bottom, pull *Memoirs of a Geisha*, then crutch back down the hall, palm concealing the book's title from onlookers. I read it in two days, then return to the shelf and pull *Call of the Wild* and *White Fang*, which I devour in one sitting.

My room shrinks. The ringing grows. I roll in bed and pace in mind, reviewing the gunfight that got me here. Here is a war story sufficient to go home with. There is no need to return to a mountain range littered with corpses, only to become one. The platoon will be fine. Everyone will be fine. Six months from now, they won't even remember me. I can go home now with stories and tell my dad and wife that I did something. Someday I can show my kids my Purple Heart. My war has been short, but I have done plenty, and the brevity of it will be lost to everyone except me. I talk myself into it, then out of it, in and out.

End of week, another doctor evaluates. I lie on a table while he sits on a wheeled stool and pedals up to the table. Penicillin has beaten the infection in my leg, the doc reports. He has a look in my ear and clucks his tongue, "Yep, that eardrum is shot. We can get you on the Monday flight."

I ask, "To the States?"

"Yes, of course."

"I need to get back to my unit."

The doctor looks stunned.

I say, "I'm going back to Afghanistan."

"It's a large hole, son. You'll need an operation to patch it, and *no* sonic pressure during recovery."

"Doc, I'll get light duty at battalion, be just as good as home."

He says, "You . . . can . . . go . . . home," as if I'm dense.

This is the wounded pipeline. Someone who wants out of the war just has to find a way in. The gatekeepers controlling flow are doctors not assigned to combat units, and thus, are concerned with patient well-being. *You want a ticket home? How about a pillow for the plane?* In combat units, on the other hand, battalion surgeons and medical sergeants want to keep soldiers in the fight. In combat units, its tough love for the injured and sick: two Ibuprofen and a slap on the ass. *Walk it off.*

In my battalion the wounded who get sucked into the pipeline are supposed to report their status to headquarters. The staffies, however, are busy with the war so no one asks, and the wounded go covert all the way home. Once at Fort Drum, rear detachment, a band of half-wits and gimps who could not deploy, scoops up the wounded.

All this goes to say that I am being flushed toward peace, and no one will get in the way.

I must reverse flow. Otherwise, battalion will give my platoon to another officer. Just give it away. Two days of cursing into a phone gets me connected to Bagram, then battalion headquarters in Jalalabad, and on to my company commander, Captain Jim McKnight, who's building an outpost in a notorious valley called the Korengal. The captain's previous assignment was with the 75th Ranger Regiment, making it easy for me to lionize him.

When the captain comes on the line, he greets me with, "Hey, Ranger," a title reserved for members of the 75th Ranger Regiment. The captain knows I want in, and it is a supreme compliment that he addresses me as such.

I say, "Sir, I'll be back, shouldn't be more than a couple weeks."

"They told me you were done."

"That's a negative, Attack Six. I'm doing burpees as we speak. How're my Boys?"

The captain says an Afghan Army platoon reinforced my Boys. They made no further contact in the Watapur. "They got pulled out and moved to Jalalabad. I've been fighting to get them out here. We are in the shit. And I mean shit. I want your platoon here ASAP."

"Got it, sir, just need a couple weeks."

"Have you called your wife?"

"I have not." My aim is to keep this a secret.

"Rear D already contacted Elizabeth," says the captain. "It's standard procedure for casualties."

"Shit." I hang up and dial Elizabeth at her mother's house in Texas, a number I'll always have memorized: 9974. Electricity shoots through me when she picks up.

I say, "Hi, babe."

"There you are. Oh my God. Tell me you're okay."

"Just a little banged up. I'm walking it off."

"They called last week, said you were wounded and evacuated to the rear." She chokes down a sob. "I didn't hear anything else."

"It's nothing terrible. Shrapnel. They didn't give you details?"

"No. They didn't say anything, just that you were wounded and evacuated."

"Fuckin' clowns. I'm going to fuck someone up in Rear D." I catch myself spiraling, draw a breath, and steady. "I'm sorry, babe. I meant to call. It's been crazy. I'm in Germany."

Hesitantly, she asks, "Everything still work?"

I laugh. "Sure."

"When are you coming home?"

"I'm not. It's not that bad."

"Are you really okay?"

"Yeah."

"This was the worst, just waiting for you to call. No one knew anything."

"It's okay now. Everything is okay. So you're in Corpus?"

"The beach . . . Oh, you should see it. The Ridley's turtles are swimming off Padre Island." She adds, "So glad I left Fort Drum. I couldn't stand it there. The snow. And just the wives picking at each other."

"I told you to make friends in the FRG." The family readiness group is a "command-sponsored organization of family members, volunteers, and soldiers belonging to a particular unit, designed to provide support."

"You should see them. It's not healthy. They look beat-up, and the high-ranking wives, the ones married to the colonels, well, they act like colonels. This general's wife, she wanted me to kiss the ring. I was like, 'I'm not in the army, you bitch.'"

"You gotta find the captain's wives, you know, the lieutenant's wives."

"I did. It's not much better. They asked me to a dinner party. They asked about my china set. *China*, Ray. I'm like, 'We live above some old lady. Our carpet is pink. Go fuck yourself.'"

"I'm sorry, babe."

Elizabeth softens, "Gosh. I'm sorry too. I'm unloading. Never mind what I said. It's just so good to talk to you. Look, I miss you, but I want you to do what is right. I still believe in this, and I will always believe in you."

"Thanks, girl. Look, I gotta run. I love you."

She says it back, and I hang up.

There are more appointments. I waste away in my kennel at Landstuhl, wounds healing while my mind decomposes. The ringing in my ear begins faintly, then morphs and climbs to a roar like ocean surf. A pillow over my head does not have the intended effect. I rue the firefight and my decisions leading up to it. Do I still have a platoon?

* * *

A week and my hobble improves to a hitch. As a vacation of sorts, the army gives me a train ticket to a German city called Trier. Thankful for something to do, I join a dozen other walking wounded. At the train station we smoke and wait on the platform. Trains rattle by. The white one for Trier arrives. The doors swish open. I struggle aboard and sit beside a window, where I do my best to look psycho to deter others from sitting beside me. It works. We speed away from the station. Germany flashes by. The countryside is clean. Knots of white-washed houses are neatly kept, the planter boxes under the windows blooming with flowers, firewood stacked with military precision against first-story walls. Seeing their villages, it becomes obvious how the Germans conquered Europe in World War II. And if neatness is any measure of national capability, the Afghans will not be conquering the world anytime soon.

The train deposits me in Trier, an old Roman city on the border with Luxembourg. A mass of colorful humanity bustles down cobblestone avenues shaded by ancient trees. It takes considerable effort to convince the lieutenant in me that this is not a patrol. Habit, I suppose.

A tornado of aromas has me dizzy. Coffee, bratwurst. I catch sharp whiffs of women's perfume. I want to charge a plump young mother and take a huge sniff of her neck. No one here seems the least bit worried about the war in Afghanistan, which I find a relief, though it stings a little. Tourists trip over one another, their necks craned at cathedrals and spires rising from the streets. Music floats out of cafés. On the fringe of Trier, I photo the Moselle River winding through emerald hills, a flotilla of tour boats gliding down the water.

It is a golden afternoon.

A square near the city center has green grass. Lying in it are European women in tank tops and men wearing capris. One couple is tied up on a blanket, oblivious to the swirling crowd. They kiss and whisper and kiss. They lie together, hands clasped, faces to the sun. Seeing them sullies my faith in my career choice.

At this moment, wounded and isolated from my unit, my reality corrodes. I have spent the bulk of my youth enamored with war, training and studying, practicing being miserable. There is no peace in the mind of a young man. There shouldn't be. I had to be ready for my test; no time for lying in the grass. For fuck's sake, on Sundays I'd take Elizabeth to the rifle range, a date of sorts with the goal being my warrior perfection. All along, I wanted to be hard. To slake this desire, I had to leave my wife and fight on a mountainside. I *had* to go to war. A good man should. The lovers in front of me are frauds. What have they ever done to earn the right to hold each other in soft grass and forget the world?

After a few weeks in Germany, my infection is defeated, and the doctor permits me to opt out of surgery for my hearing. Sometimes the eardrum can heal on its own. Best case, it will take the better part of a year. The doc warns, "Avoid sonic trauma, gunfire, and explosions."

I nod vigorously, "No. It's light duty for me. Promise."

The doc issues me enough cotton balls to stuff a pillow and orders, "Keep that ear dry."

I board the next plane to Afghanistan.

PART 2
WALK

6

VALLEY OF DEATH

NANGARHAR PROVINCE, AFGHANISTAN

SUMMER 2006

The C-130 executes a combat dive into Jalalabad Airfield, to thwart any chance of downing by surface-to-air missile, which the enemy do not possess. It is a fun little drill, like a roller coaster. United Nations bomb-disposal crews in bulky suits and blue helmets trundle in the furrows around the airfield, clearing land mines left by the Soviets. We skid onto the runway. The C-130 taxis to a stop beside the control tower. I shoulder my pack and ease off the ramp, reviewing my recovery so far. I want to run to the platoon and get back in the fight, yet the whole tour seems ahead of me. It is a heavy sense, like I've swallowed a river stone. *You can get killed doing this.*

I pull down my boonie hat against the lurid rays of noon. Aircraft exhaust rises in a faint blue haze, splintering the hooches and antennae-prickled buildings across the runway. A short walk brings me to the company area. I crunch through gravel, testing my leg. *Okay, here goes.* I pull open the door of my platoon hooch. The scent of gun oil hits before my eyes adjust to the dim light. All the Boys are lounging on cots, rifles broken apart, howling about tits and asses.

Specialist Fox, of third squad, looks at me and says, "Holy shit, it's the sir."

The Boys set down feed trays, barrels, upper receivers, springs, and trigger assemblies. They rise. "Three-six, what's happening." "LT!" "You came back." Siercks springs to his feet and pumps my hand. "Hope you enjoyed your vacation." He breaks into a huge grin. "Welcome back to the suck. Damn good to see you, sir." He reaches for the pack on my right shoulder, saying, "Need a hand?"

Cots line the walls of the hooch. We sleep twenty on the left, twenty on the right, the cots three feet apart. Some of the Boys have strung poncho liners around their cots in a feeble attempt at privacy. Siercks walks me to my cot, where squad gear and ammo cans are piled high. With a quick sweep of his hand, Siercks knocks it all to the floor. "Uh, sorry 'bout that, sir. Wasn't sure you were coming back."

I stow my gear under the cot. Right away things are different. The Boys are jubilant. They shout questions at me. "How was Germany, sir?" "You see some of them fräuleins?" "You were drinking, weren't cha?" Siercks opens a can of dip and offers me a pinch. A fire team is going for lunch, and the team leader offers, "Sir, you need anything from the chow hall?"

I am glowing. This is "the moment."

Once back with the Boys, my wounds evaporate. It is psychosomatic: the body, war, and brotherhood. I am their platoon leader, and now edified by my own mistakes, I decide there will be no more playing war. I have learned how to duck shots, and what it takes to lead.

* * *

We don't stay in Jalalabad for long. I know we have a mission when summoned to battalion headquarters. The battle captain shows me to the red phone. Captain McKnight is on the line. He starts slow, "Get your platoon out here now." He explains the unit has been under constant fire. They have made little progress in building the Korengal Outpost, partly due to terrain. The valley lies in the hinterlands of the Kush, nine miles deep and a couple miles wide, a vault of shale, accessible only by helicopter or a precarious jeep road.

The valley's tribal inhabitants are also hindering progress. The tribal men are fierce fighters, unequaled in mobility and tactic, and allied with the worst of al-Qaeda. In this valley, al-Qaeda's leadership planned the

9/11 attacks, making it the frontier in the global war on terror. In 2005 the area became notorious when militants killed three Navy SEALs near the valley's eastern divide, then shot down a rescue helicopter, killing sixteen more commandos. This was Operation Red Wings. The lone survivor was Marcus Luttrell.

In April 2006 my battalion's first major operation, code-named "Mountain Lion," speared into the Korengal. Our eight-hundred-man unit, plus a marine equivalent, launched a simultaneous attack on the Korengal and a neighboring valley to the west, the Shuryak. Fighter aircraft, attack helicopters, and artillery boosted our assault. We bulled onto the highest peaks and hit the deepest villages.

In the first forty-eight hours, the enemy faded into the population. Al-Qaeda leaders, our big prizes, were not back from wintering in Pakistan. By day ten we had hit all our primary and secondary objectives, which generated a few spasms of fire with the enemy, though nothing that ever smelled like battle. We managed to capture a few bad guys; I'd heard none of their names before. On the brigade battle map, all unit icons were in the correct places. The operation was inconclusive, as is the pattern in Afghanistan, so we declared victory and marched out, leaving two platoons from my company on the valley's west wall in a spot called "the lumberyard." These two platoons were to hold the valley, thus cementing victory.

Fighting the tribes of the Kush is like fighting water. When you raise a boot and stomp into a puddle, the water parts and then reforms when you lift the boot and walk away. In our case, the water reformed a few weeks after Operation Mountain Lion. The tribesmen dug their Soviet weapons out of hillside caches. Melting snow cleared the way for foreign fighters to stream over border passes. In a valley we had just won, my understrength company came under frequent fire. The frenetic pace of fighting had everyone turning scarlet.

My orders, the captain now explains, are to rejoin my company. The mission is to help build and hold this outpost in the enemy heartland. We will be a magnet. The enemy will mass against us, and in doing so, abandon their operations in the Pech Valley. If the Pech gets quiet, then Asadabad will follow, and if Asadabad is ours, then so is Kunar. Many say our goal is impossible in this graveyard of empires. The trick is someone must be the bullet magnet, and that *someone* is us.

I brief the platoon on the friendly and enemy situation in the Korengal. Right away I stumble over what to call the enemy. Many are from the recalcitrant local tribe, the Korengalis, some of whom are allied with the Taliban. Others have formed their own gang, fighting for a local timber baron named Haji Matin, who owns the lumberyard we have seized as our outpost. Al-Qaeda runs rampant in the valley, lots of Arabs, Pakistanis, and Chechens. There're Haqqani Network loyalists too, an offshoot of the Taliban.

The army tells me not to think too much about it, just call them anticoalition militia, which no one can say three times fast. We are not supposed to call them rebels or mujahideen, as it validates their self-image. *Enemy* is a safe name for them, but it has no flavor. In every war, the American soldier has invented fun shorthand for the enemy: Gooks, Dinks, Jerries, Krauts, Rebs. A one-syllable name is best, so that you can yell it in a fight, or whisper it in the dark to your buddy in the next foxhole. It is difficult yelling, *The anticoalition militia are coming!* when your heart is thumping and rounds are cracking by. I settle on calling the enemy *muj*, which is short for mujahideen. Siercks calls them *hajis*, which is carryover slang from Iraq, the location of his last tour.

In blowing dust we load into eight Humvees and convoy for the Korengal, me riding shotgun in the first vehicle. I am the vanguard of democracy and military power, with a cotton ball in one ear and a paper map for navigation because the computer screen in my Humvee is broken, and I haven't bothered getting it fixed. I am fond of paper maps, and there're only like four roads in the whole province, so how hard can this be? My driver is also my new radioman, Private Chuck Cigrand. Until now, he was a rifleman in first squad.

At a roundabout northeast of Jalalabad, we angle through traffic. My Humvee hits an Afghan pickup, which stalls my gallant campaign. The driver jumps out, reviews the crushed panel on his truck, and waves a fist at me. Besieged by guilt, I dismount and march toward the man, who cowers, thinking me vengeful. I apologize on behalf of the coalition. I have caused a traffic accident, and my sense is that I'm in trouble. This will get back to battalion and I will be reprimanded for carelessness. Perhaps my insurance will go up. *How does that work?*

I am quick to dispense justice. Fingering a stack of dollar bills, I say, "I'll give you three hundred dollars," which seems reasonable. When I hand over the money, the man beams and runs off, leaving his truck by the roadside.

When I remount my Humvee, Cigrand says, "Sorry 'bout that, sir. What'd you do?"

"Gave him three hundred dollars."

"Shit, sir, his whole truck ain't worth three hundred."

"So you're an insurance assessor now?" I throw in a pinch of Copenhagen. "These people need to have positive interaction with Americans."

"You're the candy man, Three-six. You wanna run over my foot?"

"Drive."

The road goes along the Kunar River. We drive past the alluvial fans of a dozen valleys. Holly trees stipple the hillsides. A footbridge spans the river, shadowing cascades beneath. The current eddies behind the bridge piers. Across the river on the right is a spine of mountains and Pakistan. We go along the river until noon and come to an Afghan outpost on a spur above the water. Two policemen stand watch in a tower with parapets.

One of our Humvees is overheating, so we pull into the police outpost to cool off. The two policemen in the tower are spotting fish in the river, yelling and pointing to another policeman on a bluff, who has an RPG shouldered. They yell and point, yell and point. The cop on the bluff jams a rocket in the tube, takes a bead on a side channel, and fires into the water. A muffled explosion splashes us bystanders. The cold shock has me panting. Dead fish rise to the surface, their bellies glinting in the sun. Two more policemen, uniform pants rolled to the knees, wade into the water with nets and collect the fish.

Cigrand says, "Must be the SWAT team."

We mount up and move again.

A little farther is Asadabad city, or A-bad, a honeycomb of shops and tumbledown buildings, in which we pass a traffic cop wearing white gloves, directing cars and jingle trucks—large cargo vehicles done up with sashes, chains, and flowery paint jobs. The traffic cop is a surprising gasp of government in these hinterlands. The American military camp within rifle range might have something to do with it. The smell of Asadabad, like all Afghan settlements, is of creatures and humanity without filter.

Beyond Asadabad, we swing left to follow the Pech River, our vehicles creaking under five tons of retrofitted armor. My heart thumps. Here is the frontier where the battlefield begins, and worse, there are mines in the road. We hasten to forty miles per hour, listing around a bend. There is a white boulder ahead, lying on a hillside above the river. The road is built around the boulder, a village built around the road. The enemy can come from anywhere. An hour drips by before we pass the Watapur Valley, where I was almost blown off the planet in early July. I do not look up at the ridge. Cigrand does, then at me, and begins to say something. The look I give him puts a stop to that.

A six-hour voyage brings us to the maw of the Korengal Valley, a gateway of rock into more rock. Slicing out of the mountains here is a protean stream of the same name, which in spring and early summer is a ribbon of whitewater fed by a massif of twelve-thousand-foot peaks. By summer's end, the peaks are naked of snow, and the stream slows to a dribble. I am no lover of rivers, only a field commander who has to cross them.

Above us is a village, a congeries of hard-baked mud, wood, and stone on a sun-dried hill. Villagers peek out their windows at my convoy. Above the village the boulders are goblin-like. Snow and ice have etched screaming faces into them. Above the boulders a thunderhead rakes a rocky altar with lighting. We nudge west, beyond the junction of the Korengal and Pech Rivers, to a ford marked on my map. Here though, we find the river swollen and no obvious ford. There is wood in the channel.

Scanning the banks allows one to gauge flow. Standing water shines in the floodplain on the far side. This river has crested in the last day or so. Not good for us. The crossing is impossible for the Humvees. I radio the captain on our company's FM frequency, saying, "We made it. River is too high. There's a storm up the Pech. Lots of rain. We'll wait, let the water recede. Shouldn't be more than twenty-four hours."

When the captain keys the radio, there is gunfire crackling in the background. He says, "Push across. Accomplish your mission."

I say, "Sir. We are going to lose vehicles, and maybe men, if we try crossing."

When he keys the hand mike again, machine guns are chugging. "Continue mission," he says.

I answer, "Roger," then curse my mulish commander. I tell the sergeants we're going to try for it. They look at each other and me, then say, "We are going to try for it?"

I say, "Our company is in the shit right now. We are fording this river."

I breathe in burst-mode as we line up on the bank. Riding in the lead vehicle is customary for platoon leaders. I must be the first to try crossing. After all, I can't tell the Boys, *This is fucked, so someone else should have a go.* Crossing first is the right thing to do. I am not scared. Not really. Maybe sort of. A little.

My vehicle crew has the unfortunate task of being my vehicle crew. I tell the sergeants piloting the seven remaining Humvees to wait for me to make it before attempting. I push the cotton ball farther into my ear, which does not steady my constitution the way I had hoped. The Afghans see what is afoot and stream down the hillside below the village. Wrapped in drab colors, they gather on the bank; there's maybe seventy of them, lots of men, some boys, all wearing a blanket over one shoulder.

In my Humvee, Cigrand grips the wheel with both hands.

I say, "Too easy. You ready?"

"Roger."

"Cool. Don't fuck this up."

Cigrand guns it, and we dive over the bank and smash into the current, brown water gushing over the hood. We slice out to fifty yards, about halfway, when the engine gurgles and stalls. Cigrand slaps at the controls with fright. Smoke pumps as the pistons turn over in their greasy jackets. Cold water is pouring into the cab, soaking my legs, then crotch. I jump onto the seat. The current pushes our Humvee sideways.

I yell, "Everyone out the hatch. Go, go, go."

We clamber from our seats, and one after the next, squeeze out the gunner's hatch. Now on the roof, I evaluate the next move. Rushing water sweeps beneath. The Humvee pivots, and the current takes us broadside.

Water rushes over the hood and roof, soaking our blouses and vests. The Humvee slips downstream, then gets hung up again, anchored by the up armor lashed to the cab. We are a few feet from the main channel, where the water is deepest. If we drift into it, the river will flush our bodies into the Indian Ocean.

I ditch my helmet, vest, armor, and gun, then bowline a rope to my waist, dive in, and stroke for the near shore, where the rest of the platoon is pulling security, mouths agape. I stab the water with both arms, doing my best to keep the right ear from going under. Waves crash over me. Logs roll by. The Afghans cheer. Between splashes, I glimpse them jumping on the bank. The weight of water in my uniform and boots has me in slow motion.

Made it. I slosh up the bank. A hush falls over the locals. They were cheering for the river. My cotton ball is gone. Brown water drains from my ear. Everything sounds like it's coming down a long hallway. I squish up to the nearest Humvee, water oozing from the vents in my boots.

Corporal Ainsworth, of first squad, is waiting with a winch hook in hand. He says, "Should we shoot the Hajis?"

I untie the rope around my waist and secure it to the winch line. Still midriver, Cigrand pulls the rope back out to the truck, hand over hand, then grabs the winch line and secures it to the tow hook. The winch soon brings our Humvee back onto the bank. Water drains from it in sheets. The engine ticks. I say to Cigrand, "You fucked it up." He throws up his hands, and we laugh. On the far bank, the sullen Afghans trickle away.

Waiting for the current to recede, we circle the Humvees like a wagon train might do against Indians. I pull off my camo top and T-shirt and spread the pieces over the Humvee hood.

The day bleeds out. The shadows go long. I tell the Boys we will bivouac. Before my radio watch, I unfurl a sleeping bag in the sand beside my Humvee and try a nap. Within a quarter hour, sandfleas have launched an offensive. I scratch my legs raw. I scratch off my hair. Commingled with the fleas are lice. Inside my helmet they begin a banquet. I abandon my sleeping bag, sit in the Humvee, and doze.

The radio squawks to life. There is action in the Korengal, south of the company outpost. The enemy has ambushed a squad patrol from Second Platoon.

My sergeants gather around the radio in my Humvee, their eyes expectant. Looking toward the fight, there are mountains, a roof of clouds, and beyond, more mountains. Orange flashes light the cloud bottoms. The patrol leader of the men ambushed, Lieutenant Jae Barclay, reads off the battle roster, numbers of his casualties. I write them down. One KIA (killed in action). Two WIA (wounded in action).

The sergeants turn confidential when I read off battle roster numbers. Each code contains the first letter of a soldier's last name. Using the first letters, we manage to narrow down who has been hit to a handful of candidates. Of course it is not productive to guess who is dead and wounded. It is tradition. If you know them, you can get the grieving over with now. If you do not know them, all the better. Soon helicopters buzz over us and hook into the Korengal to ferry away our casualties. Wind keens from the valley mouth, carrying the smell of high explosive.

Dawn finds the river down, the banks visible once more. We ford without incident and follow the dirt road around a ridge. Water bottles and Copenhagen on the dash bounce as we navigate rocks and craters in a road that appears perfectly designed for fiery crashes. The valley streaks south. Here and there, the natives have carved the riverside hills into terraces, where they grow beans, clover, wheat, and corn. Women in black cloaks harvest the crops. As we pass, they stash their faces. My Boys wave to them and blow kisses, but no one gets a date.

There are no men in sight.

We pass mud huts astride the road, a spavined village. A shirtless boy pulls a bucket up from a well. He sees us, drops his bucket, then sprints out of view. Beyond the huts the road leaves the river. We climb in four-low, crawling over rocks, the Humvee radio antennae whipping against cliffs on the flank. As we navigate loose rock, my Humvee fishhooks, sending stones plunging over the road edge to bounce and spin, bounce and spin, before splashing into the river far below.

I tell Cigrand, "Do not look down."

We grind south. Dotting the uplands on my left is a hive of mud houses. The windows are black eyes. The houses lie across the valley, same elevation as the road, and well within machine-gun range, though it would take hours to descend, cross the river, and climb to them. On my map the place is labeled Comersa Bandeh—*bandeh* being a summer settlement for shepherds. A look backward shows that the valley mouth has disappeared. Above, there is just a wedge of sky. We are inside this thing. I turn ahead, eyes raking the rimrocks above, and call to my gunner standing in the hatch, "You awake?"

"Roger, sir."

"Barrel to the twelve. Split that ridge."

"Roger, sir."

In rules-of-engagement legalese, I should now say, "If you perceive hostile intent, or witness a hostile act, then you are authorized to return fire. I am delegating my judgment for interpreting the Laws of War to you, young man." All of this I manage to reduce to, "You see anything squirrelly, just shoot."

The Humvees protest as the path climbs. The slope steepens beneath us, in some places falling eight hundred vertical feet to the river. Our outside tires keep pushing sloughs off the edge. Just ahead rain has washed out bits of the road. Twice, we stop and dismount to shove boulders over the side. Progress is excruciating, the sense of commitment absolute.

Four hours later we arrive at the lumberyard, which clings to a hillside at fifty-eight hundred feet in elevation. The position is compassed by mountains, some topping out at eleven thousand feet. Sun on the rocky slopes makes them appear galvanized, like the entire valley is metallic. In our perimeter, there are no bulwarks, towers, or trenches. The usual trappings of an outpost have yet to be built. Exposed is an understatement. It is our job to change that.

Near the company command post, Lieutenant Jae Barclay, Second Platoon leader, looks spent. He is sitting against a sandbagged bunker, his uniform soiled and torn. Blood speckles the body armor resting at his side. Last night he had been leading the squad that was ambushed.

"Jae," I say, "My man." Last time I saw him was Fort Drum, and he is badass, so I'm blathering. "You look like hell, brother. I tell ya, we had to swim for it yesterday. The river crossing tore us a new one. How you been, dude?"

Barclay takes a slow sip from a canteen. He looks far, far away, toward the drainage where the fight had been, the place he had lost men.

I say, "Sorry about your Boys."

"They had us the whole way," he says. "From the second we left the wire, they had us."

"Sorry, man. It's great to see you. Looks like you guys could use some help."

"Yeah."

We circle the Humvees, adding the heavy weapons in our turrets to the perimeter. We call them heavy weapons because they are heavy. From now on, we will have little use for vehicles in this jumbled, roadless backwater. Our mode of war will be on foot.

In the center of our outpost is a flat spot the size of a couple of tennis courts, the only place in the valley where a Chinook helicopter can land without difficulty. This will be the heart of our outpost, the LZ. Without helicopters we will shrivel.

The captain welcomes us by showing me where to start digging fortifications. We get to it, swinging, stabbing, and spading the hillsides with our entrenching tools. Shirts are off. Scorpions dart. Sweat flies. Skin burns. The ground shivers. Officers and enlisted commingle. I do not have to fill bags, technically, but what kind of officer does not pitch in when his platoon is at something? *Sorry, men, I've got a meeting in headquarters.*

Next, we deepen the mortar pit beside the LZ. In the pit two 81 mm tubes stand ready, each on a baseplate and bipod. These tubes are the core of our firepower. The aiming stakes around the pit are striped like candy canes. *Fun.*

Time drags. Prickly heat is fulsome on our backs and flanks. Lice feast on our scalps. With blistered hands we attack the earth until army bunkers take shape. Our scheme is to form a star-shaped perimeter around the landing zone. The two key positions are Observation Post One and Three. Observation Post Three is at the tip of a rocky finger that points south. It is our closest position to a clot of enemy villages. Observation Post One sits on a bench eight hundred feet above the LZ, a half-hour climb.

These two positions are satellites. Holding ground in mountain warfare is a game of primary positions and their satellites. Primaries are situated near key points of military supply, like bridges, railheads, and road inter-sections. Satellites protect primaries, and to be of maximum value, they must be located on high points. Finding high points in the Kush, however, often means climbing thousands of vertical feet, so that the satellites them-selves are isolated, and for efficiency, those assigned remain for days at a time. There is no light duty here.

Masters of defense we are not. In the six-month infantry officers' course at Fort Benning, I remember just two days of instruction on defense. Our instructor, Captain Scott, was an infantry officer who had fought with the 82nd Airborne in Iraq and Afghanistan. He blew past the classroom lectures on defense, eager to get to bolder topics. "Good units," he had said, "are aggressive. They ambush. They raid and attack by fire. They don't create bastions of safety and wait to be attacked. They assault and destroy. You do defense only so you can catch a nap, then you keep assaulting."

As we dig, the enemy snipes.

Rockets crash. Mortars plunge. Heat cracks our lips. For target refer-ences, we name the nameless summits around us Titty Ridge, Monster Mountain, and so on. Here and there, a pulse of machine-gun fire sinks into our maturing outpost. The muj are firing at maximum range and none of it is terribly accurate. The issue is regularity. Every day we are in contact, some days three or four times. You throw enough munitions at a small area and your statistical chances are much improved.

It is three in the afternoon and I am heading for the shower, an open-air plywood stall. Inside is a bucket with holes in it, held up by parachute cord. Beside the stall is a cistern with river water. The way this works is you fill the bucket with icy river water, hoist it over you, and suck in breath as cold cleanses your filth.

I scramble uphill, wearing flip-flops and a towel over one shoulder. The *snap* of a round takes me by surprise. A second later comes the *pop* of the rifle. The bullet, traveling at supersonic speed, is well ahead of the report. I am caught unprepared, no armor or gun, and haven't thought of where to run if fired upon. I charge for the shower, remember it's made of plywood, then veer left, falling in my flip-flops before ducking behind a tree. I take a few hard pants, assess the tree as too thin—no more hiding behind skinny trees—and run for a boulder, my sandals flapping. *Snap*. In comes another round. I veer again and succeed mainly in running in a desperate circle, losing a flip-flop, tripping over my towel, and splitting my chin. Cowering behind a thicker tree, I picture the sniper laughing at me. Enraged, I get up and stomp to the shower and get in. I yell at the sniper, "It's shower day."

The sniper is an opportunist, and in the following days, he takes shots at a squad filling Hescos beside the LZ, a soldier stretching concertina wire, and another wrenching on a Humvee, who catches it in the chest and must be evaced. Our snipers have trouble getting a bead on the enemy sniper because he varies timing and locations. Sometimes he shoots at dawn, sometimes dusk. Sometimes he shoots from Titty Ridge, sometimes from Monster Mountain.

The company first sergeant frets over our safety inside the wire. His name is Combs. We call him *Puffy*, as in Puff Daddy Combs, though First Sergeant is not Black and would die in place if he ever heard hip-hop. In any case, Puffy decides we are too exposed, so everyone will wear armor at all times, unless we are in one of the newly erected canvas tents, which are made of canvas. We will wear full armor to eat, work, shit, patrol, walk to the shower (he is glaring at me), dig, pull guard, check the oil level in a truck, and for all meetings at company. What did I miss? And I am supposed to set a good example for the Boys.

* * *

In our low-tech war, the key to victory is aggressive patrolling. A static unit invites disaster on itself (see lectures on defense). We must prevent the enemy from moving freely and massing his forces. If we are lucky, we will get the drop on them. To be of value in this campaign, I must lead patrols to kill muj. Any slapdick can sit in a bunker.

One morning, my platoon serpentines in the stream bottom, trooping south to search Darbart. On both sides, the stream banks rise sheer. Orchids grow in the weeps between rocks. Thorny shrubs blossom over us, branches hanging like banners, obscuring our field of vision. There is only a gasp of blue sky above. The terrain is ideal for an enemy ambush, and I am hyperalert.

From up ahead comes the chirp of women's voices. Laughter? *I didn't know they did that here.* And gossip, well, it sounds the same in every language. Our point man, Correll, raises a hand to signal halt. I jog forward and join him at the head of the column, where we push aside branches to see a dozen women in gowns sitting at the river's edge. Their hawklike faces are exposed. Some have legs dipped in the river. Vases, buckets, and washboards are scattered about. One of the women is lithe. She sports long black hair and eyes like fire. She is womanly and slender, but there is nothing soft about her. Here is my own wife, Elizabeth.

Correll, Mr. Bombs-and-Bullets, grabs my shoulder and shakes. "Sir, I said, do you want to go around?"

Ideally, a patrol moves without being seen. Stealth is the reason we are wiggling over the stream bottom, rather than along the village connector trail or the jeep road. I study the neck of rock flanking us, which the gun teams would have to climb using hands and feet. That or we double back and lose an hour. The practical choice is to blow right past the laundry party. "Move out." We emerge from cover and press ahead. Maybe the women will hang out. Maybe we will have a tender moment with them, the ghosts we never see.

I'm really a nice guy.

Correll is within ten feet of the women when they see us. The beautiful one stops cold. Pretending she is my wife, I smile at her. She flings a scarf over her face. They all go silent, as if flipped into mute by the same switch. Then they run, sandals clapping against their feet, vases and buckets in hand, water sloshing onto the rocks as they disappear into the willows.

Correll says, "Did you see that hottie? Shit, sir. Too bad she's gonna rat on us."

"Step it out," I tell him. We go another kilometer along the stream before my walkie-talkie bleeps with enemy radio chatter. It is vague enough that I cannot make any decisions from it. The muj want to attack. That much I can tell. Adrenaline pulses through my tissue. My body is a drawn bow. I can hear the bugs.

Enemy fire bursts from the rocks, about three hundred meters left, on the brow above Darbart. Bullets geyser the water just ahead. I whirl left and blast on semiauto. The Boys jump for cover, and everyone has a pull. Remembering my job, I key the radio, ordering the 81 mm mortars to shell the heights above. I call for white phosphorus—or Willie Pete—the mutant brother of napalm.

Kilpatrick's machine-gun team pounds down the trail, ammo belt jangling. I say, "Yo, Kil, there, there," pointing to a flat-topped boulder. Kil cuts left, climbs to it, and jams down the bipod. His 7.62 fire echoes in the river bottom. The sonic pressure beats on my good ear. The bad ear whistles. I jam in an earplug. Kil's face becomes a rictus. He doles out a belt of ammo before his assistant gunner can clip on the next one.

White phosphorus mortars dive in. The explosions are a hundred white streamers that melt holes in rocks, trees, and bone. The soundtrack to this fight is high-pitched ringing.

The captain breaks onto the radio. "Three-six, there's an Apache inbound, call sign Reaper. Two minutes."

We are lucky today. An AH-64 Apache had been escorting a medical chopper down the Pech River. The Apache was less than ten kilometers away when the shooting began. Soon comes the distant thump of its rotors. Enemy machine guns trickle off. The muj have heard the rotors and are making for cover.

The radio bleeps. I crank the volume. "This is Reaper," says the Apache pilot. "Mark your position with panels. Advise how you'll mark targets." The Apache swoops into the river cut.

I tell him, "Ground force marked with VS-17. Confirm visual." I display a neon-orange panel the size of a baby blanket.

He confirms.

I say, "Marking targets now with green smoke."

"Copy," he says.

Our grenadiers lob green smoke. It plumes on the high points. The Apache loosens two rockets that tear over the river before exploding in a shower of fiery tendrils. The Apache banks and comes back. The trees beneath quiver in the rotor wash. The pilot reports, "I've got multiple pax moving south from your smoke."

"Engage," I say. "Engage."

The pilot strafes them with his bushmaster chain gun then launches more rockets, *whish, whish, whish*. The detonations, masked by terrain, sound far away. Soon a column of smoke climbs over the ridge. The pilot reports, "Target destroyed. Enemy casualties in the draw to your southeast. Reaper going off station."

Enemy casualties. *Bang a gong*. I remember we must search the dead for intelligence, which sullies my elation. We call this search a battle damage assessment. The platoon reforms and heaves upstream to a footbridge, which oscillates as we stomp across. We dogleg and march past a cataract, then struggle up a drainage hemmed in by soaring ridges. Sweat has soaked my uniform through. My eyes burn with it as we come upon a field of tumbled boulders. Explosions have blackened some of the rocks. We spread out, balancing between boulders, going beneath some.

A smell like burned bacon draws me to a splotch of hillside. I pass a burning tree. Coals crunch under my boots as I scout east. Cigrand trails about thirty yards back, his radio antennae flapping as he scrabbles. Pointing right, I tell him to keep on a different line so we can cover more ground.

I look down for my next boot placement. That is when I find it—or rather, him.

At my feet there's a head wedged between rocks.

No body, just a head, face up at the sky. The jaw is hanging as if he had been screaming at the helicopter when it killed him. Viscera is smeared around the head. Half the face is missing, his eyeballs melted. His teeth are visible and likewise their sharp roots in his jawbone.

Already I am sure this image will remain with me forever and ever. My culture has fed me images of warriors lying nobly in death. This exposure is far from it. The enemy dead are vermin. We have exterminated them, reduced them to parts. And this is war. I am not supposed to fight fair. If someone shoots a pistol at you, you fire back with a bazooka. You kill your opponent in spectacular ways. You kill him ten times over. If you want to win, you never fight fair.

I search the girding boulders, finding no body. His friends must have carried the rest of him off. There is nothing more to see here. I turn back and link up with Cigrand.

Seeing me, Cigrand asks, "Three-six, you all right?"

"Yeah."

"You find anything?"

"No."

As we return to camp, the sun dives and the valley turns cinder. We follow the river trail, then cut a hillside and catch the jeep road. The moon-dust we raise while marching produces hacking coughs. Our canteens are dry, uniforms filthy. A black lens rises in the east. What emerges in me is a creeping guilt about the gunfight, like I've organized the killing of despicable, poor guerrillas with a $6 million helicopter. I wonder how this experience will be useful in the rest of my life. The thought leads me nowhere worth going. Before long I'm pondering how I might look if killed on the battlefield—the noble death-pose atop a hill, hands locked to my rifle, or like the man we killed today, unrecognizable, in a gully with scorpions, my skull smoking and eyeballs melted.

We trundle into the wire. The Boys shed gear on their cots in the tent. First squad reports for guard on the outpost perimeter while the rest of the Boys lounge outside in a cranny of sandbags, seeing to their feet and refilling magazines. Their shirts are wet, and they are slat-ribbed from endless labor. Mail Bird came during our patrol, and a sergeant from company headquarters brings up a yellow mailbag and drops it for the Boys. At once they rip into it and divvy up packages. Patterson holds up a long, narrow box for his team leader, Correll, and asks, "What's this?"

"That's probably my knife," says Correll. "Told my mom the exact specs for it: four-inch blade, matte black, serrated. 'Bout time she got it ordered. You gotta have the right knife. A bayonet ain't worth a shit unless you're doing a charge. And it's gotta be matte. Can't have shiny metal out here. Hell, I've seen a watch face catch sun from a mile off."

Correll opens the box, digs into wrapping paper, and lifts out a sword. Thing is shiny chrome, hilted, and almost takes two hands to wield.

Patterson goes, "Your mom bought you Excalibur."

From across the tent, Berben, the grenadier, exclaims, "Sarr, you gotta kill someone with that."

The yellow mailbag will carry our outgoing mail, so I pen a letter to Elizabeth:

Babe, I was just staring at the picture you sent me, the one where you look sad. I like it when you look sad. I'm in the Korengal now. My dudes are good dudes. Before the army they were delinquents and hooligans. Those types are usually tough fuckers. I would never want to go to war with Boy Scouts. There is this one machine gunner, Kilpatrick. He is 6'3" and skinny, with red hair. Very Irish lookin'. He used to be a drug addict before he joined. Every time shit goes down, this dude lets it go on the M240B. It's the most beautiful sound cuz we have the rate of fire turned up on the guns, and his string of tracers, which come out every five rounds, looks like a laser beam. Anyhow, Kil just sprays everything, and it's confusing cuz I see tracer rounds goin' everywhere, and I ask him if he sees muzzle flashes or the RPG poof and dust, and he is like, "I'm just shootin', sir," and I'm like, Okay, well, at least he is shootin'. So then I tell him where to fire. He is in the zone, and it's loud, and deep down he is a killer and that makes him special. There's something hypnotic about machine-gun fire. I don't know if that's a strange thing to say. I'm not trying to sound cool or crazy or whatever. I love my job. I love you. Write me back something dirty. And send more pictures of you, and cigarettes, and tell me what's happening in the hood.

          —R

* * *

The fury of summer is upon us. I will lead the platoon on an incursion south. The mission is to search the bullet-blistered hamlet of Donga. Speed is a weapon, so today we will go light. I carry a compass, map, chest armor, helmet, bleeder kit, water, and ammo. In the duffel bag under my cot I have stashed gloves, knee and elbow pads, crotch and shoulder armor, neck armor, ballistic eye protection, a hand-held GPS, a throat-mike for radio, a bayonet, and a pistol, which weighs 2.6 pounds and has a max effective range of thirty-five yards. Now kitted up, I jump a few times to ensure my gear rides the way I want.

    My platoon forms up and leaves at 0300, needing the full two hours before first light. We cruise the road, then cut down to a shepherd's trail and follow it as it rolls across the valley's west wall. When we get to the village fringe, we kneel in corn terraces, catching our wind before the push. "All squads move out."

We spring from the corn and charge past cracked mud hovels with attached barns. Up we go, clomping over rock, hands locked to rifles. Dirty children flee down alleys. We flush chickens and goats. It is farm sounds and smells in this village. Sewage runnels the paths between houses. Squads radio from cordon positions. "First set." "Third set." I ascend a ladder, then a neck of rock, which dumps me out near the top of the village. At last, we gain the high ground. With the cordon in place, we start into the houses, clearing from top to bottom.

The mission is a knock and search, meaning I am coming in, but I'll be polite about it. Going house to house, we find only black-toothed old women. One of these fossils cracks open her door and out of the breach flows the cool dark of her stone habitat. The woman's hands are desiccated, her eyes defiant. She shrieks at me. "No. You can't come in. No men here. No weapons."

I ask, "Where's your man?"

Tell us, you wench, so we can kill him.

She says he has gone up the mountain with the goats. In the next house, a woman says her husband is in Pakistan. Another says the men are all working in the lumberyard, which we have seized as our outpost. We are supposed to be nice to the locals, which means not smashing every door and bouncing women off the wall, so at one house, when a woman refuses to let us in, we climb in a back window and toss the place for weapons and fighters.

What bothers me is that many of the houses are dry holes. No one is home. There is simple furniture, cooking ware, and firewood, all signs of occupancy, but no people. We search and move on, finding a half-dozen more houses with abandoned possessions. It dawns on me that the Afghans are fleeing the valley.

* * *

We have crossed a geographic line that amounts to striking a match to this place. The next few weeks we range the hills in constant gunfire, crawling, fighting, and scaling. Machine guns call cadence. We forage for water and food. Our uniforms and faces look to be graphite. Electrical storms build black towers overhead. We drop gear and march on bruised feet. Combat distills us. We shed fat, then muscle. We shave our heads to ward off lice.

We shoot and bleed and die. We hit Chichal and Qualagal, chasing an al-Qaeda leader known as Objective Indian, a top commander that has long eluded the coalition, and who reportedly directs the ground war in the Korengal and Pech River Valleys. A flurry of raids and airstrikes gets us no closer to Objective Indian. More men fall. I am drunk on no sleep. We smoke in daylight and dip at night. Tobacco is a flimsy consolation in this war, where the fighting is personal. The enemy has a face, a name. Every day we hear the same muj commanders on the radio. There is Sleepy Muj, Grumpy Muj, and Jumpy Muj. Another yells at his men, tells them they are slow and weak. Another sings battle hymns terribly. When we hear Arabic and Chechen voices on the net, the enemy fire is disciplined.

The enemy contests everything. On the radios they speak of repelling invaders from their home. What is home to them is battlefield to me. Their valley is stamped in my brain. With eyes closed, I can pivot this three-dimensional image to see the trail we will take to the ambush and danger areas along the way. Every draw, hill, and creek is known. Without glancing at a map, I call for artillery strikes and medevac choppers. Strangest of all, I begin taking pride in our killing. That's not to say we're cutting off ears for necklaces. Mine is a quiet pride, one that comes from tapping the instinct of all warriors who have preceded me.

* * *

Corpus is fun. I went with my mom to the bingo. And my dad took my car to get repainted and to fix a dent I made this week by running into a tree—oops. I wish you could drive me around. I got a job at Sunseekers Tanning Salon. One of the sisters that co-own the salon is married to Art Gonzalez. Do you remember that fool with da lisp? He still dresses like he did in high school, a polo shirt and slacks, or jeans with a braided belt—yikes! And always the puka-shell necklace. He's a nice guy but he needs a fashion intervention.

PS: I love to think about you suckin' my tits when I touch myself.

—E

* * *

Sex by mail aside, it feels splendid to hear people's names, people that are not here, and to imagine my wife at leisure. Right now, in this valley, it seems there is no other place. I am here. I have always been here. My age, mother's first name, and the street I grew up on all escape me. Everything before seems lost to oblivion, and nothing is true beyond these mountains. All I need is a letter from Elizabeth to know there are good people and beautiful things, and this is not forever.

On patrol, we fire M14s from ridgeline to ridgeline. The M14 is a .308-caliber weapon, perfect in form and function. In a single shot, it has the range and accuracy of a sniper rifle, and when switched to full-auto, the firepower of a machine gun. At 44.3 inches in length, the M14 is cumbersome on the urban battlefield. It is perfect, however, for the long-range fights of Eastern Afghanistan. We give an M14 to the best in each squad, the dude who can shoot, the dude we know will blast off in a gunfight. Carrying an M14 becomes a point of pride for the Boys. You see a combat infantry platoon, you don't talk shit, especially not to the devils with M14s.

Occasionally, we get confirmed kills, like the night we spot armed fighters three klicks south of the outpost. In the optic of a thermal sight, the fighters appear glowing red against a purple-black mountainside. From a tripod in Observation Post Three, we fire a wire-guided missile designed to destroy Soviet tanks. In a half second the warhead crosses three kilometers and explodes in a white fireball. I scream, "*Yaaa!*" to exercise the growing beast in me. A curtain of smoke lingers. We dispatch a squad to comb for bodies. They find a puddle of a man, and, in the goo, a pair of PVS-14 night-vision goggles, the same model as our own. The enemy has technology, a fact most disconcerting. After that, we use our lasers and blinking strobes only when necessary. When it's dark, it's dark.

Now, in the dark, I have time to think, and I think that if I could see the future, I'd be braver. And that gets me thinking we can be many things in a single fight, brave and cowardly and bold and bumbling, especially if the shooting drags on for a bit. And if you like a guy, you remember the good he did in a fight, and if you don't like him, you remember the bad, and none of it is fair and that's beyond me.

What makes this all so hard is that anything can happen at any moment. Embracing it is delicate. A combat leader who overthinks the gravity of his situation will burn out. On the other hand, the enemy will outwit a man who does not take it seriously. Thinking for forty-three men is exhausting; a mission involves a million individual and collective decisions. Which way do we flank? How much water to bring? Should we split up by the river? How do we climb this part? Left or right around the tree? Is the prisoner lying?

All these decisions must be framed with a combat lens. Any of these decisions can get us killed. Worst case is I get my entire platoon wiped out. *Did you hear about that one lieutenant?* No one wants to be *that guy*, the one the cadre at Fort Benning sneer at in the never-ever-do-this lecture. Patrol after patrol, I learn to stop staring at decisions. Be cool and make a call. The worst thing is being indecisive.

The Boys are indolent at the outpost, lazing in the patchy shade of hollies between shifts of sentry duty. In the platoon tent, I notice the Boys touching each other, though at first, not in sexual ways. They hug and put arms around one another and sit close together, very close. When under extreme stress, it is normal to crave physical contact, and after all, there are deep bonds between us. Two privates, clowning around, are touching each other's faces and gazing into each other's eyes. Another is photographing them. Everyone laughs. Another two, both having serious girlfriends, lie together on a cot and take up an intimate position, as shy lovers might. They pose for a picture. They get up laughing as if they didn't mean it. They might have meant it.

No one does push-ups, weights, or jujitsu. Calories are stored for fighting. We strip more gear off our kits. We drop grenades, carrying two at most, for the engagements have yet to be within grenade range. Ounces make pounds. We take the gangster grips off our rifles. Of course it sucks because the grip looks badass. It is handy in Iraq, where one has to pilot his barrel around tight corners and up stairwells. Out here it is best to lay the barrel on something to steady the shot: a rock, a downed bough, the top of a wall. Standing to fire the M4, one hand on the gangster grip, is mere bluster. We are here to kill bad guys.

By August there's been no whiff of tribal capitulation, so we close the jeep road into the valley to isolate them and cut off enemy resupply. The remaining locals fulminate. They say the old ones are starving. The children are crying. I say it's simple: join the others who have left. Our strategy is to separate the enemy from the population by encouraging the population to leave. Anyone who remains is muj. *Pretty simple.* Our message to the tribe: *Fuck you, big time.* We set a night curfew too. No skunking around in the dark. You fire up a flashlight on a hill and we will make it rain artillery. Plus Correll has a sword.

This is total war.

Energy and optimism are crucial, I remind myself. What keeps me going is that I believe muj numbers are finite. We can kill our way to victory. Battalion estimates the muj at company strength, equal to our own numbers. And if they just have 150 men, then it is possible to kill them all. Secretly, I keep score with notches on the trunk of a holly tree above the LZ. So far I count thirty. That's for the company.

7

THE BEAST

KORENGAL VALLEY, AFGHANISTAN

SUMMER 2006

If I sound a little distant on the phone, I'm sorry. Most of the time I got a lot of shit goin' on, and I'm in a tiny corner of a tent with two other phones. So, it's hard to be intimate and talk to you the way I want in front of my Boys. They would think we were crazy if they heard some of our conversations. I like to think of us driving around and getting coffee. I'll drive you to get coffee anytime. Sorry I used to say no, that we had the same shit at the house. When I get home, just give me a big hug, babe, and a kiss on the cheek. Let me relax on you, lay my head in your lap and stuff. Remember that. Okay? I'm sorry about a lot of things. I love the pictures you sent, but your letters are not long enough, neither are your emails. I need your words. What are you doing? What is more important? I want at least two paragraphs when you write.

—R

* * *

My shrapnel wounds are pink divots now. Since returning from Germany, I have led increasingly difficult missions. Captain McKnight has been pleased. So has Colonel Cavoli. They have prepared letters of recommendation for my submission packet to the Ranger Regiment. When I had told Cavoli

I'd like to try for Second Ranger Battalion, he said, "I know Kurilla, their commander. You know, it's all about who you know." His words left me buzzing. I cannot stop fantasizing about being a Ranger officer, a leader of commandos, a megawarrior.

The fact remains, that day is a long way from now. Out here, it does not matter who you know.

A new mission demands attention. It is a bold operation, and I am the main effort. In the last few months, our endeavor to build the outpost has grown perilous. The enemy has shot up helicopters bringing supplies. Rock slides and bombs festoon the jeep road, making ground resupply almost impossible, and we suspect the enemy is far more numerous than original estimates.

In company headquarters, Captain McKnight and I stand before an acetate map marked up with grease pencil. The captain flashes his laser pointer at the valley mouth while explaining, "To survive we have to open a ground route. The engineers have just built a bridge over the Pech River, here, at the fording site. Now we have to secure the road, our umbilical cord. Second Platoon will do this by driving it twice a day in Humvees, ferrying supplies to the outpost, and thus interdicting enemy operations on the road. Your mission, Three-six, is to seize Comersa Bandeh."

Comersa Bandeh commands the terrain over the road. If we hold the village, we can lock down eight kilometers of road, from the valley mouth all the way to the outpost. Watching a road is not a histrionic mission, but the good news is we will not be static. We will also patrol the eastern rise of the valley, setting ambushes, launching search-and-destroy missions. This array of duties could soak up a rifle company, even two. I will do it with thirty-five men, plus an attached squad of our battalion scouts, led by Sergeant Badman.

An officer with Ranger Regiment aspirations does himself no favors by arguing troop levels with command. So I say, "Roger that," and stuff five days of food and water into my pack, along with radio batteries, socks, a poncho, a woobie (a poncho liner), a bivy sack, and a camping pillow. For the gun teams I take seven hundred rounds of machine-gun ammo and other stuff that goes *bang*.

I do some math and round up. My ruck weighs 110 pounds. Shouldering it, I find it heavy on the right. I let it crash to the ground and redistribute. Close by, Cigrand is doing the same. He has everything I have plus the radio and other communications paraphernalia. He barely looks up to the weight.

Hours before the operation, a helicopter deposits Sergeant Langmesser and Sergeant Haff back in the valley. Langmesser is coming off weeks of bed rest and surgery. I tell him he can sit this one out. He looks at me like I'm an asshole.

Good man.

Haff, on the other hand, is returning from midtour leave, a full two weeks off. In the corner of the tent, the Boys gather round him. Haff speaks of a conquest at Bagram Airfield on his way out of country. The girl is a mechanic in the Air Force. As Haff recounts his exploits, the Boys lob questions:

"She got big titties, don't she, Sar'nt?"

"Oh, yeah. Torpedoes."

"And a nice soft ass, right, Sar'nt?"

"So soft."

"And blond hair? She's definitely a blond."

"Definitely."

"But, Sar'nt, you told me it was red."

"Oh, yeah, when the sun's on her, it's red."

"And what about down there? What color is it?"

"Shaved, of course."

The Boys all whistle. New spectators trickle into the gathered crowd.

"She likes it rough, don't she, Sar'nt?"

"Animal rough."

"And from behind?"

"After a few drinks."

"Oh, boy, Sar'nt. You gotta get us a picture."

"I will. I will."

* * *

In darkness and light rain, we begin marching down the jeep road for Comersa Bandeh, spaced at ten-yard intervals beneath spitting clouds and the stone visages in the hills. The rain hushes our bootfalls. We do not stop to rest. After four kilometers, the rain ceases and we follow a path down to the river.

We set a one-rope bridge, muscle across the channel and slosh into the terraces. The climb warms us. Progress is heavy. My rucksack, wet from the crossing, feels like a bank safe. The Boys are quiet, save the occasional rattle of arms and equipment. We do our best to hold formation. The terrain still breaks us into fragments. We lose each other. The Boys whisper as they navigate. *"This way." "Dead end." "Left or right?" "Wrong way."* We are never lost in a big way, only in small ways. Our movement is punctuated by bursts of cuss words. The Boys are silhouettes, no faces. By now I recognize them by their gaits. Cigrand with his choppy steps; Haff walking on his toes; Correll with his chest out, head on a swivel; and Patterson, a hunched slave to a bad vertebra.

The fuck is that?

South of our column, a gaggle of monkeys screams in the runt trees above the river, at each other and the rocks and the gibbous moon just beginning to pierce the thunderheads. As we climb, the monkeys keep screaming, and I suppose the valley has that effect on all life.

We keep on up the hill.

The captain is on the horn for me. He says, "Status."

"Climbing."

He says, "You're behind."

"Roger, sir."

"Go faster."

"Roger, sir."

"You don't want to assault a village in daylight."

"Roger, sir," I reply. "Just keep those mortars pointed this way. We'll make it."

"Roger. Attack Six out."

We battle more terraces and slippery rock. At one point, I stop and check the map. When I look up, I am alone. I hiss, "Cigrand," and get no response. Besieged by childlike fear, I charge ahead, crashing through hollies and thorny shrubs and emerging, face slashed and bleeding, branches hanging from the camo netting in my helmet, to find Cigrand and first squad wrestling up a crag. "Just checking the map," I tell Cigrand. "That is the way. Well done and keep at it." At 0300 the moon shows us the final ramps to the village. An hour later we take our objective, finding no resistance and feeling thoroughly let down.

We commandeer a baked-mud house with six rooms and expansive views of the road, spread out on its earthen floors, and maintain 50 percent security. One room I designate as command post. It has a ceiling of timber and dried grass and feels like it could take a shelling.

A steel morning begins. A snake of fog hangs over the river. The monkeys have screamed themselves to sleep. Cigrand joins me for reconnaissance. We weave the slope above the house. To the north, a thorny divide blocks the valley mouth from view. I reference the topographic map. To get a full view of the road, we will have to set an observation post north of the divide. The post will be isolated, though within a fifteen-minute hike. About 0700 I take Haff's squad and a machine gun across the hillside and over the divide.

Obsessed with the tactical, I have failed in self-care, a common problem in field leadership. I skipped a sock change after the river crossing. Now my feet are raw. I can feel the wrinkled skin on my heel tearing. And I should have had a bite in the village. There is a hot feeling in my stomach, and hunger has me dizzy. Thoughts are cloudy. *You know better.*

The valley mouth appears. Far below is the road, a brown ribbon beside the river. A short hunt for a position reveals a fin of shale flanked by trees and boulders. The spot is ideal. I leave the details of squad and machine-gun emplacement to Sergeant Haff, then move out of sight to collapse against a tree, where I whisper motivations about when this is all over. I finish by imagining all the hamburgers I have ever eaten. It is a lot of hamburgers.

* * *

Each day in Comersa Bandeh, we launch ambush patrols onto the high ground above the village. My squads are short on men, and with simultaneous missions, the most we can muster for an ambush is seven to eight bodies. The patrols double as reconnaissance, mapping goat trails and paths used by woodsmen and shepherds, though we find no one in the hills. All this time we watch the road. Second Platoon, led by Lieutenant Barclay, uses Humvees to make resupply missions to the outpost. They complete a handful of missions without enemy resistance.

Though we are not ready to scream victory, I have a growing sense of success. Our operation has repaired the umbilical cord, and the enemy has not mustered an attack. I attribute this to my platoon's aggressiveness. By day six, we exhaust our supplies of food, water, and radio batteries. Second Platoon arranges a supply run to us, hiring Afghans from the Pech River Valley to carry everything. It buys us four more days. In our mud command post, Cigrand conjures up his hometown in Iowa. He tries to convince me that small-town Iowa is cool, cornfields are beautiful on a dewy morning, farm girls are hot, deer hunting is fun, and a hunter should cold camp if he's serious about stalking.

I remain unconvinced on all accounts.

* * *

It is six in the evening. Far to the south comes the tap of dozens of machine guns. The enemy is whipping the outpost. The thunderclap of explosives and mortars bowls down the valley. Assault rifles crackle. The barrage is volcanic, unlike anything I have heard. Cigrand, Siercks, and I stare at the radio and imagine. At the outpost the radioman estimates over two hundred fighters have surrounded them. Siercks rocks back and forth with this news. Bullets fly in droves. An enemy mortar starts a fire in the perimeter. An RPG splinters a hooch. Bullets pepper the tents. The enemy inflicts a handful of casualties on our sentries and the Afghan Army unit just flown in as reinforcements.

Siercks says to me, "Who are these dudes?"

The attack has us rattled. In the Kush outlands, the only way to learn about the primitive enemy is to fight them. We have just learned that we are far outnumbered, and worse, my platoon is off the company tether. A series of hillocks and folds, combined with distance, block us from receiving direct support from the outpost. The slopes above us are broken and near vertical. Seamed by intermittent creeks and shale ribs, the mountainside offers dozens of routes for the enemy. It is not lost on me that our current position is less than two miles from the helicopter wreckage from Operation Red Wings. The more we patrol these lines, the more sure I am that we do not own this ground. Our position is not as defensible as the outpost. Our advantage is stealth. The enemy does not know exactly where we are.

The least likely window of enemy attack is late at night. In this interval I permit myself a respite from tactics. There are dates to work toward, goals for survival, the next letter from Elizabeth, a chance for internet access in company headquarters. Little consolations keep the endless labor bearable. Rest and relaxation is the big prize, as it means a trip home. Once during the tour, each of us gets a plane ticket to anywhere in the States and two weeks off. I have elected to go on R&R in October. Imagining that time, I order up a scene of my old lady waist-deep in the Gulf of Mexico. It does not come easy, like the little things: Elizabeth snores when she sleeps, mouths the words when she reads, and always keeps a cache of essential oils in her purse, ready for deployment on any of my ailments. Important, too, she could go pro in eye rolling.

Memory latches on to little things.

The date that most inspires me is spring 2007, when we will return home. Some of the Boys count down. Some count up. Some don't keep count, saying twelve months in the field is too much to track, and dare look no further than the next mail drop. But we all feel the seasons—the swollen rivers and freezing nights of spring, then the rising heat of summer, when the hills brown and we bake in our armor.

* * *

We are ten days into the mission when the captain summons me to the radio. Second Platoon, he says, is running a convoy next day, bringing supplies and two medics to the outpost. One of the medics is a female. Her name is Wakkuna Jackson.

Jackson will be the first female soldier in the valley, surrounded by 150 sex-starved infantrymen. I make a note to worry about this later. For now we have intel saying an enemy platoon is staging in a *bandeh* three kilometers above us, about three thousand feet higher. The enemy aims to attack Second Platoon's convoy. My orders are to attack the enemy before they get the chance.

Tactical demand exceeds supply. I do not have enough men to watch the road and mount an assault, for which army doctrine says I should have a three to one numeric advantage. Thirty men is the most I can muster, which makes it one to one. If we go in the dark and hit the village at 0200, maybe we'll catch them sleeping. That is our best shot at this thing. I order Haff's entire squad, and Kil's machine gun, to collapse the northern observation post and join us. No one will watch that stretch of road tonight. I do not tell the captain, as I do not need him meddling in how I deploy the platoon.

We gather at the house and ready for assault. By now the Boys know of the convoy and its passengers. I overhear a ribald exchange:

"I heard there's a girl coming in."

"Yep. Black girl. She's from battalion. Got skin like a Hershey bar."

"Goddamn, I can't wait."

"You fucking racist. You don't like Black people."

"Fuck you, man. I'm gonna ask her to marry me."

They ask me, "Is that true, sir, there a girl on the convoy?"

"Yes," I say. "She's a medic."

"Oh boy, we better protect her then."

Sergeant Patterson breaks in. "This whole platoon is about to go on sick call."

We move after dark and gain the village at about 0300. The Boys wreck the place. No one is home, though the rooms have signs of recent activity: ash in the stoves, trash, footprints. This is another *bandeh*, a shelter for shepherds during grazing season, and without obvious signs of the enemy, there's nothing further to do. I report, "Nothing to report," and we make it back to Comersa Bandeh by morning. Siercks tells the Boys, "Smoke 'em if you got 'em."

Everyone has 'em.

I plod into my command post in the mud house and refill canteens.

Haff marches his squad across the hillside and reestablishes the northern observation post just as Barclay's convoy rounds the spur at the valley mouth. Four Humvees rumble up the road. The gunners swivel their turrets.

The convoy draws toward us, covering two kilometers, before fire and smoke swallow the lead Humvee. The harsh bang of an explosion bounces between the valley walls. The trailing vehicles halt, unable to pass the first vehicle, which remains aflame. From the hills above the road comes the tack of machine guns, then streaking RPGs. The convoy is pinned.

What is happening on the road is not action; it is failure, for me and the platoon. What emerges is bloodlust. This has nothing to do with my job. The enemy is making fools of us. I grab Cigrand, "*Go, go, go!*" and we charge out of the house and race across the hillside toward my northern position. My heart booms in my head. Coming to a stretch of naked hillside, I pause and scan uphill, then radio Haff, "Three-one, this is Three-six. We'll be coming up from the village. Hold your fire."

Gunfire almost drowns Haff's response, "They're right above us, Three-six. A shit ton."

"Roger. Don't shoot us." I examine the hillside before me and then turn to Cigrand. "I'll go first, cover me. Once I'm halfway, you come on. Don't get too far behind."

Cigrand blows a few hard breaths and says, "Roger."

I spring up and dash across the open, pumping my rifle in one hand. Halfway, I twist around to ensure Cigrand is following. He is thirty yards behind, radio antennae swaying over his helmet.

Gunfire erupts from a scrap of woods two hundred yards above. Bullets zing by my nose. The enemy is shooting downhill, and their first shots are high. I drop to my belly. More shots. Turning right. Cigrand falls then tumbles down a steep wedge of rock and disappears. *Please no!* The suddenness of his fall has me sure he is hit. I yell, "Cigrand," and turn uphill, shoulder my rifle, and spray half a magazine. The enemy answers with an RPG that hisses by and detonates in a tree. Shrapnel saws the air.

Cigrand raises his head and grins, his teeth white against his dirt-smeared face. "I'm good."

"Quit fucking around," I yell. "Get up here."

Rolling back toward the enemy, I burn through the rest of a magazine to cover for Cigrand, who clomps up and drops beside me and starts shooting. Behind us, the jeep road streaks across the opposite slope. From here the view of it is perfect. I judge Cigrand and I have hit the same linear ambush on the convoy. It is much bigger than I first thought. The enemy has laid into more than a mile of hillside. The attack on Barclay is only the beginning. The enemy, however, had not expected my platoon within rifle shot. When we join in, we force the enemy into retreat.

Clarity is a new feeling for me in combat. In the early fights, I was reacting to survive, my thinking scattered at best. This time there is no ivy in my mind. I radio Siercks, "We've got a linear ambush running from Omar to somewhere near you. Take everyone and get uphill about three hundred meters. You do it fast and they'll run right into you."

He says, "Roger."

I tell him, "I'm linking up with Three-one. We'll advance from north to south."

Armor smacking my stomach, I slog across the remaining hillside and link up with Haff. The valley is a farrago of shooting and explosions. Down below, the Humvee hit by the bomb is still aflame. At this range, the soldiers in the convoy are figurines; one races up to the Humvee carcass, his legs like scissors. Over the radio, he reports, "We've got KIAs. Two-six is fucked up. Two-six is fucked up." Then he charges into the flames. Seconds later he emerges, dragging 2-6 (Barclay) from the vehicle. He bulls back into the fire and grabs the driver, Private Bratland, and drags him out.

Jackson, the female medic riding in the back seat, has burned to death, along with Specialist Chris Sitton, who was riding beside her. In the second vehicle, Specialist Robert Drawl, the turret gunner, took a bullet in the head, killing him instantly.

I grab Haff, saying, "About four hundred yards back, we ran into more of this ambush. They broke contact south. Leave your packs here. We're chasing these fuckers down." Haff orders his men onto their feet, and we advance. The lead team moves abreast to maximize frontal firepower. Veering south, we pursue the enemy uphill, spewing suppressive fire as we go. I am desperate to close the distance. We come upon a dry watercourse that gashes the hillside. Thick trees hug it, making perfect cover for a withdrawal. I tell Haff to follow it. The grenadiers thump M203s into scrub hollies to discourage any rear guard for the enemy. Gunfire breaks out a kilometer south of us.

Siercks gives a clipped report, "Contact."

The machine gun with Siercks works the hillside. Tracers skip. I hear the natter of an enemy PKM machine gun returning fire. Siercks's group has hit another part of the ambush line. Judging from the sporadic exchange, the enemy is still breaking off. Siercks reports again, "We hit them, probably flank security. What's your pos?"

The fight has my platoon dispersed. By now we have a Dustoff inbound for casualties. An Apache will be escorting the Dustoff. I want to use the Apache but cannot if we are scattered. I say to Siercks, "We're four hundred meters north of you. There's an Apache coming on station. Stay where you are. Coming to you."

Ten minutes later we link up in a finger of woods, just as the Apache buzzes into the valley. With tracers, I direct the Apache higher into the watercourse, all of me throbbing for revenge. The pilot begins with the chain gun, firing just as he passes overhead. The sound is like a runaway buzz saw. Four-inch casings rain down, clattering off our helmets and the rocks. Our forward observer, Specialist Castiglione, jerks then falls down, yelling and slapping at his back. A searing casing has wedged itself against his bare skin. *Quit being a bitch.*

Hellfire missiles are mounted on the Apache's wings. I direct two into a ravine ahead, guessing the enemy is using it for retreat. Not until the detonations are in full bloom do I realize we are too close. The very air seems to be sucked away, and for a few seconds, only the ground and space are left. The Boys get to their feet. The Apache breaks off, and I switch to mortars, keeping the rounds five hundred yards at the fore, and as many feet above. We keep up the advance. The forest is a ruin of skeleton pines. There are downed trunks riddled with bullets. We skirt tree fires. Powder fumes are bitter on my tongue. Embers crunch beneath our boots, but we have found no bodies. I am not sure we are still on the enemy when the mortar team asks, "You still in contact?"

I say, "No."

Hearing this, the captain comes over the radio, asking, "They're gone?"

"Yes, sir."

"You were supposed to be watching the road. Second has three dead. Three."

"Sir, we only pulled off observation once, for the raid."

"You pulled off?"

"It was just one night. I needed bodies."

"I did not clear that. This happened on your watch. Attack Six out."

I smash my rifle buttstock against a stone, over and over. It was our mission to keep Second Platoon intact. I failed, and the enemy is gone. Revenge denied. And the captain's words were clear: he is prepping me for crucifixion. Dry-mouthed and low on ammo, we plunge downhill to provide security for the recovery of the destroyed Humvee. This is our atonement, watching the army wrecker lift the hulk from the crater. Burnt grease and oil memorialize the deaths. The enemy had supplemented the mine with a can of diesel fuel to melt everything and everyone, reminding me we shall kill each other in spectacular ways.

* * *

In the evening, we return to Comersa Bandeh. The Boys try laughing at the usual things, and when this does not work, silence sweeps over the village. A grave undertow pulls me down. I attempt a mental burial of the dead, which ends with their stiff arms protruding from shallow graves. Their fingers are claws. I ask what I could have done differently, which turns into machinations of redirected blame: the chain of command, the terrain, and the army are at fault. The war in Iraq has drawn too much focus from Afghanistan. The blame is on the secretary of defense, and for that matter, the president of the United States.

Having manufactured a sturdy excuse, I nod off.

Guilt is stabbing my gut. I wake with a jump, sure it is all my fault. I am the worst kind of buddy fucker. I rebuild the excuse, looking for ways to make it impregnable while monkeys scream beside the river. It is not just guilt that hectors me. This fight is not over. The enemy now knows my platoon holds ground on the east wall. Musing on the two-hundred-man attack on our outpost a few days earlier, I imagine a similar one on my own force, which produces fulsome fear, and then, a resurgence of my predictive power. Tonight the enemy is regrouping. Tomorrow the battle will resume right here at this house.

Certainty drives a reexamination of the surrounding terrain. Beneath a full moon, I dash around the village, scouting likely attack points and our own fields of fire, seeing things as the enemy might. When the reconnaissance is complete, I am sure of two attack positions: a sub-ridge right above us, and a knob five hundred meters east. I convince the captain to aim the outpost's two 81 mm mortars onto my two targets, which is no small achievement, given recent attacks on the outpost, as well as his anger with me.

At 0300 I dispatch the scouts to an ambush position eight hundred yards uphill, where they will watch a trail that leads to the sub-ridge. The scout sergeant, Badman, musters his eight men and departs. He calls in terse reports. "Rally point." "Ambush set." "Radio check." At seven in the morning, sunlight rushes down the west wall of the valley. Watching the line of day advance, my skin prickles with intuition. "I can feel 'em in my bad knee," as Ole Sarge used to say.

The radio squawks to life with activity at the outpost: supply reports, sentries rotating, a summary of enemy radio traffic in the night. I check our machine-gun positions, find them in good order, then return to the house, where I radio the outpost to ensure the mortars remain fixed on my targets. Cigrand boils water for coffee. I cannot summon an appetite.

The shooting starts around eight. Jumping for the radio, I kick over Cigrand's coffee, which he protests before firing at the coruscating hills. I call the mortars, "Fire TRP Six and Eight. Repeat. Fire TRP Six and Eight. Enemy troops in wood line." I lean into the doorless doorway and shoot. The enemy fires in cyclic mode, an attempt to overwhelm us. One of our M14 gunners, Specialist Fernando Robinson, is prone in a hillside position. Eye pressed into his scope, he spots a fighter running at a crouch, only the tops of his shoulders visible behind a rib of stone. Robinson takes a bead on a notch in the rib, where the fighter stops and levels his weapon.

Robinson fires and scores a hit, then yells, "Five-hundred-yard shot," as if we'd all been watching him.

The enemy infiltrated on a different trail, bypassing the scouts. Badman moves his M240B machine gun east and brings it into action, hitting the enemy flank. Within a minute, the first mortar shells smash into both enemy positions. I call, "Fire for effect." In comes a salvo of ten shells. Mushrooms of smoke and fire spring from the mountain. Remembering yesterday's burning vehicle, I switch to "Willie Pete." The mortar crews hang the shells, and seconds later call, "Splash." White streaks of five-thousand-degree liquid shower the mountainside. The destruction is ineffable.

The captain reports we have fixed wing inbound, so the mortars must stop firing. The two inbound planes are French fighter jets. The valley is too steep and tight for jet support; this will be a diversion. I protest, "Attack Six, I've got them. I've fucking got them. Turn the mortars back on." My violent fantasy is that I am about to kill everyone. These planes are ruining it.

The captain orders me, "Calm down, Three-six. You have control of the Fast Movers. Use them."

I make contact with the pilots, hearing broken English. Terrain disrupts our line-of-sight communication. The pilots circle at a thirteen-thousand-foot altitude, well above the valley, making laps half the size of the province. First, the pilots can't spot the smoke marking our positions. Then, they can't figure out which gully I'm telling them to bomb. I try relaying through our fire-support officer, which is no better. The pilots say they will not fire unless they are 100 percent sure of the exact disposition of all friendly and enemy forces on the ground.

"Goddamn you," I say, "That's not even a thing."

Their profession is one of risk-aversion. In a sterile cockpit beyond enemy reach, there is no need to do anything that makes you uncomfortable. At last the captain breaks in, telling me, "I'll call them off. There's an A-10 inbound, one of ours, two minutes out."

There must be an airshow today.

An A-10 Warthog streaks between the valley walls, tipping its wings to me as it skips over the village at three hundred miles per hour. The pilot bumps down to my radio frequency. I tell him, "We've got two enemy elements moving south, spread out. We'll mark targets with red smoke."

The pilot says he will use rockets. We launch smoke. The A-10 disappears for a few seconds, then crests the west wall of the valley and dives straight for the eastern rise, looking as if it will kamikaze into the mountain. Six rockets *whish* from the pods to end in red flames on the slope. The pilot blasts his chain gun. *Burrrrrrrr.* Bullets shear the forest. At the last moment, the pilot jerks the stick and barrel rolls toward the sun. We are all following the plane, necks craning as it gains altitude and clears the ridge.

Cigrand says, "Fucking badass."

I give the pilot another target, talking him onto a gully behind the rocky knob. The pilot says he'll drop a five-hundred-pound bomb. I say a five-hundred-pound bomb is a great idea. The scouts are still in position, and this bomb will land four hundred meters from their flank. I radio Badman to verify he is still where I think he is.

"Roger," Badman confirms. "Same location. Squad's accounted for."

"Good," I say. "Five-hundred pounders inbound. Keep your heads down."

Badman's voice is a few octaves higher than usual. "Danger close?"

I say, "Not danger close, but close."

The pilot calls, "Bomb released." The five-hundred pounder crashes into the mountain. The explosion blurs the form of the village and forest above. The mountain trembles. Dirt rains from the ceiling overhead. An anvil of smoke blots the sun. For a few seconds, our tracers seem to burn brighter.

I radio Badman again. "You still there?"

"Roger . . . uh . . . that was pretty close. We got hit with debris."

"I'll adjust south."

I aim for obliteration. *Burn, burn.* I direct another bomb south, just shy of Kandalay village. The A-10's twin engines roar as it banks and arrows west to disappear behind a nearby peak. Reappearing, it levels and streaks toward the target, passing so close I can read the pilot's name lettered below the cockpit. *Brrrrp. Brrrrrp. Brrrrp.* The chain gun tears a swath of forest to pieces. Trees fall. Cigrand yells, "Fuck you," to anyone caught in the path. The pilot circles and comes back around to release the second bomb. The mountain shudders. Flames lick the trees still standing.

The distant summits are smoky silhouettes. The pilot calls, "Targets destroyed," and flies toward the valley mouth. The rise above me is a black pall. Fire skips through the woods. The ringing in my ear is back. I am transcendent, the center of a Tesla sphere. Enemy radio chatter is frenzied and confused. One group is carrying four dead on litters. They speak of a dry creek. I guess which one and lay on the mortars, applauding myself. *Willie Pete on your heads.*

About then, Haff staggers through the doorway with eyes wide.

I snap, "Why aren't you with your squad."

He says, "They fucking shot me," and points to his arm. An enemy bullet entered at the elbow. Bone splinters protrude from the exit hole. Blood streams and spatters the dirt.

I tell him to sit, then yell out the window, "Doc!"

Doc runs in, flings off his medical pack, and goes to work.

Haff says, "It hurts."

I ask, "What happened?"

Haff rocks back and forth. "They caught me in the open, that terrace above the house. Must have been three machine guns firing at me alone. Aw shit, Doc. Be careful!" Haff goes on, "Rounds going everywhere. Shit hurt so bad. I had nowhere to go so I played dead . . . You're welcome."

"For what?"

"For me drawing all their fire."

* * *

After a Dustoff for Haff, I heap thanks on the captain for the air and mortars. The response time was lethal. We might win the war like this. The captain responds, "Battalion's worried about us getting overrun. They've been gathering assets."

Today we have killed a handful of muj. Their radio traffic reveals a dozen more wounded, and combined, this is a big win in our little war. In the afternoon, a bevy of tribesmen carry one of their own into the company outpost. A 7.62 round pierced the man's torso, just above the heart. Our medics commence treatment, handling the Afghan with the same skill and professionalism as they would one of our own. Our first sergeant summons a Dustoff to evacuate the man to Bagram Airfield.

Siercks scolds the Boys, "You see what happens when we wound bad guys."

Next day, the captain orders us back to the company perimeter. There have been attacks on the outpost and patrols heading south, plus the attack on the convoy, and now us. The enemy's ability to launch large attacks, in different locations, in spate, suggests their force may number near a thousand, more than quadrupling our own. The chain of command is whispering, *Overrun*.

Overrun. There is that word again. To us, it is a curse word, one we don't believe in, because at the platoon and company level, we are too proud to let ourselves believe the enemy could kill us all in one swoop. At the colonel level, having one's small units overrun is a career killer, so there is lots of incentive for avoiding it. And in the wake of such events, politicians go headhunting for generals, so no echelon of the military wants American Boys overrun.

We leave the village after dark, picking toward the river. My feet sting as we jump down between terraces. My mind is turbulent because the dead on the road insist on being remembered. What will happen when I face the captain? I recall his words, ". . . on your watch." I remember the gunner killed in the second Humvee, hit square in the forehead at five hundred yards, as if it were destined to be that way. A diamond bullet, I decide, one that had always been for him. I picture Barclay and his wife, Sierra, a lovely woman I met once. I cannot help imagining her chasing me with a hatchet; I'm running down a sewer pipe, splashing through shin-deep water, and she pursues with the hatchet, her teeth glistening like the blade.

Our bunkers appear first, then the outpost. Exploded sandbags and bullet-pocked Hesco walls gird the perimeter. As we cross the last hundred yards, the wind picks up, drying my neck and rustling fallen holly leaves. Dust swirls. Already it is hot. No one speaks. We drag ourselves into the perimeter. The captain is standing at the wire with hands locked on his hips. I freeze and summon courage.

When he sees me, the captain says, "There's my hero."

He slaps me on the back and walks beside me, smiling. "Good to have you back," he says. "You read them perfectly. Kicked their asses. Tell your platoon to drop gear and hit the chow tent. We've got hot breakfast for ya." He says nothing of the dead from Second Platoon. There is no more blame or anger. We speak of what is to come, and from this day on, I tell myself, *I'll die for the captain.*

8

CHEST CANDY

KORENGAL VALLEY

SUMMER 2006

Babe, if I were in the Karate Kid story, I would be one of those dudes from Cobra Kai dojo. They are all dickheads and shit. Not true but sort of true. You made me a good person, but I've been a dickhead for a long time. I regret it. I'm sorry for what I used to be. I was selfish. I'll be different when this is over.

It rains more now. Summer storms count as a shower. We have been fighting a lot. I don't know what else to talk about. In your last letter, you said Danny got selected for infantry. I wish he didn't. I know that's what he wants, but I just wish he didn't. Can't believe he's graduating. There's a war on, and he knows it.

A few letters ago I said machine-gun fire is beautiful. Do you remember? Hypnotic, that's the word I used. That was stupid. Wannabes say shit like that. I miss you. My electric razor broke; please send another Norelco with the flat head, and cigarettes. My midtour leave is in October. Can't wait to see you.

                                                    —R

                        * * *

In the following weeks, the jaws of war snap. Streaking metal finds men in tents and clots of trees, patrols wading the river and cresting ridgelines. Ours is a war of attrition. We lose a man here, a man there. Sometimes we fall in twos and threes. We trade bad days and good ones with the enemy, dying under heat lightning and beaming stars.

By September our company has had more casualties than any other in theater. In my platoon, we are nearing 50 percent. I do not know whether to be ashamed or proud. Causalities can be framed many ways: fighting intensity and enemy prowess, or poor leadership and tactical blundering.

Many casualties are from terrain. We have broken ankles and torn anterior cruciate ligaments. We have herniated discs in our spines. Even the captain falls off a cliff and shatters something, forcing six weeks of convalescence.

This is a shooting war, and many of our casualties are from bullets, which do things both incredible and random. Sometimes bullets pass through cleanly, and next day, the soldier is back in the fight. Sometimes bullets scoop. Sometimes they gouge. Sometimes a bullet chops off an entire limb. One bullet penetrates a guy's helmet at his forehead, follows the inside curve of the helmet, and exits at the back, leaving him with little more than a deep scratch.

One way or another, everyone becomes a casualty, from terrain, dysentery, lead, shrapnel, or too much action. And in the ashes, I am promoted to first lieutenant. I begin to take pride in my durability as a platoon leader. Many of my peers have become casualties or are rotated away from the field. Some have cracked up. Others have been fired, like one lieutenant who lost his pistol on patrol and spent a week with his platoon hunting for it. *I mean, seriously, dude, why are you even carrying a pistol out here?*

Energy and optimism, I remind myself. For the vast majority in the military, it takes a decades-long career to amass the kind of fighting experience I have. Many battalion and brigade commanders, even generals, have never been shot at, their careers built after Vietnam and before 9/11. I have bundled a lifetime of fighting into seven months. As a first lieutenant, I am only getting started, a fact that makes me tremble.

Part of me still believes we can kill our way to victory. All the same, I need something better to feed the Boys than, *Today we are going to walk around and start a fight. We'll kill a few of them, and they'll kill a few of us. And tomorrow we will do it again. Don't worry, though, the Pech has been quiet. Let us not forget strategy.*

The clarity of the invasion is long gone. The army has equipped me with smart phrases to make this stage of the war sound fancy: We are separating the enemy from the population. We are conducting key leader engagements. We are winning hearts and minds by distributing humanitarian assistance. Or most commonly, we are engaged in nation-building. During mission briefs, I pump out these phrases, yet when the Boys are alone, they murmur their own explanation:

"We're going out to draw fire again."

I correct them in the open, while secretly admiring the purity of their viewpoint.

We are holding the outpost, for now. The thing to do is make it to fall, then comes the winter lull, and with spring, we'll be rotating home. Our battalion accounts for 80 percent of the munitions shot in country, and my company, A Company, accounts for the majority of that. We *are* the war. Our enemy kills are higher than any previous unit in this region, though we have few bodies to show for it.

Colonel Cavoli sees the combat figures and becomes upset about our company's lack of awards. *I mean those granny panty dudes in 1-87, our sister battalion, are putting guys in for the Medal of Honor every time a mortar lands within a thousand yards.* My company and platoon are too busy fighting. We have not had time for awards.

Three ingredients are critical for awards: a brave act, someone seeing the brave act, and a decent writer with time to pen the citation. In September I am thinking of awards when we do some cowboy shit into the holiest of holies, the enemy village of Yakkah Chinnah, the deepest in the valley. While there, I suggest to the captain that we clear Ratfuck Ridge. Festered with enemy positions, this rock citadel connects the heights over Yakkah Chinnah to Hilltop 1705 and the enemy villages below. The washes on the ridge are deep, providing perfect cover for resupply of the al-Qaeda camps near the crest. Clearing this ridge with a platoon is a perilous, almost suicidal, mission. To me, it is a chance for a grand slam, a chance to kill them all, and so put to rest our dead.

We do it.

Atop the ridge we find camps, fire rings, and debris. The enemy evades us, and after three days, we head north, out of water and food, in the pounding sun, edging across cliffs and benches, the gendarmes rising like forgotten statues.

Back of the column, the Boys report enemy movement. I sprint to the rear, joining Sergeant Robinette, our acting platoon sergeant for Siercks, and a machine-gun team. Robinette points to a wooded draw six hundred meters out, where ten Afghan men are descending. They are not brandishing weapons.

I confer with the captain, who has joined us for the mission. We decide the men are bad. They have cached their weapons and are attempting to reposition. Who else would be hanging around up here three days into the offensive? These men have gone civilian while on the move, a common muj tactic.

The machine gunner at the rear is Specialist Pickron, of weapons squad. I point to the target, telling Pickron, "Shoot them."

He says, "Where?"

"In the draw."

"I can't see 'em, sir."

I jump behind Pickron, slap him on the helmet, and point over his shoulder, "Right there. By the boulder, just down from the summit. Got 'em?"

"I can't see 'em, sir."

Enraged, I shove Pickron aside, yelling at him, "You stupid ass." He is playing dumb, unwilling to fire on unarmed men. I shoulder his M240B and squeeze off a burst. Tracers stitch the wash, hitting low. My targets move in a frenzy. I fire three long bursts that rattle my brain. One of the men falls and disappears from view. I wait for him to pop back up. He does not. The others dart over a creek into cedars. The scout machine gun comes into action, and we slash a ribbon of trees to bits.

It occurs to me that I may have just machine-gunned someone to death and it feels splendid.

I set down the 240 and glare at Pickron over the smoking barrel. "That's fucking bullshit, Pickron. You saw them."

He insists, "I couldn't see 'em, sir."

Pickron is supposed to shoot people, not think. An infantry unit breaks down when everyone thinks. Still I wonder if he is right and I am wrong. Will I look back on this as the day I lost my humanity? I decide Pickron is being simple. He is not evaluating context. Pickron wants the world to be black and white. Decision-making in this war is about gray.

Gunfire has given away our position. The elusive enemy comes to life over walkie-talkies, speaking in numbers I did not expect. A dozen of their area commanders muster their men, which forces another decision. We can keep going down to the villages. If we do, we will likely hit a multisided ambush. We could climb back up three thousand feet and fight them in dense forest, which does not seem prudent because we can't keep ourselves supplied. Whatever we do, I expect casualties. The trick is to inflict more on them than they will on us. This is combat decision-making.

I make the call: we will dig in on the most defensible terrain in the area and wait for night. The captain agrees. It takes an hour to find decent ground, where the ridge falls away precipitously on multiple sides, limiting options for enemy maneuvers against us.

When we are done digging, we lie down and squeeze shade from the spare trees. The heat has us speechless. The scouts hold our northern flank, the downhill side of the ridge. Weapons squad and first squad hold the uphill side, the most obvious direction of enemy attack. Second and third squads are thin, so they tie together our oval-shaped defense, watching the fingers that extend off the main ridge.

At last light, we get to it. An RPG passes overhead like a shooting star, launched from the uphill side, just as I expected. Our machine guns bark in cadence. The enemy is about four hundred yards uphill, on the same shelf where we had fired at the men earlier in the day. I expected something like this.

Bullets whack into rocks beside me. The angles are wrong. I am processing this when another train of bullets zips in. *They are behind us too.* I did not expect the second enemy position. When the first enemy group opened fire, they drew our attention and counterfire. Almost all of us instinctively turned uphill. A second enemy group used the chance to sneak within thirty yards, cresting a finger off the main ridge. The scouts hold this leg of our defense.

A third enemy position crashes into us, from an opposite finger on the east side. For the first time in the tour, we are surrounded. If I don't do anything about it, we might be overrun. The enemy bounds, attempting to close the distance on the scouts. Barrels glow. Brass flies. The radio is silent. We just fight. From my rifle pit, I aim at a muzzle flash. On the enemy line, a head bobs between rocks. Someone is running laterally. I flip my selector to burst and fire. My barrel jumps. The head drops. That's a hit.

Sergeant Badman, with the scouts, radios, "They are thirty meters." We are about to do bayonets. Vaulting over a rock, I charge for second squad. A ricochet pings off a stone beside my boot. I fall and rise just as an RPG splinters a holly in front of me. The superheated gas shoves me off my feet and knocks me from a ledge. I land on my back, helmet whipping off a rock, causing a strange squeak in my neck. I rise again, determined to maneuver a squad. I run and process. In most muj attacks, they aim to inflict a few casualties while avoiding decisive engagement. This is a choreographed assault to wipe us out.

Far below, on the rises near Ashat, are farming terraces. A dozen farmers are hunched over, minding their crops. They have not bothered to watch the battle or even look up. Above them, Democratic Capitalism and Radical Islam are having a Super Bowl. We punch holes in each other. The mountains shudder as we make big rocks into small rocks and big men into small men. Still, the farmers farm.

Holly branches snap. Leaves rain down. Rocks explode. Smoke balloons. I charge across the open. My eyes are burning, watery from smoke. The valley seems to be jiggling through my tears. I dive into position next to Robinette, telling him, "I need grenadiers to reinforce the scouts." I pick up a few grenadiers, and we keep moving. At last we get to the scout position. I order the grenadiers abreast, and they loosen off every frag grenade they have. *Bloop. Bloop. Bloop. Bloop. Bloop. Bloop. Bloop. Bloop.* The attack falters as the grenades detonate. The enemy assault group ducks behind a finger. My grenadiers aim into the sky, for arc. We keep shooting.

We kill six fighters this day, and take just three wounded in my platoon. I led soldiers across the open in a battle that was no-shit, but also one that ain't worth a movie. Anyhow, it is enough for a medal. I did my job so that we would live. The captain saw it, and we had to get off our ass about medals, so I got one.

Back at the outpost, the captain wants to do an awards ceremony on the LZ, in a pitch of open ground that is a magnet for fire. We are going to line up every American in the valley, four ranks deep, so that the captain can give awards. I tell him, "Talk about giving the enemy a target. C'mon, sir. What's with the dog and pony?"

The captain says, "I am not going to let the enemy dictate where and when I give awards to my men. We will line up in formation, and I will give awards, including one to you, for valor. You will stand there, with discipline, and the enemy will know we are not afraid."

So we form up on the landing zone, 140 men, in full battle rattle on a Saturday afternoon, everyone squirmy, like we've become allergic to the open. A couple dozen awardees line up at the fore of the gathered company. We have our florid ceremony. The captain says stuff about being brave then paces the line, pinning an award to each man's armor and squeezing his hand. When it is my turn, I snap to attention and salute, firing off the battalion motto, "Against all odds, sir."

The captain returns my salute, saying, "Chosin," in reference to our unit's battle at the Chosin Reservoir in the Korean War, where, by the way, we were annihilated. Then he pins the medal on my chest, and I say, "Thank you, sir." This goes on for twenty minutes, and no one takes a shot at us. Afterward, feeling a bit chickenshit, I unpin my award for valor and stick it in my duffel bag in the tent, next to dirty socks and torn uniforms.

9

RECESS

The army has issued me a plane ticket to the States with two weeks off, my precious midtour R&R, a pause for which I'd trade my firstborn. Corpus Christi, my hometown, is where I will meet Elizabeth. She has been living with her parents. Elizabeth and I could go somewhere exotic and make a vacation of it, except I like the idea of my hometown. I want to melt into a bed and let family take care of me. I want to mooch off my parents.

I am jamming items in my assault pack for the trip: headphones, an iPod, the book *King Solomon's Mines*, which I have been meaning to read in downtime but keep falling asleep. I run across a letter from Elizabeth, which she started with, "Bruno got bit by a rattlesnake. He died. My dad buried him in the backyard. I miss him so much." She went on to ask questions that made me mad. The questions were no doubt from a magazine with a celebrity on the cover. The exercise went like this:

Fill in the blank:

   Rivals for your love or mine were

   _____

   These things symbolized our growing love (special song, place, poem, etc.):

   _____

We shared this vision for the future:

_____

We had these differences to work out:

_____

Some of the things we both believed in were

_____

To which I replied, "I don't like these questions."

To which she replied, "Whatever."

And I answered, "This is a cheap game."

Now with her letter in hand, I renew my vow not to answer such questions.

A fusillade of shots echoes across the valley. Everyone in the tent looks at each other. That's incoming. We jump into armor, snatch up weapons. *Go. Go.* A hundred helmeted men run for the perimeter, dropping into foxholes and rifle pits.

The enemy starts smoking our outpost. I sprint for Observation Post Two on the east side. Once inside, I glass a gully, catching two fighters clad in woodland camo running for a position four hundred fifty meters distant. They disappear in a crevice and reappear on a little ridge. The two look to be heading for the gully below us. They weave. They bound. I order a shell from an 81-millimeter mortar, giving distance and direction, then, "Two dismounts in the open." One of the fighters disappears, and moments later reappears, sprinting for the next island of trees. I cheer him on, "Yes, keep going, keep going, a little right . . . there." The mortar seems to detonate on his head. Instantly, he is mist.

The evil in me yells, "*Yes, yes, yes!*"

* * *

An hour later a Black Hawk lands. On the LZ I am with a group of eight who all have orders for midtour leave. The others jump to their feet, don their dust goggles, and honk about cheeseburgers and booze. Slowly my hands begin to shake, and the more I order them to stop, the more fierce the shaking. I get on the bird and drop into a netted seat. My hands will not stop. We dive north, following the river channel. We hook right at the Pech, and soon I'm at Bagram, then Kuwait, and onto Texas. My hands won't stop.

It is war to peace in twenty-four hours.

I fidget as we pass into the cavernous terminal of Dallas International Airport, the last stop before my hometown. Up ahead is a cheering crowd. People are pressed together on both sides of a roped aisle. They have come to root for the military. A plane like mine arrives every day, sometimes two or three, whisking service members home from Iraq and Afghanistan.

All veterans—mechanics, financial clerks, infantry—get the same outpouring. Much of the crowd is composed of old men with lettered hats saying VIETNAM VETERAN. Likewise, there are GULF WAR VETERAN hats. Was that even a war? A guy in a wheelchair, oxygen tank lashed to it, has 82nd Jump Wings on his blazer. Other men have the names of naval ships on their hats, USS *Such-and-Such*. There are old ladies with blue hair, waving little American flags. A handful of younger women and kids are among them, but the crowd is retiree overall. Today is Monday, and the vast majority of Americans are at work or school. The old folks assembled have driven to the airport, paid for parking, gone through torturous security lines, then stood here for hours to cheer on a plane-full of veterans whom they do not know.

Their supreme patriotic gesture pisses me off. I am loath to participate. I do not know why I am mad at them. Maybe it is because I just vaporized someone and they seem to be cheering, *Attaboy, you really killed the shit out of him.* Quiet is all I want. I need my private life with Elizabeth. To hell with their ticker-tape ambush.

I finish *King Solomon's Mines* on the flight to Corpus. Just before landing, I survey the Gulf of Mexico. I will be in it soon. At the terminal, I hurry off the plane and catch the scent of brine. Elizabeth is waiting near baggage claim. She is festooned in turquoise and wearing cut-off denim shorts. Her bosom and legs are deeply tan. Her hair is blue-black. To me, she looks like the Aztec princess Corpus *vatos* get tattooed onto their arms.

My first thought is that I am missing my own life.

She hugs me. We couple perfectly. Rubbing my stomach, she says, "We've gotta get some food in you."

I have lost twenty-five pounds and right away my old lady has seen it, so we cruise to our favorite Mexican restaurant, Acapulco, where I devour two baskets of tortilla chips without saying a word. Tejano music blares from speakers mounted to the wall. A fajita plate arrives. Elizabeth asks questions. I chew and nod, my fingers dripping grease. She keeps asking, "What about this?" and "What about that?" shotgunning me with eight months of pent-up conversation. My eyes are in my food.

Elizabeth says, "How the hell can you go to war and come home and have nothing to say."

"We don't got to say everything in the first five minutes."

"Are you okay?"

"Yes, now that I'm with you."

She smiles.

I attack an order of gulf shrimp.

Soon, our table looks ravaged. I sit over two empty plates. Accordions bellow from the wall-mounted speakers. I look at Elizabeth. She nods, "That better?" I look out the window at passing cars and people going in and out of a barred pawnshop. Before the check arrives, I am sick from the caloric overdose. I run to the bathroom and shout into the toilet.

We leave and drive for Elizabeth's parents' house. Oil refineries pass, the stacks smoking and flaring, making fuel for an army at war and a nation at the mall. The main strip in Corpus is an assemblage of flea markets, taquerias, car washes, and more taquerias. Our town's claim to fame is the highest teen-pregnancy rate in the nation, and it seems every teen mom has left a dirty diaper along the highway median.

We ramp off the highway into Elizabeth's neighborhood and park in her driveway. Elizabeth's mom, Maria Teresa Vasquez, sees me looking skeletal and gives me a hug, "Oh, *mijo*. I'll make you something to eat." I sit at the wood table in the kitchen while she ferries beans, rice, and carne asada. I eat without getting up. Flipping tortillas at the stove, Maria Teresa Vasquez is clucking about the washer and dryer she got from Sears. I don't have to say anything to her, so long as I nod and make eye contact once in a while. When done, I run to the bathroom and shout some more.

Then I melt into the cradle of Elizabeth's body and sleep for eighteen hours.

It is two in the afternoon and hot when Elizabeth and I make it to Padre Island, where we sweep into a hotel room overlooking the ocean and throw open the balcony door. I stand outside, listening to the pounding surf, that ancient rhythm telling me something I can't yet decipher about the war and warriors. Just north, a jetty reaches into the gulf. A mahogany-skinned fisherman stands at the end of the jetty, wearing shorts, sunglasses, and an unbuttoned shirt which flaps in the breeze. He casts a spinning line. *Now there's a guy who's got it all figured out.*

At night we drink beer. My tolerance is shit. Dizzy, we head for the beach, half dressed and barefoot, canned beer in hand. While riding the hotel elevator, I notice Elizabeth's blouse is unbuttoned down to her breasts.

Pointing to the buttons, I say, "We're in public, girl. You need to go one up."

"One down?"

"Up."

"Okay, down."

The gulf is argentine in the moonlight. We anchor our beer cans in the sand then wade into the water and splash. Elizabeth looks glorious, her hair shining and stomach hard. We walk down the beach, warm surf lapping our ankles. A half mile down from the hotel, alcohol has me faint. We sit in the sand.

Elizabeth asks, "What's it like over there?"

"Beautiful. Savage."

"I wish I could go, just to see it. I don't want to shoot anyone."

"I'm seeing what humanity used to be. No rationality. The women are basically slaves."

"Slaves. Yeah, tell me about it."

"Please."

She laughs. "Seriously, how's your job?"

"I'm so, so tired. And I won't bullshit you, babe, we've lost good people." I gulp my beer. "A few were my fault. One was a medic. Her name was Wakkuna Jackson. She didn't do anything to anyone, and she's dead."

Elizabeth sits behind me and rubs my shoulders.

I say, "Sorry."

"No, it's fine. Say what you want to say."

I can't put my finger on the black inside me. I venture, "I don't know if I can go back."

"What?"

"I'm just tired, that's all. And drunk."

"You wanted this." She stands up and takes an officious posture. "You volunteered. Don't be crybaby vet. Man up."

I can't help my smile. "Yes, ma'am."

I finish my drink, splay out, and watch the sky spin.

She asks, "You still want to go to the Rangers after this?"

Haven't thought about that for a while. It feels like cheating to think ahead, and who wants to jinx the future? I tell her, "Yes. The plan is still the plan."

I grab her and pull her down next to me, and then we have sex in the sand like wild beasts. When we are connected, she repeatedly slaps my ass.

* * *

I count days, tracking hours and minutes until my flight leaves at 3:52 p.m. Not one second can be wasted. I want it all. One day, Elizabeth disappears to Target, her so-called happy place. I cannot remember how long. It is too long, so when she returns I scream at her. I grab her by the shoulders and squeeze to let her know I'm crazy and mad. She hasn't seen the beast in me. Maybe I'll show it to her.

She flings my hands away, screaming, "I don't care what you've done. Don't ever grab me like that."

"Right, okay, okay."

She says, "I was getting stuff for you. Asshole," and reaches into her bag and flings wool socks, a wristwatch, and a portable PlayStation onto the living room floor, then storms away.

To an empty room, I say, "Sorry, babe."

Time at home is a hard recess. All my base needs are met. It is unsettling. I keep waiting for something to happen. Idleness corrodes my sanity, and I go looking for the war, in crowds at the mall and traffic and trees in my parents' backyard. A muj with a machine gun made of gold is in my dreams. The sun is at his back. He readies his gleaming weapon and aims at my platoon. The Boys are climbing a hill. They can't see him in the blinding sun. Watching from the outpost, I scream to warn them, mouthing, "Contact front," but make no sound. In one long burst, the gunner mows them all down.

Between this recurrent dream and the bliss of seeing Elizabeth, I toy with the idea of missing the flight back. This sin is called absent without leave, AWOL. I think of excuses for not showing up. Elizabeth would corroborate any story: family illness . . . taken hostage . . . caught in a revolution while visiting a beach in Central America . . . car wreck, yeah, that's a good one. I'll have to wreck a car and hurt myself. Perhaps my dad's Ford Focus. It's a piece of shit anyway.

Knock it off. I am an officer, a leader who wanted this. Going AWOL is desertion. It is for pothead draftees sent to Vietnam. I miss my Boys. I even miss my job: the sting of Copenhagen in my lip, the bleeping radio, marching at midnight, lying on the ambush line, the smell of my poncho liner. Truth is it feels wrong pissing in a toilet; I'd prefer the yard. Worst of all right now is a feeling of endless space around me. In the war I have unity of purpose, am always part of something. There are no private quarters or moments. We march together and live in formation. I am a link in an assault line. In the infantry there is no solitary, isolated action. Leave has me aimless.

* * *

It is raining when Elizabeth tells me goodbye outside the airport. I issue a hug that brings her to the point of suffocation. She rasps, "Okay, okay."

I let go, telling her, "I'll call ya," and march for the terminal. I do not turn back. *Game face.*

A day later, I land at a military airfield in Kuwait for a layover. To kill time I head for the chow hall. A few hundred service members, coming and going to war, are jammed in the place. No one is here for more than a day, so all are strangers at the long tables where meals are stabbed with plastic forks. I cringe.

I pick up a tray, stand in line for lunch, and scan. It turns out I have one ally in this sea of strangers. Sergeant Major Carabello, my battalion's chief enlisted man, is sitting alone. Relieved, I set down my tray across from him. He looks up and breaks into a grin. "Attack Three-six." Carabello twists the top off a can of Copenhagen fine cut and offers it.

I decide I will dip and eat at the same time. "Thanks, Sar'nt Major."

We are part of the same tribe, and I know his mannerisms. The heavy look he wears tells me he is doing a windup. Carabello likewise takes a pinch of Copenhagen and lips it. He says, "My wife keeps telling me to stop dipping. But you know what, dip . . . tastes . . . good, so I don't." He drops the can in the arm pocket of his uniform before saying, "Maybe when the war's over."

"How's Chosin?" I ask, using the battalion nickname.

"Good." He exhales long and loud. "Sir, I've got bad news."

"I knew it."

"Your platoon had KIAs."

With jaw clenched tight, I take in the story. Sergeant Major spares me no details because I will write the awards for the living and the dead. The captain ordered my platoon to Ashat, one of the supreme enemy villages near Yakkah Chinnah. My platoon, ravaged by casualties, stepped off with twenty-five men plus a few squads from the Afghan Army. Their mission was to set up a firebase in Ashat.

Hold on, a firebase?

They would separate the enemy from the population, which in Ashat means everyone—so, not sure how that works. Shortly after arriving, my platoon came under fire inside the village. Chunking grenades, the platoon fought from house to house, killing three muj. On a naked hillside beside the village, Specialist Fernando Robinson was shot in the chest, just left of his armor plate. The round hit his heart and exited the opposite armpit. Cigrand, my radioman, dragged him to cover. Blood pumped out of the holes in Robinson, and soon, his life flickered and went out. Cigrand, soaked in Robinson's blood, did CPR because Robinson was his friend and they both believed in one another. He did CPR well past Robinson's death. Cigrand did CPR even after being told a Dustoff was not coming.

The platoon took defensive positions in the village. The enemy coun-terattacked. A short round from an American howitzer landed in a knot of Afghan Army soldiers. Five died. Many more were wounded. They screamed and screamed. Back at the outpost, the captain gathered a quick-reaction force. Our long-time medic, Doc Anthony Vaccaro, and platoon sergeant, Siercks, were both at the outpost—Doc awaiting midtour leave, Siercks with a torn ACL. Hearing the platoon had taken casualties, they volunteered to lead the quick-reaction force. Three Humvees launched with reinforce-ments, Siercks and Vaccaro in the lead vehicle. A few kilometers south of the outpost, the enemy ambushed the convoy with a volley of RPGs. One hit the lead vehicle and pierced the soft back panel before ripping through the cabin and decapitating Doc Vaccaro. His brains sprayed all over the passengers.

Now we have seven dead. This was enough to wrestle an AC-130 gunship from the Joint Special Operations Command. By 2200 the gunship took orbit over the valley and started banging targets. The muj had been listening for helicopters and did not seem to expect the gunship, which killed a dozen of them lying in ambush on another hillside. The enemy faded into the landscape.

The idea died for a firebase in Ashat.

Someone had to clean out the Humvee that Doc Vaccaro was riding in.

When I finish writing the awards, I pen letters to the parents of Doc Anthony Vaccaro and Corporal Fernando Robinson. In my letters I say they died with valor in a fight against evil men. I do not write what is true: I should have been there. If I'd have been there no one would have died. They died because I went on leave. Without me to talk to the captain, the platoon got pushed into something dumb. I am no Rambo, but I can nego-tiate risk with my commander, and I think that saves more asses.

10

HEARTS AND MINDS

KORENGAL VALLEY, AFGHANISTAN

FALL 2006

The marching shadows of winter come early in the Kush. When I rejoin the platoon, a grave pall hangs over the Boys. Lingering shell shock from the battle in Ashat still grips them. Compounded with constant field time and exposure, the effect has been caustic. And though not our first casualties, Vaccaro and Robinson were both brave and popular. When men like that die, it hurts more. Isn't brave and popular what we all aspire to?

I miss the good old days before anyone was hit, though I wonder if any time in war should be remembered that way. By now new guys have mended the holes in the platoon. Replacement troops dropped in the middle of a war are not to be envied. Technically, all of us are veterans, but we array ourselves in two cliques: old guys and new guys. For many new guys being new is their only sin. Old guys find ways for new guys to fall short of the best in their dead brothers. It is easy.

During my leave, more good, noncommissioned officers were lost. The second squad leader, Patterson, had ruptured a disc in his spine and is now gone. Far worse is the loss of Siercks, already on his way home with a torn ACL. He was a fount of optimism and a friend to me. What Siercks has done amounts to abandonment because he was not wounded; he got hurt. Privates get hurt, new guys get hurt, and fucking pogues. Platoon sergeants are not supposed to get hurt. They are supposed to be in control. I get to thinking I will hold it against Siercks.

On a computer in company headquarters I tend to my own career. A half-finished application packet for the Ranger Regiment has my attention. There is a seed of doubt in me about an elite trajectory, and more combat. I have this recurring fantasy of comfort, seeing myself as a staff officer or a company executive officer, busy with logistics and conqueror of ice cream sandwiches. *You've done enough*, part of me reasons. No one joins the Ranger Regiment seeking personal safety. Rangers are storm troopers launching raids and attacks; no hearts and minds, no guarding roads or traffic checkpoints. The missions will matter in the Rangers; they die for good reasons. A commander of Rangers is a superman.

I finish my packet and submit.

* * *

Subduing the hermetic Korengalies has been far more difficult than expected. After the July battle in Comersa Bandeh, we consolidated and used our concentrated power for incursions south of the outpost, boring deeper into enemy territory. We can celebrate tactical victories and a swelling kill count. Our logistical woes, however, have reemerged. The stores of food, bullets, mortars, batteries, and IVs are near depletion. In pushing south, we abandoned the north, and once again, it has become obvious our foothold is flimsy. To survive, we must turn our island of combat power into a peninsula, which means extending the bubble of control from the valley mouth down to the outpost. We tried this in the summer. It ended in flames. We will try again.

My task is to secure the valley mouth, about five square kilometers of foothills and terraced river lowlands, from the Pech Road south to Comersa Bandeh. I insist on doing it without vehicles, telling the captain we can range the entire zone on foot. Vehicles and convoys will confine my combat power to the road. We will set patterns that the enemy will target. I have no appetite for enduring an ambush like the one on Lieutenant Barclay's convoy.

Within this broader mission is a salient subtask. The US Army has hired an Afghan construction company to widen the Korengal Road. Design specifications call for drivability for the army's ubiquitous deuce-and-a-half supply truck. I am to recruit the local Afghan police unit to provide security for the construction.

If we are going to win the valley's north end, the sprawling village of Omar is the crux. On my topographic map the village is labeled Taliban, which is subtle. It is the same place where the enemy ambushed our Second Platoon convoy. The easy thing is to assume Omar is all bad and to charge in with guns on full auto. As we prepare to depart, the captain tells me, "We just need one elder on our team. I want you kinetic down there. Be aggressive. But don't forget the villages. The only way we are ever going to win is to get them on our side. Baby steps. Find me one elder, one village."

I say, "Roger, sir."

"And remember. Don't ease up on your men. You drive them hard, right onto the plane home. When we land in the US, you can sleep."

At the outpost we assemble in the dark. The Boys wait with cigarette coughs. I spot-check weapons, radios, and night vision. We go by moonlight, slaving under armor and rucks. Two by two we file down the road, stomping the long shadows lying on the path. Our voyage is six miles, and we do it without rest. The valley opens into a terraced floodplain a kilometer wide. The river twists through the bottom, sixty houses straddling it. There are no lights. We take a position near the jeep road. In the morning the Omaris wake for prayer and find us digging in.

I am not sure how to start this off, so I act like a soldier, and the natives act like natives, and we have ourselves a standoff.

* * *

Two days pass before a boy scurries up to our position, saying a delegation of tribal elders requests a meeting with me. In Afghanistan a gathering of elders and military commanders is called a *shura*. I agree.

It is four in the afternoon and drizzling when we gather in a house of mud and straw in eastern Omar. I sit cross-legged, which I soon discover is excruciating in armor. A dozen tribal elders sit on my flanks. War and sun has turned their skin lizard-like. They wear vests colored olive, dun, and charcoal. Some have adopted the peculiar practices of dying their beards red with henna and lining their eyes with antimony.

In the center of the Afghans is the chief of Omar. He wears a magnificent black beard. The scar on his cheek, just above beard line, makes him look every bit the villain. He could be seventy or forty. His movements, graceful and limber, betray no old age. Word is, the chief is a bad guy, but also calculating and pragmatic. He has flirted with the coalition before, if only for a very brief time. To me, he seems worthy of investment, for in this land, only men with blood on their hands have gravity.

A boy brings in a platter topped with chai cups and sets it down in the middle of us. We suck up chai. Introductions follow. Then the chief of Omar pontificates. I listen and make smudgy notes on a write-in-the-rain notepad. The chief blames the Korengali for the Second Platoon deaths in his village, an accusation that triggers a cascade of blame between the elders. Suddenly, no one in the room is Korengali. Every village elder blames every other village for the fighting; every valley blames every other valley. All the Afghans blame the Pakistanis. The Muslims can at least agree that Christians are entirely to blame for evil in the world. I stop making notes.

At last, we arrive at infrastructure. The chief of Omar wants water pipes for his village. Upon hearing this, my heart thumps. This is the angle. Striving to appear calm, I ask what for, what type, and how many, then make notes as he answers.

When the meeting ends, I struggle to my feet, vowing never again to sit cross-legged. We shake hands and leave for our corners, where we watch each other at length.

The next move is mine. It is daybreak when we post up near the chief's house, which sits atop a long stone stairway east of the river. I tell a rabble of village boys that my medic can see anyone injured or ill, and to spread the word. It does not take long for men, teenagers, and boys to form a line stretching a quarter mile. In a little room in a little house, our medic, Doc Goff, treats the Afghans one by one. Goff, a high-school graduate, sees everything from stab wounds to flu to depression and broken molars. He is gentle with the young boys and rough with the men. In America he would need forty years of medical schooling to do what he is doing. After an hour, Goff says, "Sir, if this keeps up, I'm not gonna have shit left if one of us gets hit."

I check the line of Afghans. It looks to be growing. "Keep at it."

In the third hour, Doc exhausts his aid bag and resorts to the army cure-all, eight-hundred-milligram tablets of Ibuprofen. I assure Doc we can go thin for a little while. More supplies are available from convoys driving the Pech River. Today we are good men winning hearts and minds. The way into the tribal heart is through the kids.

* * *

Many days in November the valley is socked in by fog. The menace of winter is upon us. Swollen storm clouds arrive, then howling cold. To maintain a tactical advantage, I move the platoon to a different position every night or two, and in the gelid predawn, stalk our perimeter for infractions: a cigarette on watch, sentries dozing. I want to see night vision down, thermal optics powered up. *And for fuck's sake, get your hands out of your pockets.*

Some of us have been living out of rucksacks for nine months. Every week we climb ten to twelve thousand vertical feet, lugging enough armament and weaponry to kill a fleet of mules. We nap between missions. On patrol we forage corn and beans. We scrounge naan from the locals and overpay for their mangy goats. We crawl, scrabble, and run. Cold cracks our knuckles, and they bleed. Rocks shred our uniforms. My languor is marrow deep. Anything can happen at any time, a fact that grinds us into effigies of ourselves, into brave scarecrows.

A helicopter delivers a batch of Boys just back from leave. The group has four men. It is supposed to have five. One man, Private Yunke, disappeared during R&R, meaning he is now absent without leave. The squad boys say, "Yunke fucked us," as they cross-load his gear. Without him, their sentry shifts get longer, their loads heavier. There is no isolated action in the infantry. The four others who have just returned should look rested, but appear far from it. Shock is on their faces. Their systems are in disarray. Going to war for the first time is easy; coming back to it is the hard part.

* * *

Sniper fire from the Omar Divide has us crabbing through the lowlands, then clamoring up a draw. We reach the divide and begin clearing. The sergeants troop the line, "Stop bunching up. Pass it back. Spread out. Pass it back. Skirt that clearing. *I said, stop bunching up!*" With little warning, a specialist flops onto the ground and refuses to go on. The specialist says his foot is broke and that he needs a helicopter. All he needs is a helicopter. The specialist looks at me with dumb, trusting eyes, thinking perhaps that I am still civilized. Doc Goff, his squad leader, and I kick the specialist around. "Oh, my foot," he keeps saying.

I shake the specialist so hard his teeth rattle. This is bigger than him. Our ethos is fragile, and it will shatter if I start medevacing quitters. The beauty and terror of this war on foot is that we are trapped. We must march because we have no other choice. The road is several thousand feet below us. Even a litter carry is impractical for more than a kilometer in tough ground. *You want a medevac? Then I've got to see battle wounds or bone sticking out. Otherwise, kid, you're gonna walk that shit off.*

An idea takes hold: shoot him. This will set a good example for others thinking of quitting. I pat the kid on the left leg and say, "I'm going to shoot you so we can get a helicopter. How about I shoot you in this leg?" He seems confused. He turns to Goff, a betrayed look coming over him. I say, "Left leg it is. In the meat, right?" as I stick the barrel against his thigh. "I'll try not to hit bone. I mean, at this distance . . ."

The kid gets up.

I keep the platoon roving after midnight, bouncing back and forth across the valley, sometimes going deep, sometimes waking near the mouth. Constant movement sounds smart in the Ranger handbook. It is momentous to execute night after night in the mountains.

My ears are already stiff with cold when I tell the noncoms we march at 0300. When 0300 comes, the hills are frosted, ice rimes the river, and snow clouds smother the ridgelines. The Boys dally, cold and half dumb with lack of sleep, making space in their rucks for bags of food, clothing, and winter supplies, which we call HA, short for "humanitarian assistance."

I hiss at the sergeants, who wander bleary-eyed, cursing and kicking the Boys into formation. I storm the line, "Let's go. Let's go."

The Boys limp with old injuries as we scale down the terraces, edge a wall, and descend a staircase into the river gravel. At a ford, our boots crack the ice along the bank, then we splash across, water filling the cargo pockets on my trousers. We climb, sleet pelting our faces. The contours, darkness, and sleet break us apart. I have lost a squad, and I say to no one in particular, "Where's third? Where's fucking Three-three? Stupid fucks. Break in contact. Everyone halt . . . break in contact. Fucking amateurs. I said halt. Fucking Three-three, there you are. Whaddaya doing? Where's your head?"

"Sorry, sir, I thought we were going right."

We gain the river trail and follow it north to meet the Afghan police on the Pech River. Their station is a bombed-out house. We sweep into it, finding a lump of forlorn policemen sleeping under blankets on the ground. The woodstove has gone out. "Rise and shine, boys." Grunting, they cast aside blankets and lurch to their feet and greet us.

The police wear a smattering of wool uniform, traditional Pashtun dress, and Adidas tracksuit. Together we sip chai in a battle against morning cold. A policeman relights the stove, and I stand before the licking flames to dry my trousers. Next to me stands the police chief, a big man who some maintain was once Taliban. Now reviewing him, I decide by birth and upbringing he is a pirate. I tell him of the coming road construction and ask if he is willing to provide security for the project.

He shakes his head, "We are very busy. Very busy."

We drop bags of sugar, beans, and rice at his sandaled feet, which does not elicit the response I had hoped for. I appeal to his sense of honor and community, and the method falls equally flat. Next, we break out the winter gear, gifting them thermal underwear, balaclavas, beanies, and Gore-Tex. At once, they leap into it and model.

The police chief, pirouetting in his hand-me-downs, says he could help, if only he had some DVD players for cold winter nights.

Next day we linger in the hamlet of Omar. Two squads hand out coats, blankets, and bags of sugar and beans to shivering Afghans stride the Korengal Road. The Afghans are a proud and defiant people, but like anyone, they go crazy for free shit. I join a squad and the Afghan policemen in a position in the boulder-strewn hills overlooking the road. Today we are protecting construction crews, and *feeling* like we are protecting construction crews. Bulldozers, backhoes, excavators, and dump trucks have launched into the project. They rattle up and down the valley. Steel teeth bite the cliffs above the road. Men with jiggling cheeks operate jackhammers. Rocks avalanche onto the road where hydraulic arms load the rocks into waiting trucks that haul it away. The road gets wider. We stand by, unaroused.

One of the policemen with us, Abdul, is switched on. He is young and fit and has an aquiline nose. Abdul watches my Boys and mimics them. First, Abdul fashions a sling for his AK-47 so that he can carry his weapon across his chest like us, both hands always on it. In our overwatch position, Abdul digs a rifle pit then constructs a low rock wall for cover, just like the Americans. He smokes with my Boys. With borrowed binoculars, he glasses the nearby hills.

After a few joint patrols, Abdul offers his home to us, saying we can rest in an extra room that once belonged to his brother. I accept. Next day the sky blackens with weather. We follow Abdul to the north end of Omar. His home is a two-story deal with a mulberry in the courtyard. Abdul shows us to a room with a glassless window overlooking the Pech River that we cover with ponchos. We roll out sleeping bags and nap.

In the afternoon a storm smashes into the mountains. Along the river we get rain. I watch it sheeting from the eaves as if looking at the world from behind a waterfall. For dinner, Abdul brings out argentine plates heaped with rice, beans, and goat. We eat in T-shirts, sitting on the floor, everyone laughing and dry, Abdul the policeman and a platoon of American infantry. The trick with eating, Abdul demonstrates, is to break off a piece of naan, cup it in your hand, and pinch at the rice, beans, and other filling you want. We show Abdul how to do it up burrito style.

After dark Abdul retreats across the courtyard to tend to his wife. Rain turns to snow. The wind is whistling when Abdul returns, lantern swinging in his hand, to find me. We sit in the light of his gas lantern, the pungent smell of kerosene filling the room, and talk about America. We talk about shining cities. Abdul likes cities. He calls himself, "A mountain boy."

"Cities aren't so great," I tell him. "The problem with cities is they make you feel like you're always supposed to be doing something."

Abdul says, "But you never get bored? Yes?"

"Yes, well, I don't know. Bored in a different way. A hollow kind of bored."

Abdul asks if I am married. *Yes.* He asks if I have kids. *No.*

I show Abdul pictures of Elizabeth. One shows us together on Ruby Beach, the rocky coastline of Washington at our backs. Our faces are shining. The picture is a treasure to me.

He takes the photo, studies it for a long time. Smiling, he says, "She looks Afghan. Very beautiful."

I laugh.

Abdul does not offer a picture of his own wife. I ask Abdul if he wants to talk about his wife, and he withdraws. I say I am sorry, and he says it is fine. We are the same and we are different.

At five in the morning, half a foot of snow covers the ground. Curls of smoke rise from nearby houses, mingling with falling snow. I trudge to our sentry positions to spot-check. The Boys have stomped little trails between the house and our sandbagged machine guns. The gunner's eyes are slits against the flaying wind. The Boys not on guard are in puff jackets, a garment too thick and warm to wear except during guard duty.

Up for morning prayer, Abdul brings armfuls of wood for the stove in our room. Kneeling, he stokes a fire to life. It cracks with wet wood. I let him finish and then tell him he should not make a fire for us. He has already been too kind. He nods and retires. The fire warms our bones. The roof over us leaks in three places. We huddle in corners to avoid the water. We are sardines against each other, so that a man having to piss must pick his way over an obstacle course of bodies, weapons, and sleeping bags, each misstep provoking, "What the fuck?" "Asshole." "Watch it."

The sun seems to have gone missing. I want to tell you a story about heroic soldiers impervious to hardship. I cannot. For three weeks the sky is despair, alternating between rain and snow. It seems as if my bones are frozen. Little things slip. I fall asleep on radio watch. I wake with a jump and walk the perimeter, finding everyone asleep. In my own shame, I chew no one out.

* * *

It is early December when we patrol to the chief of Omar's house. He receives us in his courtyard and shows me into his great room. The scar on his cheek is purple in the frigid morning. I ask him for details about the water pipes he requested in our *shura*. Surprise washes over the chief.

He says, "You remembered."

"Of course."

He says, "Four years now, Americans visit here with helmets and rifles. They sit and they ask what do you need? They take notes and go away and nothing happens." The chief rises and ducks from the room. There is shuffling in the next room. He returns with a hand-drawn engineering design and spreads it before me, saying, "You are the first to come back."

He is stroking me.

Age has yellowed his paper designs. Running down the center of the first page is the river, splitting the village and the valley. Here is a drawing for his pipe scheme. Tracing a finger over the map, the chief explains the main intake will be in a side channel upstream from the village. They will build a headgate there to divert water into a canal that ends in a holding tank. A web of pipes will feed water from the holding tank to nearby homes.

"We need pumps here and here," he says, jabbing the map with his finger. He ticks off his list, "A hundred bags of concrete for the holding tanks and headgates. Two-inch water pipes, one-inch pipe, couplings, elbows, tees," and so on. "It's got to be metal," he warns. "No plastic pipe. Plastic cannot survive winter and fighting."

I put a hand over my heart in the Pashtun gesture of sincerity. "We will make this happen. Count on me."

"I trust you, Commander, except look at your men. It's hard to believe you." He points to Castiglione, my forward observer, who pulls security beyond the doorway. Castiglione is kneeling. His cock peeks at us through the tear in the crotch of his trousers. It is very cold this morning.

* * *

I keep us moving between houses and hilltops. Enemy fire has been minimal as of late, mostly sniping, the occasional RPG, or pulse of machine-gun fire. We shoot back in proportion, answering a burst of fire with a burst of fire, rather than artillery and bombs and chain guns. I do not want to turn the valley's northern reach into a battlefield again. The war is where we make it. If it is quiet, I think that is something.

We launch ambush patrols at night, and during the day, squads overwatch the road construction project. The widening continues. Caterpillar dozers and backhoes groom the road. Without notifying us, Afghan engineers blast the mountainside with dynamite, sending us all rolling for our rifles. The construction crews have made it three kilometers. Seven more to go. It is slow, as is everything in Kunar. The worst of the road lies near Comersa Bandeh. We will wait for spring before taking it on.

A pack of young boys has been frequenting the platoon in the daytime, selling soda and cigarettes, their hearts full of swindle. These boys are filching supplies from jingle trucks on the Pech, then hitching rides and finding us. They sell sodas for a dollar. Smokes cost five. At my elbow is one of the members of this syndicate. He is about seven. Today he has brought rubies to sell, all of which appear to be fragments of taillight. Some of my dudes think this boy is a spy, and I think they are maybe right but I don't know what there is to spy about with us. Anyone can walk up and talk to me. Up close, you will get a good look at the tear in the crotch of my camo and will detect I have not showered for ages. And with the constant quest for shelter, the total effect is that I am a commander of the homeless.

The water supplies for Omar arrive on flatbed trucks. I send spy-boy to fetch the chief, who soon comes flying up the terraces, trailed by dozens of men and boys wheeling carts and barrows, leading donkeys and mules. Old and young from Omar empty the trucks. Some of the young men I have not seen before. They are fit and sharp-eyed and probably fighters. Today is a silent truce. The villagers shoulder their lengths of pipe, heft the concrete into barrows and carts, and rope the rest onto mules. The entire village works for a week, pipes on their shoulders, trenching, fitting, burying. Day and night, metal clinks off bedrock.

On Christmas Day the platoon makes for the Pech River. There, a supply convoy drops hot mermites for us. This whole day I am sure nothing bad will happen. The enemy does not celebrate Christmas but still I am sure nothing bad will happen. On a delta of sand we eat like princes. There is turkey, ham, stuffing, mashed potatoes, and pie. The war would be all right if only I could eat like this once in a while. Afterward I get the runs, some of which I eject into the courtyard of a *qalat* during a late-night raid. Merry Christmas.

The January storms are big. They collect over the high Himalayas and roar downhill like so many lions. In this cold our batteries die quickly, then the mind and the body, or maybe it is vice versa but the result is the same, a gradual wasting. In the uplands there are spindrifts on the ridges. Tree branches bow with snow. A roof of clouds hides the faraway summits. Graupel lashes our faces. My toes are frozen in my summer boots, but I am loath to change them for winter footwear. Why abandon boots that have never given blisters? Footwear, after all, is no small thing to a man without wheels.

By mid-January I exhaust the army money, having used it on food, building materials, and local supplies for the platoon. Our tour is nearing completion, and command says we cannot draw more army money. Using a satellite phone, I call my dad, Russ. I tell him, "Sorry, I know, I know, I've been a real shit about calling. Everything is fine. Please send money."

He asks, "How much?" Not "*What for?*" or "*Why?*"

I say, "A thousand."

"Everything okay?"

"It's the winter lull. Nothing to worry about here. We are hibernating."

I ask about the NFL and who's in the playoffs.

Being from Connecticut, he says the Giants are losers and girly men.

I say, "I knew that without the news. Anyhow, I gotta go. Send that money quick."

"Copy that. Hang in there."

I have already spent loads of money building a crude firebase at the valley mouth. We call it Michigan because someone from Michigan insists. Not my idea. We have four-man bunkers there and cots. Problem is, I cannot see much of the valley from the perimeter. To remain aggressive in the southern reaches of our zone, I need a house thereabouts. We could endure winter in the open, living under ponchos and tempting frostbite, but there is no sense in it. The toll of this war is cumulative. Little things matter, like a woodstove and a roof when it is snowing. The Boys sleep a little better when no one has to spoon. They march faster and shoot straighter. There are plenty of hard-asses that like to show off how good they are at the suck. The name for that condition is marine.

We have been in the field for months, and I don't stand when I can sit. I don't sit when I can lie down. And if Cigrand wants to carry his laptop in his ruck and watch music videos when he's not on mission, then shit, I'm like, "You got any rap?" As far as lodging goes, I could take over Afghan houses with force. We have many guns. That, however, is not my program. The last thing I want is to be an occupier who galvanizes the locals. The money from my dad allows for an arrangement with the elders: I'll pay ten dollars per night to shelter my men in their homes. Quietly, I reason that no one is going to light up our position if we sleep in the middle of a village.

* * *

The Omaris finish their water pipes and invite us to a ceremony where they will turn on the spigot beside the mosque. We gather around it—my Boys, the villagers, and the policemen. The chief says something stately, turns the spigot, and fills a bucket. Water laps over the lip as he raises it in triumph. Then the chief comes to me, one hand over his heart, and bows his head slightly, saying, "Thank you."

At this moment I am high on myself. Perhaps my legacy in Afghanistan will be something other than shell casings in the mountains. *Let that sink in.* After the ceremony we have tea in the chief's great room. He talks and I listen. He tells stories of battling the Soviets. The chief was a militia commander when Russian tank columns came up the Kunar River. He seeded the road with mines and launched ambushes. He talks and I listen. Together we look to be teacher and student, him tutoring me on the destruction of empire.

The chief recounts an attack where, "A tank spots me hiding in the rocks. My men have made it to the creek, but I'm stuck in the rocks. The tank swings its gun around and levels it on me." The chief acts the story out, one arm straight like the tank barrel. "I see down its black tube. I picture the men inside, blond men drunk on vodka, laughing. I tell myself, *Get up and fight.*" The chief locks hands on a pretend rocket launcher perched on his shoulder. He rises, takes a shooting stance, and fires. "The rocket went straight down the barrel of the tank."

The chief's entourage are nodding their heads at me, looking officious.

The chief throws his hands in the air in mock explosion, knocking his own *pakul* to the side of his head. He says, "My rocket exploded in the tube, which ignited the store of rounds in the tank. Only the tracks were left."

Everyone is clapping, grinning and nodding vigorously. The chief sits and straightens the *pakul* on his head. We sip more chai. We eat naan and talk of the road and the river. The chief says he is happy for projects. He wants more projects.

He asks me, "What do we need here?"

"A wide road."

"No, Commander, that's what *you* need. What do *we* need?"

"I'm not sure what you mean."

"How can we make a better life? You come from a place I have not seen. What I know is you will travel across the world and fight for it. What is it we need to make a land like that?"

I have not thought on this. Perhaps the question catches me by surprise because it cuts to the heart of everything. What system is right for a people who, at heart, despise the notion of system? In my mind, I try on a few responses, patching together smart phrases the army has given me. None of it sounds quite the way I want.

I decide that, "Education. That is the way out of darkness."

"We are not in darkness. Look," he says, thrusting a finger out the window, "There is the sun. I have been to Kabul and Karachi. I could not see the sun between buildings."

"You're right. You're not in darkness, Chief. Forgive me. I misspoke. With education, you can be more prosperous. Your kids can live longer."

"Our children learn at the madrassa."

"Yes, that is one way. I'm thinking university, Chief. Yeah, I'm thinking that type. Science, math, psychology, you know."

The chief nods and sips chai. I suspect we both hear what we want.

* * *

A day later we take a house south of Omar. The place is empty, the family having fled the fighting. The brother of this family still lives nearby and he comes to see what we are doing. He is a shepherd. Some disease has him looking and smelling wretched. He is polite with us and accepts my money to stay in the empty house. He is also prudent about mixing with us when the sun is high, and promptly makes himself scarce. We are in the house two long days, doing the hill stomp and road detail, before the chief arrives with his retinue in tow. All wear their *pakuls* way back on their heads, so that I wonder how they stay on. They look dashing.

We sit in the little den I call my command post. Cigrand is leaning beside the window, radio antennae sticking out, hand mike in his lap. I do not dismiss Cigrand from tribal meetings because he is smart, and afterward, I have someone to think with. Mostly we laugh. At any rate Cigrand watches the meeting get under way, his eyes blazing as the chief, girded by his court, does formalities. The proceedings soon turn to substance.

The chief wants a school.

"What kind of school?" I ask.

"There will be two wings. One for boys and one for girls. Come, I'll show you."

I join him and his crew, and we pick down the terraces, hop between rocks in the river, then climb to his house. Just below the stone stairs that lead to his door, the chief says, "Here," stomping one sandaled foot. "Flat ground and close to the trail."

I say, "It is very close to your house."

I am not naive. The chief is cashing in on me, and I suspect he is with the enemy in one way or several. The fact remains things have been quiet, and he must have a hand in it. I am buying peace, and that is fine. It is what you do when you cannot kill your way to peace. The thing with a school is you must have teachers. You can erect a building and call it a school, but it is not unless you have teachers.

The policeman, Abdul, says there is a girls' school near the Shuryak, so I take a couple squads and we hoof it down the Pech to ask the teachers there if they will teach in the Korengal for extra pay. They say fuck no, and I say they are fuckers. I radio company to say I'll win this war with just a few more installments from Uncle Sam, and they radio battalion, who radios brigade. Before long I have money for a school and some teachers from Asadabad, young go-getter types, willing to give it a go in this violent corner of the mountains. When I tell this to the chief, he shakes his head and wags a finger at me, saying, "City people are not welcome here. My men will be the teachers."

I say, "They need qualifications. You gotta show me. It can't just be your brothers."

He looks shocked. "Why not?"

* * *

It is February. Snow has halted road construction until April. At Firebase Michigan, I am looking for something to do, other than shiver, when I remember a friend telling me the Afghans love cricket, a game brought in by the British many decades before, and volleyball, brought in by the invading American military in 2001. I call a *shura* by sending spy-boy to muster the village elders.

The elders assemble by the Korengal Bridge. I tell them we are going to have a volleyball tournament here, starting tomorrow, my treat. I have a hundred dollars left of the money my dad had sent. I give it to Abdul, and he climbs into his Ford Ranger police truck and revs away, heading for Jalalabad.

The tribesmen are gathering when Abdul returns. He skids to a stop beside the Korengal Bridge. He drops tailgate and we pull supplies from the bed. Everything I ordered is here: One volleyball net. Two metal poles. Three volleyballs. Ten red jerseys, ten blue jerseys. Abdul also went rogue and bought professional soccer jerseys for himself and the police. There is a bag stashed under his seat too. Abdul shorts me on change. I don't sweat him.

We set up in a flat beside the river. We sink the poles. We drag heels in the sand to mark court boundaries. We use extra logs, seized from an enemy lumberyard, to build bleachers. Sitting five high in the bleachers, we watch the Afghan police play the Afghan Army. The Omaris play each other. The Korengal plays the Shuryak. My platoon plays the Afghan Army (losing, by the way). We watch and laugh, the chief and I and Abdul. For two days we play in the open, serving, bumping, setting, and spiking. No one takes a shot.

1 1

ENDURANCE

KORENGAL VALLEY, AFGHANISTAN

MARCH 2007

Fifteen days left. I can feel the plane ride home, us accelerating off the runway and nosing into the clouds. I can smell the Coke the stewardess will serve me on the plane, feel the fizz against my nose as I gulp. For a few weeks now, not one shot has been fired in the valley's northern reaches. I do not pretend I have won the war. All around, though, there is progress. The Boys feel the end of their yearlong tour. They move a little faster in the dark, pretending maybe that they are marching home.

Jingle trucks deliver bricks and concrete for the school. Once more the chief arrives with a brigade of village men and boys. They load wheelbarrows, carts, and donkeys with supplies and pilot them up the valley. For two days they ferry bricks, wood, and bags of mortar. When all supplies are piled below the chief's house, they begin work. A firm from Jalalabad oversees the technical bits. For safety, their engineer insists on my platoon's presence at the site, where the engineer paces with drawings under one arm, pointing and yelling at the villagers, who yell back. For three days everyone is stooped in labor and yelling. When the building site is ready, the chief informs me they will set the first stone the next morning.

He says, "You will set it."

"It will be my honor."

In the morning the valley is clear, bright, and cold. The sun is on our faces, and my breath is steam as I bring the platoon to the school site. I post a squad and our machine guns on the hill overlooking. The rest of the Boys form a perimeter by the school, smoking cigarettes, little knots of village kids around each position. Meeting the chief at the foundation, I shake his hand and remove my armor and helmet. I set down my rifle. I am unarmed and exposed. We are building a school, and I do not need a rifle. This is my grand finale.

* * *

Parts of our battalion are boarding planes for home. The army whispers our return date to our families. My platoon has a few nights left in the field, then we'll march back to the outpost and catch helicopters. At the outpost the other platoons are conducting equipment inventories. As it goes with inventories after a year of fighting, lots of material has been lost or destroyed, and for accountability's sake, the chain of command has to shit on everyone. *Dump your gear. Everyone. Line up and dump it. Search party. Lock down until we find those binos.*

I would rather be in Omar.

It is six in the morning, and I am checking positions when Cigrand finds me. "Sir, Attack Six on the net for you." My heart pumps hard, three, four times. Hearing from the captain at this hour is unusual. I rush to the radio, dreading whatever this is. *Probably a stupid mission. Yeah. Gotta be.* I take up the hand mike, "This is Three-six."

The captain says, "New development: we've been extended three months. All relief plans are canceled. Forward elements have been called back from Drum."

Feeling faint, I sit down. "Say again?"

"We've been extended, part of a larger surge into Iraq. Our new departure date is June."

"June?"

"Yes."

"Sir, you said June."

"Roger, Three-six. Check your radio. I have you loud and clear."

"That's three months, sir. Are we staying here?"

"Yes, for now."

I manage to whisper, "Roger."

"That is all. Attack Six out."

I drop the hand mike and wobble around. There is an art to giving bad news. I am not sure what it is. I am sure it is not what the captain did. We already have guys on the ground at Drum. They are telling those fuckers, "About face," and putting 'em back on the planes. Talk about a kick in the sack. And the captain, shit, his delivery; how could he be so fucking cold about it? I shake out my arms and ask what I wanted from him. Should he have been weeping over the radio, bitching about how silly it all is, the injustice? The captain gave it to me straight. We are soldiers. This is war.

I have to tell the platoon. Dread wells up. Cigrand, I remember, is sitting on a cot across the room. He is staring at his platoon leader, a curl of smoke rising from the cigarette in his hand. He has three-day stubble on his chin.

I say, "You hear that?"

He takes a long drag, holds it, and exhales, blowing smoke far into the room. "Yessir."

I say, "Against all odds."

Flatly, he replies, "Chosin."

Picking up my gun, I stagger outside and make for a copse of hollies to look after myself. With emotions in check, I return to the courtyard to call, "Squad leaders on me," in a wobbly voice. I clear my throat and try again with all the authority I can muster, "Squad leaders on me."

The thing to do is be sincere. I give it to the squad leaders like the captain gave it to me: direct. I do not say *Sorry* or *This sucks* or *Uncle Sam never plays fair.* They are soldiers. I am telling soldiers they have a new mission. They stare at me in silence, knowing the weather is warming, the snow melting. The unspoken fact is the fighting season is upon us. There will be blood. Some of us will die who otherwise could have lived.

We settle into the doldrums of an extended combat tour. The best I can do is set a good example for the Boys: keep my weapon oiled, uniform tidy, and rucksack tight. I blouse my pants for the first time in many months. We go to camp for a wash, and there, receive new uniforms. I order them put on at once. In our war of endurance there is much to be said for soap and fresh clothes.

In April, Specialist Chris Wilson, a rifleman from my second squad, is reassigned to Second Platoon, which is short on men. Soon after, Wilson leans against a Hesco wall at the outpost. The enemy fires a recoilless rifle, which strikes the wall and blows him to bits. His death casts a terrible shadow on the Boys. By extending our tour, the army stole his life, or so it feels. Not long after, during an ambush, one of the team leaders, Sergeant Hernandez, falls in the Korengal River and drowns.

The little details of death haunt the rest of us, because when Boys get killed doing something, that thing they were doing is cursed; whether it's eating a beef stew MRE, or riding in the back right seat in the lead vehicle, or toeing across that footlog over the river near Darbart. By now dozens of curses haunt us. It has gotten near impossible to do anything without a pang of terror.

In the dark, alone on radio watch, when the last lights in Omar village have winked off, I think of Elizabeth. I invent ways to torture myself, imagining her remarried to a guy we went to high school with, a good dude who started on the varsity basketball team when he was only in tenth grade. Elizabeth went on a date with said dude one night after I forgot her birthday. In my dreams of acid rain, Elizabeth is married to this fuck. Elizabeth holds two baby boys with full heads of hair. Cross-legged, she sings to them, one boy bouncing on each thigh. She is living the life she always wanted with me, the one I had been too distracted to give her. I despise myself for it. I despise this war and the boyish reveries of manhood that brought me here.

* * *

In April the road widening resumes. Excavators eat into a band of cliffs near Comersa Bandeh. The cliffs crash onto the road. A dozer pushes the rocks off the edge. They thunder down to the river, sounding like artillery to all within earshot. Widening this section is a victory because it is the last stretch preventing army deuce-and-a-halfs from navigating the road.

The valley is open.

Soon after, a convoy from our battalion supply company runs for the outpost and makes it. Pulling into the perimeter, the drivers blow their horns. Steam brakes *hiss*. Engines *tick*. The convoy drops ammo, batteries, and gun parts. The Boys at camp gather to whistle at the female soldiers in the convoy, who at this point in the tour are beauty queens. Two of the women shed their camo blouses to lounge on the hood of a vehicle. They have rings on their T-shirts from boob sweat, which has the Boys howling from every bunker and guard post. High-powered optics are redirected inside the wire. In fact the enemy could walk right through the gate. A couple hours later everyone gears up, and the convoy winds back down the road toward the maw of the valley.

Expecting an ambush on the convoy, I have led my platoon into position on the west side of Omar. Behind a rock on a fifty-degree incline, I watch the trucks bunching up and spreading out as they navigate the twisting road, engines groaning. Right where the valley widens, the enemy opens fire from the eastern heights of Omar, directly across from us. We fire our machine guns over the convoy at the enemy, who continues to fire at the convoy, and for a few minutes, the convoy sprays heavy weapons at everyone. One of the trucks, taking rounds through the windshield and canvas-topped bed, veers off the road and crashes down the terraces, flips, then comes to a stop upside-down with the engine on fire. The two battered drivers unstrap, fall out, and stumble for cover.

Tracers, rockets, and grenades fly in every direction, so that the fight appears as a vortex of light and flame with a curious beauty. It takes a few bursts for my crews to get the machine guns right. Soon we pelt the ridge with accurate plunging fire, which knocks the enemy off the attack. They begin a retreat, I judge, through a deep, forested drainage that slashes up a mountain called Abbas Ghar. I drop a salvo of mortars on pace with their retreat.

"Sitrep," I call to the Boys. The squad leaders check bodies and ammo then report, "All up." I say we will not pursue, as it would require climbing down a thousand feet; crossing the road, terraces, and river; then climbing a two-thousand-foot hump in the ridge and dropping into the drainage. It would take a few hours just to get on their trail. The Boys lift themselves from the earth, straighten aching backs, and wipe off. We will help with the flipped truck.

Forty minutes later we have descended to the road. An F-16 fighter jet arrives on station. Some officer in battalion is relaying locations to the pilot. Circling high above, the pilot scans the drainage, reports heat signatures, and drops a bomb. Under my night vision, I watch the jet circle. The contrails are white streaks in a moonless sky, the plane's tailpipe like a star. The jet circles at length, then drops another bomb. The pilot reports direct hits.

We are five kilometers away and four thousand feet below the bomb sites, which to battalion is close enough to justify a sweep for bodies, and I would be a fool to say I'm surprised. Looking to be nimble, I recruit a squad and one machine-gun team, leaving the rest of the platoon to help with the flipped truck. After refilling magazines at the convoy, we cross the river and scramble to the toe of the ridge. The sun rises. We stay near the spine for a couple hours, following a goat path that overlooks the drainage. At the very bottom is a seasonal creek. Dense trees obscure the slopes on either side, which are broken here and there by cliff bands. Boulders and shark-fin rocks rise from the forest. We slog up another thousand feet. By now the fighter pilot is long gone, so I am taking orders from the captain, who's talking to battalion. Both are insisting that we count enemy bodies in the drainage. Bodies. We love dead bodies.

I give it a shot. The Boys are cursing as we drop to the first bomb site, ladder style, descending a couple hundred feet through a neck of broken rock before landing on a bench in the forest. The terrain is vertical, but we are close. Using a ledge in the cliffs we sidle east, faces against rock, until gaining the exact grid where the bomb detonated. By now the Boys are soaked through and bleeding from their hands and knees. We find nothing. We bang around for a while. Nothing. I radio the captain, "I'm at the first point. Nothing."

He says, "Roger. Look harder."

"Attack Six, I'm where the bomb exploded." I let out a long frustrated breath. "I've got nothing."

"Move to the second bomb and continue search. Prepare to copy grid."

I mark the grid coordinate he reads off. "Roger. Moving now."

I throw the hand mike at Cigrand, who says, "We're going to keep looking, aren't we, sir?"

"Until we find something."

Ahead and above us is a box canyon. The grid coordinate is inside. I figure best case, I am going to lose a man to a fall, and worst case, we hit a trap in the canyon and all die at the bottom. I envision the enemy pitching grenades from the clifftops, me yelling and running in circles as they blow us to molecules. Either way, it is *Dear Mrs. Such-and-Such, your son died bravely looking for bodies so that some staffies could cream themselves.*

I am pissed. The Boys are blunted and sloppy of foot. My solution is telling them to remain here and watch the surrounding ridges. I am going alone, so mad that I'm ready to self-martyr. I laugh hysterically. Cigrand wants to know what's so funny.

I say, "Everything."

Cigrand says he'll come with. I do not wish to tell him that I am doing suicide by chain of command. I say, "Nah, I'm faster alone," but he insists, and the look of loyalty in his eyes damn near melts me. "I don't need you to protect me," I say.

"Problem is, if you disappear, we'll have to find you."

"Okay. Let's go."

We lurch up a drainage that has never seen the sun. An impossible ridge shadows it from the southeast, sweeping up and up. We claw along the creek, following a series of waterfalls and pools. We clamber on the left bank, hop over, and follow the right, picking the easiest lines on an incline of fifty-five degrees. There is a path in here somewhere—the enemy used it—but we are off, and the terrain is so jumbled we'd have to be standing on a path to see it. The cliffs get bigger. We are soaked.

I sling my weapon across my back and ascend a slab of smooth gray rock. Cigrand scales behind me. About forty feet up it's technical climbing, smear technique and finger jams. We have assault packs only, and no rope, so I take my time, stuffing my fingers into cracks until they are sticky with blood. We shuffle across a ledge to a moderate pitch and go crablike up to a shelf. The rock turns to choss, crumbling shit, and we are scratching upward, breaking pieces off as we pinch at holds. At last I come to a rock chimney, sidekick the wall, and stem up, my rifle barrel clattering as I go.

Cigrand gets to the start of the chimney, looks up at me balancing in the air, and yells, "Fuck that, sir. I'm going left."

Topping out, I check the surrounding terrain and the map. Close to the second grid. I swing my rifle off my back, into the low carry. I hop from rock to rock then squeeze through a slot between two leaning boulders, feeling like a fleck in this empire of rock. My legs are heavy. I trip and go down and bite clean through my lip. My gun clanks. The sound echoes in the surrounding cliffs.

Fuck you, Afghanistan.

I gain the second spot. There are no signs of a blast. I am swallowing blood from my pierced lip. We are alone and isolated. The building pressure of it is suffocating. The point of this ratfuck of a mission is intelligence. Find the bodies and search for intelligence, as if a muj machine gunner will have bin Laden's cell phone number in his pocket.

You shouldn't have dragged Cigrand into this.

Off to the right, Cigrand scratches upward. "Over here," I call. He comes trudging up, chest heaving, and puts hands on his knees. "This is it," I tell him. Side by side, we pant, fighting our armor and the building heat. I poke around in the rocks. There is nothing here.

I tell Cigrand, "Give me the radio and head down to the squad. I'll catch up."

"I can wait."

"Go."

I do not want him to hear this. Once he is out of earshot, I radio the captain, "Attack Six, Three-six. We've got bloodspots here."

"Roger. Take a picture of bloodspots."

"Will do." I spit blood on the ground and take photos.

"Any bodies?"

"Negative."

"I want bodies. Keep looking."

"I'm in cliffs. Can't get any farther. We may lose radio contact."

"The enemy was there. If they can move, you can move. We dropped way too much ordinance for there to be no bodies. Keep looking."

"Roger." Then I almost yell, "Attack Three-six, out."

"You don't *out* me," says the captain. "I *out* you."

"Attack Six, you're coming in weak and broken."

"You will keep looking."

"Attack Six, you're coming in broken."

I turn off the radio and climb down, stopping every so often to listen for Cigrand. I do not see him until I'm right on top of him. He startles me into raising my rifle. Leaning against a tree, his face is a mess of blood, sweat, and thorns. "Dammit, Cigrand. What're ya doing?"

"Can't remember which way we went."

"Left, I think."

His knees crack as he gets to his feet. He asks, "What happened, sir."

"Nothing. No bodies. We are going down."

"Thank God. You want me to take the radio?"

"I got it."

Seeing I do not have the hand mike clipped to my vest, he asks, "You listening to the net?"

"Radio is broke."

He gets it now.

It is noon when we make it to the river. We splash water on our faces and necks. It feels so good that I dunk myself, gasping for air when I come up. The feeling is one of renewal, almost baptismal. We make the climb on bruised feet to the jeep road above, leaving wet footprints in the terraces. I radio the captain, "Attack Six, Three-six. We found no bodies. I fell and injured my back. We aborted."

He is fuming when he says, "Say again."

"I'm injured. We aborted mission. No comms due to terrain."

Silence tells me he is thinking. I am not proud of what I am doing, but I'm sure the body mission would have gone on until one of us, maybe all, got broke or killed. I stepped in front of it and lied. The entire machine breaks down when field leaders lie; this is not a crowning moment for me. Sometimes survival and sanity collide in this war of remote control.

Fuck you, Afghanistan.

* * *

Spring grabs hold of the land. Trees along the river bear leaves. The blue orchids and the wild marijuana are back. Poppies stain the hillsides a harsh red. The days are warm. Sweat sheens our faces as we patrol the rivers and villages. I keep the platoon busy: watch the road, visit the police, raid this house. The land is alive again and so are the dead. In the predawn hours, when things are slow, my mind dredges. Crazy comes up. The dead echo. Worst of all is waking for night radio watch. The dead are watching me, their faces mutilated.

Keep moving.

We visit the school, finding the masons and carpenters at work. The building stands a quarter finished. Elbows resting on the windowsill, the chief of Omar yells down to me from his home, inviting the whole platoon up for a sip. I accept, and we climb the long flight of stairs. I crouch through a door and sit against a tasseled pillow on the floor across from the chief. His grandson brings cups of chai and sets them before us. We take up the steaming cups, blow at the tea, and slurp.

The chief reaches into his vest, saying, "I have a gift for you. Open your hand."

I do.

He drops a piece of rusted metal in my palm, saying, "From the story I told you." He makes an exploding gesture with his hands.

In my hand is a piece of tank track. I smile. "Thank you."

"You are a good man, Commander."

* * *

By early May the platoon is coasting. We are getting short again. Thirty days to be exact. We have had a handful of solid gunfights, though no casualties, and in my mind, that is the best measure of our tactical prowess.

I am sloshing in the mud of Firebase Michigan when news comes that Battalion Commander Cavoli and Sergeant Major Carabello are making surprise visits to all platoons. Their tour is one of morale. I know they will arrive sometime this afternoon, as the platoon leaders in each firebase are tracking the convoy's movement and passing updates via radio. My sergeants get the Boys cleaned up. Everyone shaves. At about 1400 my counterpart in Charlie Company, Lieutenant Riley, radios, "Chosin Six leaving my pos. Heading west to you. Good luck."

An hour later the convoy appears. Four Humvees slam around a bend near the river and tear into Firebase Michigan. I greet Cavoli and Carabello, who at once ask to address the Boys.

The Boys come trotting out of the bunkers to form ranks before the sergeant major. A few Afghan kids stand on the hillside, curious about our formation. Sergeant Major lectures on vigilance until we board the plane. He has a reputation as mercurial, so we do not mince words when he asks, "You guys have enough bullets?" *Roger, Sar'nt Major.* "Food?" *Roger, Sar'nt Major.* "Batteries?" *Roger, Sar'nt Major.* "And phone cards, everyone got phone cards? Anyone doesn't, you tell me right now, and I'll give you four a' mine." *A-okay, Sar'nt Major.* "And how's these policemen?" *Great, Sar'nt Major.* "How about the Afghan Army?" *Even better, Sar'nt Major.* "How about the enemy? Are you kicking his ass?" *Of course, Sar'nt Major.*

The sergeant major asks, "So what do you guys need?"

Grinning, gunner Rene Berben pipes up, "Sarr Major, can we have a new AO?" He's asking about our area of operations.

A rictus takes hold of the sergeant major's face. "What? What?" he stammers, so mad he has lost his words. The sergeant major looks at Cavoli, who nods. Sergeant Major orders my platoon, "You men move out. Back to your posts. Berben, stay here."

The Boys sense his building rage and scatter at once.

Standing beside Cavoli, I protest, "But, sir . . ."

Cavoli raises a finger to hush me.

Sergeant Major crushes Berben in sight of the villagers and the Taliban and a dozen crows hanging out by the piss tubes. Berben is half as tall as Sergeant Major, so the scene has the feel of someone drowning a puppy. Sergeant Major hisses at him, "You don't want to be here? You're too good for it?"

"Ne . . . negative, Sergeant Major. I just, uh . . ."

"You ungrateful little shit. Everything we do for you. Everything we do. You're fucking done. Done. Get your ruck and get in my Humvee."

As Berben sulks for his squad bunker, he begins crying. Tears cut the dust on his face. All the while I'm standing beside Cavoli, stunned by the suddenness of this calamity and not sure what to do. I manage to say, "Sir, it was a joke."

Cavoli glares at me. "That little smart-ass. You don't need him in this platoon. You have to stomp out that kind of thinking. Why am I telling you this?"

"Sir, I'm not defending what he said. It's just I need the bodies. It was a stupid thing to say, but he's a good kid."

"It's decided," says Cavoli. "Trust me, we are doing you a favor."

I look over Cavoli's shoulder at Berben chucking his gear into the Humvee. Berben begins to bawl. His chest quivers. He sits in the Humvee with his chin on his chest and cries and cries.

I approach the Humvee and set an arm on the open door, "Berben, you'll have to leave your gun."

"I'm sorry, sir. It was a joke. I'm so stupid. Where are they going to put me?" He snivels and gasps. "Are they taking me off the line? I don't want to leave the line."

"I don't know. Look, Berben, no hard feelings. You'll always be one of us. Now how about that gun."

Minutes later the colonel's convoy departs with Berben crying in the back seat of the second Humvee. I cannot stop thinking about this little warrior, crying at being removed from his platoon and squad, destroyed at being forced off the battlefield.

* * *

The code name for the last major operation is "Big Axe." We will assault the south Korengal one more time. Looking to be in the action, Cavoli drives up the newly widened but not yet paved Korengal Road. He ensconces himself in company headquarters at the outpost, which flushes out riffraff like me. Cavoli has brought along his executive officer, one of the last men in the battalion who has not earned a CIB (combat infantry badge). The XO is looking to get in the shit, though not too deep, I suspect. Just enough for the badge.

After the Big Axe mission brief, Cavoli guides me to a sandbagged nook behind headquarters. I stand at attention. Cavoli keeps me there for a few long seconds, then says, "Relax. How's the platoon?"

"Good, sir. It feels good to be on the offensive again."

"Keep the Boys focused. This is the last push." He asks, "You still want to go to the Rangers?"

"Yessir."

"Good. You have orders for the Ranger orientation program. If you pass, you'll be assigned to Second Battalion. Congratulations."

In a flush of excitement I break courtesy, "No shit?"

"It will be a break, after this."

"Excuse me, sir?"

"This, what you're doing out here. This is as hard as it gets."

I do not believe him.

He says again, "Everything will be easy after this."

I smile. "Thanks, sir. I can't believe what these Boys have done."

"I know. They did it for you, and me, and each other. No one can ever take it from them."

With two weeks left in country, we helicopter to snow-covered ridges deep in the Korengal. We are pushing the enemy back, interdicting ratlines from Pakistan, and making space for our replacements. The offensive is clean on the topographic map: blue arrows, red boxes, and straight lines from helicopter insertions to enemy positions. On the ground it is squiggly lines and torrents of cursing. In the mornings the snow is a hard crust, which has us slipping and splitting our chins. By midday the snow softens to a mushy quagmire that has us post-holing from one objective to the next. We kick steps into the snow as we climb. We heel-plunge when coming down. We grab handfuls of snow to cool our necks and brows. The high-elevation sun reflects off the snow so that even the underside of my nose is sunburned.

We hit some caves, do movement-to-contact and search-and-destroy, all the cool-guy stuff that looks good for battalion reports and the new company commanders who need maneuver time in a combat zone. This offensive is a résumé builder, and I get to thinking all offensives are. No one has died, so morale is soaring. After three days we trundle back to the outpost. We cross the surging Korengal River, using a footlog perched twenty-five feet above the furious channel. We make it across and trudge up the last hillside. We are three klicks from camp. *Spread out. Don't bunch up. Walk with your head up. Check your six.* We are three klicks from the end, and I mean *The End.*

We have just gained the village of Aliabad when fire erupts at our rear. We wheel around and return fire. The enemy is on the opposite slope of the valley. The Boys dive for positions and squeeze off well-aimed shots. The squads bound between houses, then come abreast at a rock wall and blaze away. Our machine guns hammer the enemy in measured bursts. No one balks. I do not call for mortars. We fight with the guns we carry, one last time, brave and disciplined against some of the best light infantry the world has ever known. Seeing my Boys, I realize the true measure of a warrior is not his first battle; it is his last.

* * *

Our replacements arrive, the 173rd Airborne. They are arrogant, sinewy, and florid-faced in this new heat. We are quiet, skinny, and tan. In the beginning, they are brave. They seek the glamour of total war. They are the best unit in the army, and we are the worst, which explains our casualty rate in the Korengal. Such hubris is to be expected. It is far easier on the paratroopers' psyches to attribute our high casualties to laziness, poor leadership, and all-around weak genes. The incoming company commander, who faces a fifteen-month tour here, shouldn't say, *The unit we are replacing took a bunch of casualties because the enemy is tactically brilliant, equipped with Soviet weapons better suited to this terrain than our own, has superior numbers, and is the population. A bunch of us are about to die.*

Better to say that we suck.

I am too tired to argue with them about it. First week in June we board helicopters and leave. As we fly down the valley, I have this ineffable urge, so I raise both arms and flip the bird to the mud villages below.

PART 3
RUN

12

AFTERMATH

The 173rd has a man killed within their first twenty-four hours in the Korengal. Hearing this, and still welded to the valley, I review their tactical decisions. *They got it all wrong. Should have listened to us. Arrogant bastards.* I must arrest this thinking. Disentanglement from the valley is not as easy as I had hoped. *It is not your problem*, I keep telling myself. *We are going home. We are never coming back. Never ever. I got the platoon through. If I do nothing else in life, I have done this.*

The platoon is not what it was fifteen months ago. Of the forty-three original members, just sixteen remain. Turnover is a trivial detail. The platoon is an organism unto itself, one that transcends individuals and time, one that dies only through total annihilation. So long as it has members, the platoon survives. I have earned the right to be part of this sacred organism, a link between past and future.

We land at Fort Drum and step off the plane. Tarmac greets us. No wives. No children. A general of some sort is waiting at the bottom of the ramp. One by one, the general shakes our hands, saying, "Well done, Trooper."

"Thank you, sir."

Who is this dude? Seriously, where's my wife? I step onto a waiting bus. Our families, I learn, are gathering in the gymnasium near battalion headquarters. Before we see them, we will turn in our weapons and form ranks. Our loved ones' first view of us will be marching in formation. It is a discipline thing, and torture for soldiers denied their families for so long.

A couple hours after landing, we march into the gym with the division band smashing out a battle hymn on cymbals, horns, and drums. There is a rush of life. Wives, kids, dads, and moms are in the bleachers waving signs and flags. I scan the crowd and spot Elizabeth. As soon as the ceremony is over, we trot to each other and hug. Lavender scents her neck and hair. I say, "My wife." A heaviness seizes me. My body is a thousand pounds, and I have been awake for a hundred years. I am sick of the men around me, officers, noncoms, and privates alike. They are great Americans, and I know their habits, fears, and most cherished dreams. I am sick of them, and I am sure they are sick of me.

Elizabeth and I leave at once.

At our place I feel confined. To be indoors is not yet right, so we open all the windows. Crickets chirp. The breeze flutters our curtains. Squirrels run atop the wood fence. The heaviness in me subsides. We stay up late on the couch, talking in the television light. My detox begins with Elizabeth's eyes, brilliant with life. I sit on the carpet in front of her. She rubs the valley from my neck. The world begins to feel right again. She knuckles my back until I find sleep.

* * *

The first day of summer is supposed to be our happy ending. All the officers in battalion have pitched in to buy beer and meat for a barbecue. *Free beer. Bring your families!* We seize Olmsted Park, a grassy hilltop overlooking Watertown. In summer the land beyond Watertown is exquisite. Finger lakes and rolling farms fill the valleys. Mature oaks and maples with neon green leaves shade the grills where our steaks and patties sizzle. Shafts of sun strafe the picnic tables beneath the trees. The smell of charcoal wafts across the hilltop as soldiers and families arrive.

Everyone, it seems, has bought a new vehicle, trucks mostly, with REST IN PEACE stickers pressed across the back windows. The Filipinos pull up in tricked out Honda Civics with mufflers like cannons, talking shit. "Who wanna race?" Though the officers have bought beer, the Boys still saunter up with eighteeners under their arms and fingers hooked into six-packs. Everyone wears a black bracelet for a friend lost. Everyone wants to get numb.

We drink a lot. It is quiet though, the mood restrained. I suspect we have been together so long that we have already talked about everything there is to talk about. Old guys from my platoon, the ones medevaced off the battlefield, are here. Billy Siercks, my old platoon sergeant, is wearing a Led Zeppelin T-shirt, shorts, and a knee brace. He joins me at a picnic table. He keeps tapping his beer can on the table. *Click, click, click.* I think he is nervous. We do small talk for a while before he tells me, "Sorry for leaving you guys, Three-six. It killed me that I couldn't say goodbye. I looked for you at Bagram, thought I might catch you coming back, but no luck. It was torture here on rear d. Every day I worried about you guys. All I could do was take good care of our Boys who got medevaced."

There is sorrow in him. Siercks wants me to say it is okay, that he did not let anyone down. I turn and reach into a cooler and open a beer and set it in front of him. I slap him on the shoulder. "You haven't met Elizabeth, have you?"

Platoon sergeants aren't supposed to get hurt, so I do not give him what he wants.

An hour in and Cigrand arrives, carrying a case of Bud Light and wearing a tank top that looks like it has not been washed for weeks. He saunters up to me and Elizabeth. Rapping him on the back, I say, "I knew you were a little bit redneck, but goddamn, son."

He looks down at himself and up at me, "Whaddaya mean?"

"Never mind." I introduce him to Elizabeth. Cigrand does not know he is my best friend in the world. I do not treat him as my best friend because I am an officer and it is poor form. He is though, because he was in the exposures that matter in my life. That will still be true, I believe, if we never speak again and I live to be a hundred.

Elizabeth hands Cigrand a beer. He smiles for her and she smiles back. They are instantly friends because I have told each of them everything about the other.

More of the wounded arrive. Sergeant Robinette, who was gutshot in the same fight that I was decorated for valor, now rolls up with a colostomy bag attached to his wheelchair. He chain-smokes cigarettes. His complexion is sallow. He says he has not been outside much. Roberts and Shannon, both shot below the waist, have canes. Patterson is bent like an old man from a ruptured disc in his back. A few picnic tables distant, Jae Barclay and his wife are eating. With 80 percent of his body scorched in the explosion, Barclay spent most of our tour in the army's medical burn center in San Antonio. His face is a patchwork of skin from other parts of him. I avoid Barclay and his wife. What should I do? Introduce myself to her? *I'm responsible for your husband's ghastly appearance. He's looking better though. No hard feelings, right?* Of course, I can't. I do not know what to do. *I just know that I am so terribly sorry, Jae. The muj stole your face. They did it right under my nose, and I am sorry.*

Young men, many not old enough to drink, are limping, rolling wheelchairs, and bent over canes. Neck braces and blood-splotched bandages are the new uniforms. We are the bludgeoned survivors, prostitutes of bravery. Absent are the fallen. Vaccaro, killed by a rocket; Robinson, a bullet; Wilson, a recoilless rifle. Bombs took a handful of us. One died of drowning. Another in a vehicle rollover. More in a helicopter crash. It is a litany of causes. In the end, we all die the same, no matter rank or marital status or fighting prowess.

Every man lost is a small tragedy. And I will always feel responsible for the ones in my platoon; like if I were better, maybe no one would have gotten smoked. This guilt is like a furnace in my chest. I am incapable of explaining it to others, even Elizabeth, fearing that if I try, I will smear the war on her, and so ruin the one pure thing in my life. The antidote, I believe, is more fighting. Only through force of will can I fix my chemistry. *Rangers, lead the way.*

13

THE INVADERS

The Ranger orientation program, or ROP, is a three-week evaluation for combat-proven leaders seeking entry into the 75th Ranger Regiment. Elizabeth joins me for the trip to Fort Benning. Leaving Fort Drum, I drive us through the day and night, seeing the throbbing cities of the eastern seaboard out the window, hearing songs for the first time on the radio, and feeling as if I've returned from Mars. Elizabeth and I talk about everything. The world is new, and she is lovely. I had been worried she would look older. It turns out she looks better, more like a woman, a little fuller, her hair longer, and eyes happier than before.

I ask, "Do I look the same?"

She says, "You look skinny and dirty."

I say, "Why for? I've had plenty of showers."

"I know, but you still look dirty. It's your face, I guess."

The conversation pivots to our current trip. I tell her that if I get into the Rangers, I could be deployed again any time. Is she okay with this?

Silence.

"Hello?"

She says, "I want you to be your best."

My eyes get hot and wet. "Thanks." We move onto family, talking about nieces and nephews, and while we do, I imagine laughing children and fulfilled parents. I blurt, "Let's have kids."

"When?"

"Tonight."

She laughs.

"I'm serious."

She withdraws. "Not yet."

"Why?"

She bites the nail on the index finger of her right hand, like always when she's about to string barbwire. "I'll be your widow," she says. "God help me, I'll do that, and I'll be proud of it. But I won't be a single mom."

I want to torture her. "What's this about?"

"You just got back. Why are you in such a hurry to die?"

"*I knew it.* You're not okay with this. That's great, just great. I'm going to die now?"

"Don't be a jerk."

"You're the one fucking with me."

She softens. "I'm not. I just don't want to be alone."

I soften. "In the Rangers, it's different. The missions matter. Dudes don't get killed so much."

"Yeah, right. I saw *Black Hawk Down*."

Shit. I made her watch it.

"It's not like that anymore," I say. "The Rangers run around the same places as the regular units, except they do it at night with six aircraft overhead. It's easy. The colonel even said so."

"And what am I in this? Housewife waiting for husband? I'm not stupid."

"Babe, what's up your ass?"

"My ass? Listen." She looks tragic. "Just before you came back, a sergeant in—I can't remember, Two-fourteen I think—he gets killed by a bomb and his wife is pregnant."

"I heard."

"No, you didn't. She is highly pregnant. When they go to her door and tell her, she collapses on the porch. They leave, and she's crying in the front yard, rolling in the flowerbed with the neighbors watching." Elizabeth pauses, pulls in a few breaths. "The wives, they all say, 'This can't be. It's so tragic. This won't stand. The army is at fault.'"

"I'm sorry, babe. That's not us."

"Shut up and listen," she says. "It's not that. This woman, I think she is stupid. She is pathetic. What did you think was going to happen, Miss Warrior Wife? You get pregnant by a man going to war. Everything is supposed to be okay? The Taliban don't give a fuck about your little fairy tale."

Elizabeth goes on, "And Sara . . . you know Sara. She's a platoon leader's wife, not some nineteen-year-old bimbo. I go to her apartment, and she got a little knickknack in the kitchen that says, HOME IS WHERE THE ARMY SENDS US. I mean, it's like she has no agency, no mind. All these women have had a psychotic break with reality."

"Goddamn, girl. Why you wanna shit on good people? Calm down."

"Fine," she huffs, crossing her arms tight. "I'm not stupid, you know."

The outburst has her spent, and by midnight she dozes off and gets to snoring. We pass through Baltimore, where the skyscraper lights dance on the harbor. Having seen *The Wire*, I decide not to exit for gas.

At two in the morning, Elizabeth wakes suddenly and offers a shy smile. "Was I snoring?"

"Like a chainsaw."

"Gosh."

"You feel better?"

"Yes."

"I love you, girl."

"I love you too. And don't worry, babe, you're the second biggest that I ever had. How could I leave you?"

* * *

One thing to know about ROP is that the men being evaluated are leaders who are already Ranger qualified and combat experienced. No one yells at us. Some call it a "gentlemen's course," although we are perfecting techniques for mass killing, hardly befitting gentlemen. It means a substandard candidate will be ejected without commotion. *Right this way, sir.* The cadre test us on the basics: push-ups, sit-ups, pull-ups, rope climb, five-mile run, sprints in combat gear, and a twelve-mile march laden with armament. All these events, held in quick succession, are for time. I exceed the standard on each test and resist the urge to show off, as it would attract unwanted attention.

The cadre teach the raiding arts to those who pass the initial tests. We learn fast-roping from helicopters (fun), night close-quarters combat (sort of fun), and night parachuting (not fun at all). We learn knife fighting and jujitsu. Hand-to-hand combatives are on the program to instill the Ranger spirit, but more importantly, because these skills are cool. If we have reached the point where I'm killing someone with a bayonet, then everyone is dead, and the mission is surely fucked. Once we get to the battalions, the instructors say, we will learn to hot-wire cars and operate heavy machinery.

I'm going to take over the world.

We learn Ranger weapons. One is the Carl Gustaf antitank weapon, a bazooka for commandos. It is not that I'll be shooting it. The idea is to learn how to deploy it, understand its range and capability. I must see and feel what the weapons team sees and feels. The best way to learn is carrying it and firing. We spend a lot of time at the range with rifles. There is zero nonsense about milliradians, bullet grain, and jacket types. We deal well-aimed, hot lead in volume. I practice advancing while shooting, chest plate squared to the front, so that if I catch a bullet, it's more likely to strike armor. Legs poised in a fighter's stance, I take deliberate, measured steps toward the enemy, getting better at keeping eyes on target, feet moving, barrel honed. I drop a mag, jam in a new one, thumb the bolt release, and keep firing. *Rangers go forward, firing.* We are assaulters. There are safer ways to hit a target, but our hallmark is headlong aggression. We do not prance. We do not backpedal. We invade countries.

The shooting and machismo have a strange healing property. In Afghanistan we got ambushed so much that I began to feel impotent, like I could never get the drop on the enemy, and thought somehow we were all a bunch of lazy shits. Shooting drills with Ranger sergeants cauterize these old wounds. I forget feeling helpless.

All the time the cadre scribble on clipboards, evaluating us, not just for tactical competence, fitness, and the universal skill of "being good with our hands." They are gauging attitudes: Who is a dickhead? Who is a suck-up? How does a captain respond when critiqued by a staff sergeant? *Ranger sergeants*, they tell us, *are self-propelled and fiercely protective of their Boys*. The default is suspicion of outsiders and officers who are "rotating through." The cadre tell us we will have to win trust, no matter our rank or combat credentials. I imagine my Ranger platoon sergeant, seeing him seven feet tall and barrel-chested, with the disposition of a tommy gun.

Some mornings we work out using the Ranger Athlete Warrior system. The cadre explain that traditional army exercises such as push-ups, sit-ups, and long, slow runs are insufficient to prepare commandos for war. The regiment has applied exercise science to the battlefield, and thus revolutionized its training. In most cases a combat mission starts with a low-intensity endurance event, say, marching six miles to a target house, followed by a flurry of high-intensity action much like a football game—clearing rooms, kicking doors, wrestling a terrorist to the ground.

Climbing is part of every mission, so we throw ourselves at walls, scaling ladders, and ropes. We do everything wearing armor, helmets, and fighting vests. The cadre say we must be collegiate-level athletes in running, climbing, and lifting if we want to win on the battlefield. I am supremely impressed, and a little skeptical, for one day we tour the Third Ranger Battalion gym, finding it a festival of shiny, weird, and absurd contraptions. In one corner is a device that could very well be a time machine. Everything is wildly expensive. Someone has made a fortune selling gym equipment to the regiment.

The regiment has a psychiatrist. Third week of ROP, he spends a few hours interviewing me. He explains it takes a certain personality type to enter a home in the dark and kill all the occupants. His interview is no Myers-Briggs. The questions are about social deviance, my capacity for violence, and responding to extreme stress.

A felony event in Second Ranger Battalion illustrates the breed this shrink is looking for. In 2006 young Rangers from Charlie Company returned from Afghanistan, their pockets bulging with combat pay, and decided they should rob the Tacoma, Washington, Bank of America, *because they could*. Four of them roll into the bank, wielding rifles and pistols. They are bellicose and in total control, sweeping the lobby and offices. Everyone folds. The Ranger who pulls door security calls out time elapsed. The leader of the group, a Ranger buck sergeant, boosts over the counter and collects $54,000 in unmarked bills. Less than two minutes after they entered, they slam out the front door and run to a waiting vehicle.

The security tapes of the robbery show military precision. Anyone watching the news in Seattle can tell the robbers are professionals in violence. Unfortunately for our men, a bystander caught the license plate on the getaway vehicle. Between that and the security camera footage, it does not take long to zero in on members of Second Ranger Battalion, the local commandos. Everyone involved goes down.

Long-time members of the battalion still whisper about the robbery, about its perfect execution. An old Ranger sergeant dismisses the fact that the cops bagged the young Rangers within three days. "That's what happens when team leaders run their own ops."

All this goes to say that the darkness is alive in a good Ranger. The key is finding guys who are moderate on the darkness spectrum. *High* equals serial killer or bank robber. *Zero*, on the other hand, equals pussy. We take a psychological exam, which is several hundred questions long, to see if we are pussies, Rangers, or serial killers. The thick booklet lands with a thud when the shrink drops it on my desk.

I tell the truth, and no one kicks me out.

The final test is an interview with senior regimental leaders. This is more terrifying than the physical hurdles. I have been to the worst place on earth, but am now scared because I want this so bad. Pressure, after all, is mostly self-inflicted. Standing outside the conference room at regimental headquarters, my legs quiver, and I pull at my camo top to fan myself. My biggest fear is that my face will burst into sweat, my nervous habit. This would not look good, to have a Ranger officer without control of his physiology.

I march in and snap to, finding a solemn group of the Ranger brass seated at a long table. They order me to sit in a single chair before them. Right away, sweat beads on my lip. The urge to exaggerate, to put myself in the best light, is profound as they launch the first questions. I answer with sweat running into my mouth, swallow, and press on, deciding the thing to do is tell the truth: I led a unit that was shot to pieces. I have been surrounded and damn near overrun. I have climbed every mountain in Kunar Province twice. Oh, and I'm pretty fucked up in the head.

An hour later I emerge accepted.

* * *

Right away Elizabeth and I move to Fort Lewis, Washington. We drive into a town called Steilacoom overlooking Puget Sound. My deployment scars are fresh, but this is the plan, I tell myself. *Stick to the plan.* Elizabeth is thrilled about Seattle and the big woods around us. "Anywhere but Watertown," is how she put it. We find a rental house on a hill. The apple trees in the yard are pendulant. We drop bags in the living room and blow up the air mattress.

It is seven in the morning and cold when I report for duty behind a tall brown fence near the Fort Lewis Airfield. Inside fifteen minutes, the ops officer asks if I'd like to go to Iraq. *The battalion*, he explains, *is already deployed.* He is polite. "Or you can sit this tour out. The war isn't going anywhere, and I can keep you busy until they come back. No one will hold it against you. Say, do you know PowerPoint?"

"I'll go."

I speed home and find Elizabeth on the air mattress with a book resting on her stomach. She is reading *The House of the Scorpion.* I tell her, "Uh. Hey, babe. Damn, you look good."

She flings aside the book and sits up. "Don't tell me."

"The battalion wants me to deploy immediately."

"Unbelievable."

"Yeah, unbelievable."

"You know you've been deployed four hundred and twenty-five days of the five hundred we've been married."

I muse on this and say, "You're right. It sounds bad when you put it like that."

"I know I'm right. Look, I love you and support you. I also want this to slow down."

"It will."

"When?"

"I don't know. Remember, babe, this is our plan."

"I think it's your plan."

"Hey. Look at me." I sit beside her. "Don't say that. I can't do this without you . . . Did you just roll your eyes?"

"No."

"Yes, you did."

"You're a man. Why do you have to keep proving it?"

"That's oversimplifying."

"I'm not gonna sit around this time. I'm going to find a teaching job somewhere."

"Somewhere? Somewhere. You mean here?"

"Yeah. Where else?"

I exhale. "That's good." I want her here, but not in tow. My profession forces a gypsy lifestyle, with two years being the average time spent in one place, the most being three. Constant moving dampens any ambition for the military wife. In the army community, the name for this condition is "trailing spouse." I am searching for an upside to the arrangement and falling short. New scenery, I guess, and improved map-reading. Some wives surrender themselves to it. *Home is where the army sends us.* Elizabeth does not deserve to be stymied. She is too smart.

That night I sleep in doses and wake at dawn, agitated, to scan the Olympic Range across the Sound and think of what I want for her. We are young and addicted to one another. We define happy simply as being together. I keep making that impossible. Right now I have no remedy. I will think of something.

* * *

Within three months of returning from a fifteen-month tour, I am on a plane, bound again for war. On the ride, I unfurl what Elizabeth said. *Have I done enough to be a man?*

If you have to ask, the answer is no.

Iraq passes below, village lights sprinkled in a sea of sand. I land in Balad, small as Iraq bases go, but extravagant in any case. This is the big war with all the journalists and generals. Everything is different. My first raid will be north of Tikrit, in the ferocious Sunni Triangle. The terrain is all flat and—*oh, thank you*—we get to drive.

We gather for the briefing in a domed tent. Inside there're abundant computers and a theater-sized flat screen on the wall. Playing on the flat screen is an aerial feed of last night's raid. Two Ranger sergeants are pausing, rewinding, and fast-forwarding the feed, analyzing their takedown of a house. The tent walls are lined with lockers, each Ranger having his own. In the lockers are weapons and optics I have not seen before. All the guns have tiger stripes painted on. They are beautiful guns.

Tonight's target is a terrorist cell that has fielded suicide bombers with devastating results. The mission briefing is concise, the raid compressed into five PowerPoint slides. The Ranger sergeants brief their respective assignments. Several have the physiques of bodybuilders, and with the lockers and instant replay, it seems I have joined an armed NFL team.

Under starlight we jam into seven Strykers, twenty-ton, eight-wheeled armored vehicles topped with heavy weapons. Our Stryker convoy bulls down a country road for fifty minutes and stops a mile from target, a compound inside a Bedouin village. We pad up on foot, passing houses of mud and gypsum. Out in the dark, a goat bleats. The target house appears, a two-story deal ringed by date palms. A few whispered commands bleep over the radio.

We surround the target. No one wants a hug from a suicide bomber, so tonight we will use a cutting-edge tactic known as a "call out." It is a sexy and highly classified technique for hitting a target, less likely to result in mass casualties than storming from room to room. I am not supposed to say this but I will. In a call out, we surround the house and say, "Come out with your hands up."

With a bullhorn we order the occupants, "You have two minutes to exit the house with your hands up, then we are coming in and killing everyone who remains." For the record, we are not for sure going to kill everyone, though we are going to err on the side of killing everyone.

Through a window, I spot an Iraqi man with bed head and a Kalashnikov. He comes running down the interior stairs to see about the fuss. Halfway down he pauses and squints out the window, shoulders his weapon and takes aim. The glass in front of him cracks as our sniper shoots him in the face, exploding his head like a water balloon across a tiled wall where a family picture hangs. Another man wearing a fighting vest charges down the stairs, gun in hand. A dozen Ranger weapons *crack*. This time the window shatters and the man goes to his knees, reaches at air, then falls headfirst down the remaining stairs before folding up on the landing.

Women appear on the second floor, filing from a room and making for the stairs. They wear black gowns. Seeing their dead men in the foyer, they begin wailing and clawing their own faces. We yell at the women for a while, saying, "We won't shoot you," a few different ways to get them into the courtyard. For some reason they do not believe us. We pull them behind cover.

We stampede into the house with guns up, stepping over bodies in the foyer, careful not to slip in the pond of blood. Up the stairs and down a corridor. Another armed man flashes between rooms. One of our assaulters points his snub-nose machine gun at the wall of the room that the man dove into. Plaster flies as he punches a hundred rounds through. By now I am drunk on the killing. We flash-bang the room, then charge in to find the man behind the bed, leaking all over the place. Outside the women scream their heads off. We match a photo to the man's face to confirm he is the target. *Jackpot.* We make a few more holes in the house and call it good.

Feeling infamous, we jam back into the Strykers and speed north for another building, eight kilometers distant, listing around corners and running over enemy dogs, creatures so vicious and mangy that I suspect all life on earth benefits from their destruction. We stop on the main road, dismount, and march in a staggered column, bristling with gun barrels. We follow a canal, then hook right into a palm grove. Fronds wave overhead. We brush along. Above and through my night vision, the AC-130 Spectre Gunship supporting our mission is visible. It radios us, reporting people in the grove about two hundred yards ahead. The canopy obscures their movements. A spotlight attached to the aircraft fixes their location.

Our lead squad forms a phalanx. The K-9 handler sprints ahead, wielding a Belgian Malinois that has shiny white fangs, black gums, and black lips. The dog, panting in the heat, wears an infrared strobe and a glow-in-the-dark patch with his call sign. He is our canine kamikaze. He is our fur-missile.

We creep up, then launch the fur-missile. He streaks into the grass. Seconds later there is snarling and gunshots. Our handler calls back the dog. We send 40 mm grenades and two drums of ammunition into the grass, then advance, finding two men had been lying in ambush with a PKM machine gun. One's head is spilled onto the feed tray, the other stitched with a dozen rounds.

That's a good boy, good boy. Who's the best boy?

Leaving them facedown in the sand, we advance toward the target, stalking in chest-high grass. The AC-130 overhead continues circling, one wing dipped, so that the 105 howitzer on board has a clear shot at the ground. As armed men squirt from the target into black rock desert, the howitzer on the plane flashes and pops. At this distance, the gun does not sound like a big deal, but we are blowing the runners to pieces. A sweep of the bodies for intelligence reveals only viscera and innards.

This terrorist cell is decimated. We reload the Strykers, wipe sweat from our faces with shirtsleeves, and reload our mouths with tobacco.

I'm getting off on this. No lie.

We return to base around dawn. Not far from our compound is an Olympic-sized swimming pool. During the day, instead of sleeping, the young Rangers go to the pool to tan and try for a fuck on the Air Force girls. Beside the water, the Rangers lounge about like kings, wearing just black running shorts and Oakley sunglasses. They get in and out of the pool without using the ladder, leaving no doubt about their workout regimens. Ranger battalion scrolls are inked on their forearms, but they tell the girls, "I can't say what unit I'm in."

* * *

In the fall we rotate home. The battalion commander, Kurilla, assigns me to be a platoon leader in Bravo Company. In garrison, the Boys of Bravo don their tan berets, wearing the headgear beautifully, rank patch jutting forward, the rest sweeping down the left side of the skull, nearly hiding one eye. Each beret is cocked so far to the side it looks like it must be pinned to the hair. I spend a lot of time at the mirror fine-tuning my own beret.

I go along the quad to meet the Bravo Company commander, Major Sadler, who is reputed to be the best in battalion and a rattlesnake under fire. In his midthirties, Sadler is relatively old for his position. Such is the standard for officers in regiment; we must first shine while commanding conventional army units, before becoming eligible to lead Ranger units of equivalent size.

I head for Sadler's office, hurrying down a cinder block corridor in cinder block barracks. On the corridor walls, Ranger artists have drawn skulls, bones, demons, and military armaments. It is all tattoo-style art, scary and cool and tacky.

Sadler summons me, "Enter." I click heels in front of his desk. "Relax," he says. His hair is immaculate, the lines on his face strong. On his desk is a coffee mug the size of an 81 mm mortar. He is a little soft in the stomach, as is often the case with majors and above, no matter the unit. Right off the top, Sadler says, "Welcome to the battalion, and to the best company in it. The colonel tells me you've already been deployed with Alpha. That's good. You get what the endgame is, what we are shooting for."

Sadler stops and looks out the window at a team of Rangers climbing thirty-foot ropes on the parade field. He smiles at them like a patriarch. Beside the ropes, Rangers clad in battle rattle drag three-hundred-pound sleds between orange cones. He says, "God, look at them." Then he pivots. "Where were you in big army?"

"Tenth Mountain, Af-Pak border."

"Dismounted?"

"The whole time, sir. Lots of helicopter ops though."

"You're weak on vehicles then. Absorb what you can from your weapons squad leader. He'll be your vehicle commander when we deploy."

"Roger, sir."

"We're in training cycle now. Train, fight, train, fight. It doesn't let up here. We'll run MLATs in a couple weeks. You know what MLAT means, right?"

I file through army acronyms in my head. "Sorry, sir."

"That's multilateral training exercise. We practice invading a country. Goddamn, Lieutenant, what are they doing in ROP these days?" He does not wait for an answer. "Then, we'll gear up for the next trip, probably Iraq again. Training can be hard on platoon leaders. In the rear, you won't get to be Iron Mike." He's referring to a brave statue at Fort Benning. "The Ranger sergeant knows his business. They run the platoons. Your job is easy until we go downrange. That's a good thing or a bad thing, depending on your personality. Let your platoon sergeant run the squads. Let your squad leaders run their teams. Set a good example. Do what they do, but not in front of them if you're not good at it. Does that make sense?"

"Yessir."

"Can you shoot?"

"Yessir."

"Good. Too many platoon leaders get embarrassed on the range. Let me be clear about something: Batboys aren't perfect. I've seen better guys in big army, not a lot, but some. These sergeants will tell you they are perfect, but they are not. A Batboy's self-esteem tends to be too high for his own good. That is also part of what makes them great. Anyway, I know you've been in real gunfights so you know when shit's fucked up and when it isn't."

Again he looks out the window at the Rangers ascending ropes, dragging sleds, then goes on, "You are in charge. You see something wrong, you address it. If you are timid when you must be bold, I will fire you. If you fuck up, I will fire you. And if you're weak when we go overseas, I will fire you."

"Roger, sir."

"I'm assigning you to third platoon. The Seabass. You're platoon sergeant is Locke. He is ceaseless. The noncoms he grew up with call him Little Bear. You have to earn the right to call him that."

"Yessir."

"Move out."

My platoon holds the third floor of the barracks, and after flying up the stairwell, I hustle into the headquarters office, finding Sergeant First Class Locke at his desk. He rises, grins, and points across the office. "How you doing, sir? That's your desk."

Locke has the slim build of a prizefighter. He stands five feet five and wears a shock of brown hair with streaks of gray. On the surface there is little evidence that Locke is a hardened manhunter with nine combat tours. I am relieved he is not the NFL-linebacker type I had expected. In short order, I sit, flip open my laptop, and log in, not sure what else to do. I open the top drawer in my desk to find a black dildo, a monster so big I could bludgeon someone to death with it.

Locke rushes out of the room laughing.

In the morning Locke invites me for a run. We meet in the dark, about 0540, outside the company barracks. He speaks in breathless bursts, no pauses. "Where you living? Steilacoom, nice. You were in Tenth Motown? Afghanistan or Iraq? I saw you got hit. Taliban Marksmanship Badge on the license plate. You married? Me too. Kids? I got a girl. It looks like it's gonna rain today. Always raining here. Gotta watch out for the Legs on this route." We head for a back road cut into wet, tall forest. Once on the route, Locke pounds a six-minute pace for the first five miles. I am a good runner, and still have my Korengal feet, so I keep up fine. Locke gears down at our turnaround and runs the five miles back at an eight-minute pace.

We tear past regular army units—the Legs—running in formation and singing about airborne rangers, and for a few moments, it feels like a pep rally for me and Locke. When we get back to the battalion fence, our heads are steaming. Another formation of regular army trundles past. Snickering at them, Locke says, "That's such a waste, I haven't run in formation in ten years. Okay, good run, eh? I like that route, minus the Legs. Hey, you hungry?"

* * *

We practice invading a country by parachute. Like most missions, we start with a briefing, and it is the briefing more than the mission that has me shitting. Parachuting from a plane onto a blacked-out airfield is mostly a physical enterprise, and a damn sexy one. That is the easy part of being a Ranger. The hard part comes before that: briefing forty high-performing officers and convincing them that I am an expert. For three solid days, I rehearse and guess the questions they will ask, terrified of making a fool of myself. Elizabeth, the teacher, suggests making flash cards to study. I do. At the dinner table she quizzes me. She wants to go to bed, and I make her quiz me.

We are nocturnal and it is mission night. A bunch of important people assemble in an aircraft hangar: the battalion officers and senior sergeants, C-17 pilots, some high-ups from joint special ops command, and our helicopter crews from the 160th Aviation. A map as big as a tennis court covers the ground, showing an airfield in the desert. The leader of each small unit stands on the map then moves to specific points to simulate the maneuvers his unit will execute. I brief my part smoothly and whisper thanks to Elizabeth for the idea of flash cards.

Now comes the easy part. By chalks, we gear up and toddle into C-17 Globemasters, sporting rifle and case, parachute and reserve. Rucksacks dangle between our legs. Each man is a mix of sophistication and simplicity. I have a $10,000 pair of night-vision goggles and an assault rifle with an optic the public has never seen, though I carry both in a canvas case that has not changed since World War II. Rubber bands hold my static line to the pack tray on my back. Rubber bands will ensure everything goes right when I jump out of an airplane flying two hundred miles per hour. Everything always goes right. When my chute opens, I will fall at eighteen feet per second. The impact on landing is equivalent to jumping off a two-story house, so tonight I am going to jump off a two-story house wearing sixty pounds of weaponry and see how it goes.

In the C-17 there are no seats so that we can fit more bodies. On both sides of the cabin, we crash onto the floor and wiggle against the fuselage and each other. This will be a four-hour flight. Loose items are hazards, so we can't have spit bottles. I swallow Copenhagen juice. With parachute and rig already inspected, we can't start unbuckling or unsnapping to get comfortable, which means I can't piss, so I don't drink water. I sit in dim red light and swallow more Copenhagen as the plane lifts off and jets south across the United States. There is nothing to do except look at each other and guess who is scared.

Plugged into the flight intercom, I receive tactical and weather updates. Of note, winds over the drop zone are too high for a jump. High wind means tangled chutes, scattered jumpers, and violent landings, exponentially raising the risk of injuries and death. We may have to abort the whole dance. It's leaning that way, but for now we press on.

The border of Nevada passes beneath the plane. Most of the Boys are asleep. Helmets bob. Winds are still too high. Outside temperature is four degrees, the windchill far below zero. I look at Locke, wondering if they will call this off. He nods at me and smiles. *Fuck, we're going.*

A single wind reading between gusts is below the threshold, which is all we need. "Twenty minutes." We struggle to our feet and inspect each other, looking for loose straps, hooks undone, and busted rubber bands. My rucksack swings between my legs as I check my lowering line. I inspect the Ranger beside me, slap him on the hip, and say, "You're good." Nearby are the Rangers jumping with heavy armaments—mortars, base plates, the Carl Gustaf bazooka. It takes two men to get them on their feet. They will fall 20 percent faster than the rest of us. The look on their faces says so.

"Hook up." The call echoes down the cabin. We hook static lines to the cable overhead, elbows up as we half the slack. My heart starts as the jump doors slide open. A rush of cold air fills the cabin. I stagger as the pilot noses the plane down to jump altitude.

Our jumpmasters lean out the doors, so that in the cabin, only their hands and boots are visible. The first jumper takes position, staring into the dark. As the black runway comes into view, the jump light pops green. The jumpmaster howls, "Go!" Up front, the jumpers chasing minibikes leap into space, following their bundles. I lurch into a run. Boots thud across the deck. I turn at the door, no time to think, and leap.

Winter air hits like a hammer. Cold robs my breath. The plane's roaring engine streaks by. My chute pops. The risers are twisted, which sends me into a spin. My legs swing as I come around, and the straightened risers soon bring me to a rocking stop. Below is a lake of darkness. I look up, seeing the four C-17s that follow my own, lined up one behind the other, each ejecting two rangers per second.

As the din of jet engines fades, I am bouncing in my risers. Something is wrong with the chute. There are divots in my canopy, someone running across. I order him to stop that. He runs off the edge, and floating away, says, "My bad."

When this many men jump, it is impossible not to have some midair chaos.

We have exited at very low altitude, ensuring the enemy has minimal chance to shoot us, affording us maximum surprise. For jumpers, this means almost no time to pull a reserve if the main chute malfunctions. Our common nightmare becomes real: a few jumpers back, someone is burning in three times faster than the rest of us, a victim of a cigarette roll—meaning the chute did not fully deploy—and is now dropping at thirty to forty feet per second. The plunging figure disappears in the dark.

Below my boots are parallel runways separated by a grass median. The Rangers who have already landed are being dragged across the ground by half-deployed parachutes. They look dead. Furious wind shoves me laterally over the first runway. I yank on my opposite riser, doing a pull-up to counter prevailing wind, which makes little difference. The speed is sickening. Up comes the runway. I hit like a five-hundred-pound bomb. There are starbursts.

When I wake, my parachute is dragging me down the runway. I pop one chest connector. The chute deflates. There is a bass drum in my head. I pull my rifle, mount night vision, and stuff my chute in a bag, then toss it in the median between runways so that the chute does not interfere with the landing of our aircraft.

The army has taken the fun out of jumping from planes.

The army is good at killing fun as well as people.

Around me, Rangers smash into fences and buildings. The collisions are no shit. I cannot hear them on account of wind. One of my Rangers hits the door of a truck near the terminal, collapsing the metal. Some shatter the runway lights. In a sister company, a Ranger with over a hundred jumps does a perfect parachute landing and still manages to splinter his femur. He rolls around, screaming into his throat. Ankles crack. Heads snap against runway asphalt. Half my company has landed in desert flats prickling with cactus. I learn that the Ranger with the cigarette roll in his chute is one of my team leaders, Sergeant Mac. He deployed his reserve moments before hitting the ground. The impact compressed his spine. He is having a bad day.

Even in the Rangers, there are risk assessments, decision points, and plenty of lip service to safety. In gale-force winds we still jumped. When an elite unit does a windup this big, it is almost impossible to rain check. The individual jumper pays. We are Rangers. Tonight I taste what the old wars must have felt like, when the calculus was much different: if you throw enough motivated bodies at something, you will win. The individual is expendable.

I sprint down the runway, head pounding, as I make for the objective. Words come slowly when I link up with alpha team from third squad, then Sergeant Archie—the third squad leader—and his bravo team. Another Ranger is wandering in the median like he has lost his car keys. He is from Charlie Company and very far from where he is supposed to be. He wants to know, *What are we up to on a night like this?* Certain he's concussed, I grab him and fold him into our ranks. About four minutes after landing, I am first to reach the platoon objective on the runway's north end. Archie's squad spreads out in a line of scrub cedars. We wait for the rest of the platoon. Two minutes pass before Locke arrives, a squad in tow. I step out of the cedars and signal him with my laser.

He goes from a run to a trot, asking, "You the first one here?"

"Roger," I say, feeling exultant. "I've got Archie's squad."

"Good. We've got plenty of firepower to take this building." Locke stops and squeezes his neck. "I landed in goddamn Utah. Fucking wind."

* * *

After the airfield, half the platoon members, myself included, are nursing concussions. The good news is that Locke is all right with me. Most mornings we work out together, eat chow, then hover between squad bays. Today we will inspect second squad as they conduct demolitions training. Locke walks me down the barracks hallway, laughing about some mission during the last "trip," which is Ranger code for combat deployment. Without warning, I am tackled at the back of my knees. My head bangs off the tile floor. The assailant is a Ranger private.

Two more Rangers jump from a doorway and pin my arms. Another pair comes from the right. I flip onto my stomach and mule-kick one in the mouth, spilling him onto his ass. I throw an elbow at someone's face and knock him into the wall. One of the assailants gets a flex cuff on my left wrist. I deliver a right cross to his neck. He yelps. Locke, who is watching, yells, "This one's feisty," and another fire team jumps in. Twisting and punching, I break free and run for the stairwell, thinking I've beaten the attack.

From a barrack's door on my left flies Sergeant Archie. Shoulder first, he launches all two hundred pounds of himself at me. The impact sends me into the wall, and I go down stunned. Ten Rangers pin me to the floor, flex cuff my wrists, then mummy me with duct tape. They finish by taping my mouth shut and covering my head with a sandbag. They lift and carry me horizontally down the corridor. I thrash. They bang my head into the wall. I stop thrashing. We descend three flights of stairs. They march me down the main hall of the barracks and stuff me in a closet.

A few hours later, Major Sadler opens the closet door in his office. I fall out at his feet. He looks at me and says, "Oh. They let you in. This is good."

Through my taped mouth, I plead, "Untie me."

He rips off the tape and says, "I hope you went down with a fight."

"I got a few, sir."

Some days, training is Hollywood. We fast-rope from Chinooks. We parachute off the ramps of helicopters. We blow doors with C-4 and test new weapons for the army. Most days, though, training is not much different than big army; we all do ground combat.

The main difference to me is ammunition. We have so much. I know because I ordered it. In big army, each soldier in a platoon might shoot a combat load over the course of a day. On a Ranger training range, we put ten to fifteen times that through our barrels.

I watch Locke a lot. Even his smallest actions are precise. There is no wasted movement. With his assault rifle, Locke is fluid death. On the ranges we shoot until carbon covers our faces and we can barely lift our arms. Then we eat breakfast and shoot some more. We are building reflex. The idea is to shoot straight without thinking. When the enemy cracks rounds at us, we do not duck. We go nuclear.

14

BLOCK PARTY

IRAQ

SPRING 2008

The next trip is to Iraq, and we have just been assigned a covert mission: take down a cartel of sorts connected to a foreign power. This is secret squirrel business, some I'd-tell-you-but-I'd-have-to-kill-you business, and I can't say anything about it, so I'm quick to tell everyone that I cannot tell them. From this day forward I will deal in vagaries. We need a bunch of dudes for this mission, so my Ranger company must form a brand-new strike force with a team of Navy SEALs. No one has done this before. Covert. Commandos. Cartel. I am soaring.

Locke reacts to news of working with SEALs with a sarcastic, "*Greaaaat.*"

Three weeks before deployment, the SEALs come to our battalion headquarters for a meet and greet. Supposedly, there was a row over who had to make the trip to whose headquarters, an early pissing contest that it appears we won. We jam into the battalion conference room, where our battalion commander kicks off the meeting by telling us Iraq is on fire with civil war. The capital is imploding. American casualties have surged. Iraqis are dying by the thousands. The Haji has fielded a new weapon called the explosively formed projectile (EFP), a bomb with a copper warhead which can penetrate the armor of any vehicle, even that of the fabled Abrams tank.

This is the context for our new endeavor: SEALs and Rangers working together for the first time, complementing each other in a joint mission to root out the worst of the worst. New endeavors are fragile. We are two elite units unaccustomed to sharing. We have to put egos aside for the good of the mission.

Blah, blah, blah.

After the colonel finishes, we go around the room introducing ourselves, everyone speaking one octave lower, being hard as shit. When the briefing is over, we strut up to our SEAL counterparts for a proper introduction. There is much butt sniffing. My sergeants are dropping names of missions and operations, the biggest, baddest war stories they can think of to let the SEALs know that we are hard and they are Hollywood. "Where you been? How many tours? Oh, you were there in '02. Were you part of Anaconda? Oh, that's too bad. I was. No shit, you were in BUD/S"—Basic Underwater Demolition/SEAL school—"in '03? What was I doing? Oh, that's right, assaulting Haditha Dam."

I meet my SEAL counterpart, Dan White. He is an O-2, same rank as me. The SEAL chief, or sergeant first class in army speak, is Eric Diggs. There is a third leader in the SEAL platoon, a junior officer. I cannot remember his name, or what he does, only that he is being mentored by the other two. In a world of supercharged noncoms, I do not envy the extra officer.

The SEALs brought a major too. Big guns. On paper he is in charge of this whole deal. The way this works is White and I are same rank, so we need a higher rank to babysit us in case we get to clawing each other's eyes out.

The SEALs wear mops of hair and the same type of mustache. I suspect they have a talent for self-admiration. They use first names with each other and with us, which has me wincing. First names are a no-no. In the Rangers, we call each other by last name or simply *Ranger*. We are storm troops, part of an unstoppable machine, and as such, each man is expendable. Expendables do not have first names. My first name is for my old lady and my mom.

For much of the meeting, Locke forces a smile. He seems to hit it off with Chief Diggs, though on the return to our office, he says to me with disgust, "You know what some of these dudes were doing their last tour? Security details for VIPs. I've got Ranger privates with more combat time than these clowns."

Our unit flag is heavy with campaign streamers, and Locke is not excited about being under fire with a group of nautical newbies in that most hallowed task of *the assault*. Having come from a unit shot to pieces, I relish the idea of hitting targets with dozens of highly trained commandos, no matter their branch of the military or number of previous fights. More than anything else, I suspect my job will be keeping civility on this trip.

* * *

Two weeks before my departure to Iraq, Elizabeth takes a teaching job at Tillicum Elementary School outside Fort Lewis. Work quickly engulfs her. On the day I am to leave, I emerge from the bedroom with duffel bag in hand to find her at the kitchen table with school papers splayed across, mouthing the words as she reads.

I say, "I gotta go."

She looks up. "I love you."

". . . Will you drop me off?"

"Yes. Let me finish these lesson plans. Ten minutes."

"No, I can drive."

She says, "Are you sure?"

"Yeah."

She stands and kisses me. "Be safe."

I open the front door, and with one foot out, glance back. She is back in the papers.

We have a C-17 all to ourselves for the sixteen-hour flight to Iraq. I read *Atlas Shrugged*, or like one chapter anyway. We land at a sprawling US base that takes forty-five minutes to circumnavigate by vehicle. Our compound is located near an industrial trash incinerator that vomits ash on everything within five miles. Thirty-foot concrete walls surround our compound, making us an island inside an island. SEALs and Rangers alike spread into assigned container housing units, one man to a room, and drop gear.

We outfit the ready room, each Ranger and SEAL prepping his night vision, armaments, radio, bleeder kit, and weapons for whatever. The SEALs brought their scuba gear too, should we need to attack al-Qaeda's navy.

First thing is deciding who gets to be *assault* and who gets to be *isolation* for missions. Assault means clearing houses. Isolation means holding back the neighborhood. White and I agree our respective men will rotate the duties each mission. I lose in rock-paper-scissors, so the SEALs go on assault first.

We do not wait for shit to happen to us. We go do shit. Four hours on the ground and the first mission is ready. Our target manufactures and distributes EFPs. He has buckets of American blood on his hands. I will call him the Mad Bomber of Baghdad. He lives in a place I will call Shia Town. This precinct is a stronghold for the militia. Last fall the militia fought conventional American units out of Shia Town, picking them apart with bombs, snipers, and vicious street fights. We had a choice: level it or leave it. The army chose a strategic withdrawal. Our Abrams tanks now stand on the perimeter of this warren, keeping it isolated, yet allowing it to be what it is.

The US military is fond of the containment tactic in the dense cities of Iraq, which collectively house over thirty million people. When faced with numerous hot zones and too few ground troops, it is helpful to withdraw from zones of marginal importance, isolate them, and pursue strategic objectives in surrounding areas. The problem is that the abandoned zones become bastions for the enemy, staging areas for training, supply, and launching attacks into neighboring districts. They are cancer zones. You cannot ignore cancer for long.

The situation in Shia Town is perfect for our task force: a raid into enemy-held territory to grab a high-value target. A couple hours before launch, I reach the US Army battlespace owner by secure phone, seeking more information about Shia Town. When I announce our intentions, my counterpart, an army captain, says, "Holy shit. You're hitting Shia Town?"

"Yeah. What do I need to know?"

He tells me, "The road ringing Shia Town is mined. I wouldn't drive it. And don't go into the interior. It's fuckin' tight. They'll try to take out a vehicle and trap you, brother. We had to level three blocks with the tanks to get a mech platoon out." Then he says, "I can't believe you're doing this. Freaking Rangers, man. Kick some ass, brother. Rangers lead the way."

Feeling heroic and a little soft in the bowels, I walk into the briefing room, finding everyone assembled. SEALs on the left, Rangers on the right. There is no assigned seating. Our cliques come naturally. We talk through the raid then gear up.

It is midnight when we climb into the bellies of our Strykers, which the SEALs insist on referring to in nautical jargon—deck, aft, port—a habit that has long since grown tiresome. I ride in the second vehicle as we surge into Baghdad, the turbocharged engines growling. We come to forty-five miles per hour. On the bench seat in the troop compartment, I have the fidgets. No traffic rules apply to us. Because of night curfew, there are no cars. We have free reign of a city home to five million people, and in our machines we are gods. All have eaten a good dinner. Everyone has had a shower and a shave. After Afghanistan, fighting fresh feels disingenuous.

The RPG cage rattles as my Stryker barrels down a potholed boulevard. Lampposts cast domes of light that we avoid. We serpentine the stinking streets of North Baghdad, minarets and rounded mosques going past. As we navigate roundabouts, Sergeant Reese, my weapons squad leader, issues commands to the driver. "In at the six, out at the twelve." Then, "In at the six, out at the three." Even though he has eaten a few IEDs over the years, Reese stands tall in the commander's hatch.

We hit fifty-five miles per hour. The sweet scent of diesel combustion stirs me. The crude streets race past, trash choking the curbs and gutters. A couple klicks out, we raise hatches and stand up, torsos exposed as we sweep guns and lasers across palm-lined streets and black buildings.

Exiting the highway, we ramp onto a cratered arterial and rumble west. Shia Town is on the right flank, a labyrinth of tenements, mid-rise apartments, and power lines. Rubbled buildings are interspersed. Ahead, barbed wire blocks the road. Reese spots a break near the sidewalk and orders the driver, "Shoot the gap, there. Don't slow down," and we don't.

Just beyond are pendulant electric lines, strung between houses, criss-crossing the road. We duck in the back hatches to avoid being clotheslined. Reese's Stryker turret rips down the first few lines, which twist and knot over the hull. Flashes, sparks, and cracks of electricity light up the street. More lines snap off and whip about. On we go.

What the turret misses, the Stryker's antennae does not, and after a quarter mile, there's a few dozen electric lines wrapped around Reese's Stryker. Some drag behind. Reese raises in his hatch, saying, "Everyone up," through the intercom.

"Rally point in thirty seconds." Then, "Ten seconds."

A ball of fire swallows Reese's vehicle. Building windows shatter. Pavement flies. My vehicle shudders from the concussion while shrapnel *pings* off our armor. Smoke and billowing dust spew over the street. "Push through," I say. "Push through." My head snaps as the driver guns it. Through the curtain of smoke, I see Reese's vehicle intact.

"All elements push through." I yell into the radio. "Three-four, sitrep."

Reese coughs, coughs, then answers, "We've been hit. Motor sounds funny. Standby for sitrep." Sergeant Williams's squad is in the belly of the vehicle. Williams reports, "We're good. Shrapnel came through the cabin. Fuck, we're good?!"

A bomb six hours into the trip has me thinking I'll need meds after this.

My job is to stay focused on tactics, make decisions. I wear a quarterback sleeve on my wrist. Inside the sleeve is a map of the target house and surrounding blocks. We have already reached the rally point, the place where we planned to dismount and walk the last mile to target. The element of surprise is lost, and there's no rule for what to do when bombed at the rally point. I make the call, "Dismount. Continue mission."

The ramp on my Stryker is stuck. We climb out the hatches, adrenaline surging, and jump off the top. It is about ten feet to pavement, and midair with forty-five pounds of battle rattle, I regret not scooting off the top like the others. Spine rams brain. Knees buckle. I go down, roll, and stand up. Smoke from the bomb is still heavy in the air.

I find my legs and run for a dark alley, following Archie's squad. Bootfalls on pavement give way to measured steps as we ease into a sleeping neighborhood. Guns at the high-ready, we march down an alley, threading cars. This battlefield is vertical. A hundred windows look down on us. It is no big thing, I think, as the streets are dark and we have night vision. Coming to an intersection, my platoon divides into four blocking groups. I join position one.

We move beneath a portico, past an electronics shop and a bullet-scarred wall, to seize the intersection north of target. The SEALs blow the door on the target house and funnel inside. Right away, AK-47 fire begins nearby. It is hard to tell, maybe five blocks away. We have a drone overhead that reports Hajis jumping into the beds of pickups and moving toward us. Narrow streets and mid-rise apartments interrupt the drone's view.

I elbow the hood of a car, barrel pointed north. West of me, another AK-47 cracks off, maybe three blocks away. More shots echo to the east. Soon gun flashes fill the district, lighting the building facades. The militia is doing reconnaissance fire: shoot down a street, hope we will shoot back. Once they find us, they will try to pin us and mass. They want us to blow their precinct to shit. When Americans leave a string of civilian bodies and gutted houses, it boosts the militia's political maneuvers.

White, the SEAL platoon leader, radios that they have taken the first house. No luck. They are going to hit adjacent houses. In commando parlance, we call it a "block party." Houses, apartments, and shanties of corrugated metal are commingled here, none having logical floor plans. We must keep at it, room by room, house by house, smashing kneecaps, elbows, and chins on the hard edges of Baghdad.

In the course of a half hour we exchange a dozen bursts of fire with the militia. No decisive engagement. The heat has us reeling. I radio for White, then meet him in the foyer of the first house cleared. In this maze of dungeon-like buildings, our guy can move a whole block without exposing himself to the street. We need more assaulters, which I volunteer. At first, White objects to help, perhaps thinking this is a scheme to undermine America's navy. I argue about stretching into daylight and the probing fire. He concedes. In short order, Locke pulls a squad and leads them to a breach, and if he thought about what to do, he didn't stop for it.

One good crank on a pry bar gains them entry into a low-rise apartment, where they start kicking doors. We wake up a lot of Hajis, some scared, some pissed. The raid goes on like this until 0400, and we are no closer to bagging our man. We have lost the element of surprise, and the longer we are static, the more likely the militia can draw us into a street fight. This is not the mission, so we call it.

* * *

Upon returning to base, we study the hit on Reese's Stryker. It was an EFP. The projectile pierced the hull and engine compartment before breaking into fragments. Under the bench seats where Williams's squad had been sitting are jagged holes and shards of copper. Had the pieces hit a few inches higher, the story of tonight's raid would have been far different.

Driving around knowing the enemy has bombs that can defeat your armor makes you feel stupid for having the armor at all, like wearing chain mail after the advent of the rifle. War is a technological race, and at this moment, we are behind. The action-reaction sequence started with the invasion of Iraq. The bulk of the infantry traveled in unarmored troop carriers. In the aftermath, the enemy deployed roadside bombs, inflicting casualties, instilling fear. We armored our vehicles and regained the advantage. Then the enemy deployed remote-controlled bombs, which we defeated by installing radio-signal jammers in our vehicles. And so on. The latest development in this race is the explosively formed projectile. The militia is killing our tanks with ten dollars' worth of copper.

Our man is still out there, the Mad Bomber of Baghdad. Capturing him is one act in this multiyear arms race. My strike force has a routine, and like any routine, it casts normalcy over what we are doing. During the day, the intelligence shop finds targets while the ground force sleeps. I wake at 1500, work out, and head for the ops center, where I study intelligence reports and the latest enemy movements. About 1730 Locke and I head to chow, where he talks shop with no periods. Early evening my squads barge into the ops center, hair still wet from showering. "What are we hittin'?"

With Copenhagen in our lips, we curse and jab fingers at satellite imagery. White and I figure out the big-picture maneuvers and where subelements will go during tonight's mission: Strykers, snipers, assault and isolation teams. We squabble over who's *isolation* and who's *assault.*

"It's our turn."

"For real, dude? It's our turn."

"Last night didn't count as a turn."

"Bullshit. You hit a house so it counts."

"That was a shed."

"No. It was a house."

"Shed."

"House."

After midnight we leave the airfield and hit targets. We shotgun doors and flashbang rooms. We throw Haji on the ground and cuff him. We drive back with our sensitive information and lay it out for the analysts, then gather for an after-action review, or AAR. What went right, what went wrong, what can we improve?

No talking shit about the SEALs in the AAR.

We do this every day: Wake. Prep. Brief. Load. Roll. Kick doors. Exploit. Debrief. Chow. Weights. Sleep. Repeat. We keep missing the Mad Bomber and going back again. The dude is turning this into a matter of ego. Other targets are ripe for action, some less than two miles away. We keep going back.

The way this works is we must bang targets every night. A strike force that does not launch looks bad, either dumb or lazy, or dumb *and* lazy. Other commandos will talk shit because each morning, staffies roll the missions of each strike force into a twenty-four-hour operations report. The report summarizes target location, enemy killed and wounded, whether the target was caught, and special notes on enemy tactics. Though not intended to be, the report has become a measuring stick between Ranger units, so that when I call a fellow platoon leader in Charlie Company, we are both looking at the report and we say something to this effect:

That was you guys on Objective Knight?

Yep, two targets and a follow on.

Not bad. We hit four.

How many KIAs?

Three.

We had five. Objective Baker.

Women don't count, dude.

Fuck you, neither do dogs.

You guys can come up here if you want to hit real targets.

Real targets? I saw you hit a fucking disco last week.

It was a night club.

Each morning, as we keep missing the Mad Bomber, the operations report stings a bit more: *Strike Force Two reports dry hole.* Six raids. Six misses. One attempt on our man, led by our sister strike force, turns into a running gunfight with bullets skipping down the streets, RPGs splattering on Strykers, shot dudes falling from rooftops, and room-clearing with frags. I watch the raid as it happens on the aerial feed. I want to be there and I don't.

A shootout is fun to a point. Beyond that point, you wish to have chosen a career with the Department of Motor Vehicles. Anyway, we have a big shootout for this guy and that doesn't work either. The raid that succeeds is unremarkable. All the pressure in Shia Town flushes the Mad Bomber north of the district, into an isolated country home. We hit at 0300 and catch him sleeping.

He is an Iraqi cop.

1 5

NIGHT CRAWLERS

IRAQ

SUMMER 2008

I love teaching. I had a girl in a class I was subbing for declare she was a lesbian. It went something like this: "Hi, Miss, my name is Teddy, and I'm a lesbian," to which I replied, "Hi, Teddy, nice to meet you, and that's a little too much info. Please sit down." These middle school kids don't know their heads from their asses! They are like, "I'm emo." "I'm punk." "I'm goth." Geez, whatever happened to just being a kid? I miss you. Don't be a hero.

—E

* * *

The sun torches the desert. City streets bake. Body temperatures surge. Egos get in the way. Choices lead to animus between army and navy. Who hits what house, whose snipers get to climb that rooftop? We argue over equality, like who wrenches on the Strykers when we get back from missions. White and I fight a little war inside a big war. So do Diggs and Locke. When out of earshot, we find ways to undermine each other.

One night Sergeant Archie puts it like this to Sergeant Lacion, my first squad leader: "Yo, that SEAL, Chief Handlebars, he's got a tramp stamp."

"No," says Sergeant Lacion morosely.

"I swear," says Archie. "He was shaking down Haji on target last night. I saw it, right under his back plate. How do you like that?"

"I figured he was a rear-entry type."

"For real."

"From now on, I'm ordering buddy teams to the showers."

Pointing at his crotch, Archie says, "Chief Handlebars can't have this."

I cannot confirm or deny this tattoo, for I never saw it, and I am not proud of all my ink, though it is a matter of content and trying too hard, rather than location. All the same, we go on hitting targets every night, army and navy storming Central Iraq by Stryker and helicopter. In our shared purpose and shared danger, we learn to get along. None of us will admit to learning from the other branch of the military, though I notice it on targets: my Rangers using soft, careful room-clearing; the SEALs mastering tactical aggression.

When the big targets are not up, we go for the small guys. We will kill anyone, semibad, superbad, financiers, foot-soldiers, IED movers, IED makers, Iraqi cops, their nephews. We will launch on the sister's boyfriend's cousin if there ain't shit else to do. The paradigm is that they are all part of a network, and I start to wonder if every Iraqi is bad, like somehow we aren't looking at it right; like if we dig deep enough, to the roots, we'll uncover that the majority of Iraq's population is Shia, and that the Shia don't want us in Iraq any more than the Sunni do. I suppose I could have told you that before we got here. This is intelligence.

For us, it is bombs and bullets every night. The Shia are in full uprising. The militia parades. Sunnis are pissed that the Shia are consolidating political power. Al-Qaeda is killing anyone it can. Foreign actors are protecting their own interests. Everyone shoots at everyone.

One normal thing in Baghdad is wealth—air conditioners humming, a Mercedes in the garage of the target house, emerald jewelry hidden in a dresser. I grew up middle-class, so raiding the rich has me feeling criminal, more bandit than commando. One night we blow a gate and charge into a walled garden, discovering fig trees, beds of hyacinth, and a bird fountain.

Shooting people who keep a bird fountain is hell on the conscience.

On another raid one of my team leaders, Sergeant Gerling, nicknamed

Raindrop, is the lead for breach. He is five feet three and might weigh 140 pounds with grenades stuffed in his pockets. It is ten in the evening, and Gerling is sticking explosives to a door when the charge detonates prematurely, the dreaded short fuse. The blast throws Gerling onto his back while blowing out the barred windows beside the door. Looking like a chimney sweep and still smoking, Gerling struggles to his feet, saying, "They've really got it coming," then shotguns the door.

We bull into a three-story house. The windows are curtained with velvet. A young woman is sitting at the dining room table, thick textbook spread in front of her. Gerling, still smoking, throws her on the ground and restrains her. All the while she is raving about this burning man who's come from the dark. She goes on to protest that we have interrupted her studies for an exam on internal medicine, claiming to be in med school, and by deduction, innocent. Meanwhile her dad bails out a third-floor window and onto a neighboring roof, where our sniper shoots him in the hip and stomach. Downstairs, Gerling tells the future doctor, "You can practice on him."

Upstairs we find another male, an uncle of sorts, whose name is not on the blacklist. The Boys swab the uncle's hands with an explosive test kit, a device prone to false positives. He fails the test. "Sir," reports Gerling, "he popped hot. Should we take him along?"

I say, "Either he's been making bombs or handling baby formula, motor oil, WD-40, or fertilizer. Or maybe he made a salad with vinaigrette for dinner. I'm over these kits."

Gerling replies, "Sir, just look at him. He's a bad guy."

I look at him. "Yeah, he is a bad guy. Let's take him and use him as a shield."

* * *

It is late July. I call Elizabeth at our home, and she picks up. I say, "How's it going?"

"Good . . ."

"What's happening?"

"Not much . . ."

"You're awful quiet."

"What. I'm here." There is a coldness on her tongue. I plod ahead. Her laughs are dull, slow. I tell her this much.

She says, "What do you expect, a party when you call?"

"No. I just want to feel like you miss me."

"I do."

"Tell me something good."

"Listen, can you call back in a few hours?"

"What the fuck?"

"I've gotta get ready for parent/teacher night."

"Fine." I slam down the phone. This could be a gamut of things: she is numb to separation, tired from work, has a secret swain, or really is preparing for parent/teacher night. In any case, our calls aren't what they used to be, like during the first trip to Afghanistan, when we were oxygen to each other and every word was electric. In those days I had only a handful of chances to hear her voice. Now I've got a phone at my desk, so admittedly, I take calling for granted. And I suppose we have both succumbed to the combat lifestyle, the notion of a long-distance marriage. A marital therapist would probably say that we just need to communicate expectations of each other. That's not our style. We insist on reading each other's minds.

Moving on.

The heat is blinding in Central Iraq. Dust cakes the palm fronds along the Tigris, giving them a decayed look. Our newest target is inside Shia City, which measures five-by-five kilometers. Shia City used to be called Saddam City. That ended with our invasion. The city is headquarters for the militia, and these dudes like to get crazy. Many years before, Saddam had the city's thoroughfares widened for tanks, so that he could subdue their crazy. Once off the thoroughfares, Shia City is a rookery of alleys, tight turns, and dead ends, all watched by multistory tenements and sties of sheet metal. The militia wields a complement of Soviet and Iranian armaments and claims troop strength in the tens of thousands. This is their stronghold. Shia City is Shia Town times ten.

Our target's presence in Shia City is problematic. Just before our arrival, two Ranger platoons launched a raid into the interior. Things went to shit. The op was a standard capture/kill mission, in and out, but the Rangers got bogged down, giving the militia a chance to mobilize everyone. And by everyone I mean *everyone*. Granny. Cats. Dogs. There were casualties, many of them civilian, although it is hard to tell how many of those "civilians" were in the fight. The drone recording of the battle is mesmerizing, like a pyrotechnic show on a planetary scale.

For five days with my Shia City target it is *stand up, stand down, stand up, stand down, stand up, one leg, no the other leg.* We even convoy to the brink of Shia City, waiting in strike position for twelve hours, before command says, "Stand down." On day six, our target breakfasts at a café then jumps into the passenger seat of a pickup. By midmorning political sensitivities have prevailed. There will be no ground assault to capture our target. The new plan is to kill him from afar.

Gathering in the ops room, we feast on the aerial feed. The air is charged with nervous excitement. Locke, Reese, and I are sitting on one side of the table, laptops in front of us, the wires winding between empty water bottles filled with spit from plug tobacco and Copenhagen. The SEALs are sitting on the other side, facing us. At the head of the table is a large screen, and on the screen is the feed from a surveillance plane. They are following the pickup truck as it corners through the alleys of Shia City.

An Apache helicopter comes on station and readies Hellfire missiles. On-screen, a reticle splits the truck, showing where the missile will hit. The reticle glides along, never leaves the hood. Watching it, I have this sense of omnipotence. The Apache pilot is waiting for the vehicle to drive into an uncrowded area. There are formulas for these things. If fewer than ten civilians might be killed, the approval for a remote strike can be given on a much lower level, which is far more efficient than what happens when you might kill more than ten civilians. Fewer than ten, it is, *Meehhh, go for it.*

Watching the reticle makes me giddy. I say to White, "This guy is so dead."

The pickup stops and the passenger, our target, walks into a store. I am holding my breath, willing his reappearance with every fiber of my being.

At last he exits the store and jumps back into the passenger seat. The truck eases into traffic. Civilians jam the sidewalks beside the road. I issue silent commands: *Move. Outta the way. Get out of the road. This is never going to work.* The truck crosses a bridge over a canal, and joy, there isn't another vehicle for a hundred meters. No pedestrian bystanders. In the ops center, eyes are riveted to the feed.

White says, "This is it."

Typing stops. Phones click off. Emails cease midsentence. It is absolute silence.

Command says, "Cleared to fire."

The pilot says, "Roger. Engaging."

No one sees the missile come in, just the flash and jetting black smoke. The truck goes to pieces. The blast ejects our man through the roof, straight into the air, and instantly, I can see his limbs are broken. The force of the explosion has shattered his bones and liquefied the organs. The body begins to spin, arms and legs out in a hypnotic death twirl. Spinning and spinning, he seems to float in the superheated summer air. Then he drops and lands in what is left of the truck bed. The flaming hulk smashes into a guardrail and sparks to a stop.

Everyone cheers.

I pump one fist in the air, *"Fucker."*

I notice some of our guys are cheering because they think that is what they are supposed to do. Other guys are killers and they mean it. We keep on watching the feed. Civilians flock to the burning vehicle to help. Flaming gasoline drives them back. They surge forward and back, looking for a way in. The feed zooms.

There is a head on the sidewalk.

"Goddamn. Did you see him fly? Is that a head? Dude, that *is* a head. A *head.*" We slap high fives. I sit down and grin at White. He asks, "Chow?"

We go out laughing and eat hot dogs.

A head . . .

16

THE EDGE OF ME

IRAQ

SUMMER 2008

The heat is claustral near the end of our tour. The mission pace has been breathless, and now I wish for soft targets, easy compounds in easy areas that are best suited to my emotional arc. We get the opposite. Our targets are talking to each other, adapting. Our raids have them afraid of the dark and now word has spread inside the enemy network. With each telling, the tales of our strike force grow more fantastic. One enemy commander insists to his bosses that we parachuted in during the night. How else could we have slipped past his men in the Iraqi police?

The problem with our success is daylight raids.

It is seven in the morning and already the sun is tyrannical. Our target today is a chief financial officer of sorts. Mounting Strykers, we launch at 0800 and wade into the city's rush hour. Trucks, sedans, and motorbikes clog the roads. The Iraqis honk for fun. A riot of smells fills the rude streets: exhaust, trash, bread, decay along the Tigris, and sewage, always sewage. We run the medians. We run the sidewalks, dodging Jersey barriers, and the side streets. Locals jump against storefronts as we speed past. We keep eyes on the cantilevered balconies overlooking the road. We ram down a choked blacktop, my Stryker skidding as we hop the median and angle into oncoming traffic. A mile from target we stop and regroup. Heat shimmer has the Iraqis dancing on nearby rooftops. *Proceed to breach.*

We start the raid by smashing our lead Stryker through the compound gate. We pour out of the vehicles. As we race across the courtyard, I spot more Iraqis on a roof across the street—a man collects a boy in his arms, and they flee down a stairwell.

When we blow the house door, it flies inward and knocks out a man who'd been waiting with an AK. The remaining rooms are cleared without incident. Command radios us, saying we have another target a few blocks away. *Might as well.* Locke and I grab two squads to hit the second target, leaving a few vehicles and an isolation team with the SEALs. We jam into three Strykers, speed to the next house, crumple the gate, and ransack the place.

Command reports a red sedan has just exited from a nearby house and orders us to interdict the vehicle. "Everyone out." We reload the Strykers and lurch south, taking directions from the drone aircraft that is following the car. The drone pilot is relaying to command at the airfield. Our strike-force radioman tells us. We tell our drivers. The delays are maddening.

The troop compartment in my Stryker is a kiln. From the driver's hatch, wind swirls inside, feeling like jet exhaust. My ballistic glasses fog. Sweat beads on our cheeks. Screeching around a corner, we see a red sedan. *Ramming speed.* My driver surges ahead to pinch in the sedan. A dozen of us pour out, rip a Haji from the car, and throw him on the pavement. He squirms and yells in Arabic as we toss the groceries in his back seat. Oranges rain on the sidewalk. I grab one and stick it in my cargo pocket. Now command is yelling, "Wrong vehicle. One block east."

We load back up and hop a curb and smash down a sidewalk. Locals jump out of the way. We furrow the roadside stalls selling produce. Rounding a corner, we come upon another red sedan and rear-end it. The trunk wrinkles. The driver gets out and runs between buildings. We dismount and smash a door into a house where two children sit before a television under a creaking ceiling fan. *Sorry.* We sprint down their hallway and kick out the backdoor into an alley. I vault over a gate, catch a boot on it, and fall on my face. *Goddammit.* I get up just in time. The man slams around a corner and runs into us. He puts his hands up, falls to his knees, and begins weeping.

"Wrong vehicle," says the radio.

I am boiling with desert heat and rage as we break into teams and charge down another block on foot, looking for a red sedan, finding them parked along the sidewalk, in traffic, alleyways. We rifle through an empty one, then stop another by jumping in front of it with guns up. The Boys rip the driver out and put him facedown on the hood. I gather the collar on the driver's *thawb*, lift his head and smash it down, saying, "I . . . know . . . you're . . . a bad guy," as I bang his cheek off the hood in cadence.

Guilty of having a nondescript sedan.

The Boys are searching the trunk when Locke motors up to me. "This is fucking stupid."

He is right.

I radio the Boys, "Load up. We're gonna consolidate on the first target."

Command says, "The red sedan is one block west."

"That vehicle description is half the cars in Baghdad," I answer. "We are consolidating on target." The radio does not like that. I ignore the response. We reload Strykers. As we nose ahead, I take out my orange, bite into it, and suck until my neck is sticky with juice. Six blocks brings us back to the target house, where we find the SEALs wrapping up their search. A couple of them ferry bags of sensitive items into the courtyard.

A scan of the rooftops and streets reveals no one out. It does not feel right. Beyond the house is a vacant lot. Hot wind rustles the tattered netting on a soccer goal. The lot ends beside a long industrial building with awning windows on the second level.

Our air cover reports low on fuel and breaks away. I radio the platoon, "Air cover signed off. Just us now." We form a perimeter, strongpointing the corners of the house. I radio White, "How long you need?" to which he replies, "Five." In the far distance runs one of the highways through Baghdad. Cars streak up and down. Around us, it's silence. I kneel beside the compound gate.

One of our machine gunners is first to fire. In response, across the vacant lot, a slew of automatic weapons rip into action. Muzzles wink from dark enclaves. Bullets shatter the awning windows of the industrial building. The enemy tracers are hard to see in the lurid daylight. Sergeant Reese pilots his Stryker into the vacant lot, allowing a second Stryker to get in line beside it. They fire up a grenade launcher and a .50 cal.

Concrete explodes on the industrial building. Our machine gunners rake the second floor. Enemy bullets raise puffs of dust around the Strykers. A string of bullets snaps by. I radio my SEAL counterpart.

He says, "Three minutes."

We keep pumping rounds into the industrial building. From the southeast side of the house, Archie reports contact, then likewise Gerling on the southwest. An RPG streaks overhead to detonate against a parapet next door. Another rocket rubbles a wall on the street. Just left, a black-clad figure pops around a corner with an RPG shouldered and lets loose. The rocket explodes against the cage on Gerling's Stryker. My squad along the wall turns barrels on the RPG gunner and folds him onto the street, where he flops around before a tracer disappears in his head. Bright-red blood spurts, then ponds on the pavement.

I turn back to the industrial building. Rounds crisscross the vacant lot. In a nearby alley runs an Iraqi man carrying a body. Dirt and concrete explode in all directions. The man gently sets down the body, rips off his white shirt, and waves it overhead. A tracer streaks by, sending him ducking into the dirt. He rises and again helicopters the shirt over his head. I yell, "Don't shoot him," to my Rangers along the wall, who keep shooting. The man picks up the body and runs toward us, hugging a row of low buildings.

Our gun team fires the Carl Gustaf bazooka into the second story of the industrial building. The explosion launches bricks all over a soccer field. A piece of the roof collapses into the building. Dust jets. A spire of smoke rises. There is a pause to admire the devastation. Our man keeps running, closing to fifty yards when I see he is carrying a boy. Bare, dangling feet bounce as the man runs. Twenty yards out, the man stops and waves to us. His moves are desperate. I wave him into our lines. Sweat streaks down his dusty face and chest. His eyes are glistening. Locke grabs the man and ushers him into the courtyard, where he lays the boy in the shade under the eaves. In hysterics the man explains the boy is his son, and that we shot him.

White emerges from the house and, seeing me, says, "Let's go."

I'm looking at the boy and his father. The boy's shirt is black with blood, as are his father's pant legs. Locke yells for our medic.

I say to Locke, "Seven, that's a negative with Doc. We're done. This isn't our problem."

Gunfire cracks everywhere. On the edge of the courtyard, my Rangers keep firing, squeezing rounds between the Strykers. Another RPG crashes into the street.

I grab Locke. "We are leaving."

He looks at me sidelong. "Give Doc a minute."

"This is not the mission."

"Just a minute."

"Seven, listen, dude, we are not a rolling hospital."

By this time Doc is kneeling at the Iraqi boy's side. Blood gushes from a hole in the boy's chest. There is no exit wound. Doc says, "I need time."

I say, "We've got no time. This isn't our problem."

Locke says to me, "Let's get him stabilized. Then we're out of here. I'm not ordering you, sir. I'm just saying."

I am thinking of our Boys, and admittedly, I am thinking of me. *Fuck these people and their stupid red sedans and their sandbox of a country.* I glance toward the street. Above the compound wall, the gun turret atop one of our Strykers glides east. The engine growls. Metal groans and glass shatters as the Stryker smashes into a parked car. The Stryker stops, radio antennae swinging, in the intersection south of target. Enemy bullets *ping* off the armor. The militia started this. Why should I put Rangers in further jeopardy to save this kid?

I swing back to Locke. "Goddamn, Seven. Let's go."

Doc looks up at both of us, one finger still inside the boy's chest, and says, "He's done unless we get him to a hospital."

Death has grabbed hold of the boy's eyes. The distance is growing. A tongue of blood spreads beneath him.

Locke says, "Let's take him to the airfield."

I say, "Not our mission."

"Sir. That's not who you are."

Locke never talks like that. The words hit me, so out of place in this gunfight.

I pace.

"Sir!" says Locke.

"All right, all right," I say. "We take him."

Doc lifts the boy, saying, "Hospital," to his father.

The father points to himself, asking if he can come.

Locke looks at me.

Over Locke's shoulder rises a plume of fire as an RPG detonates.

I say, "Why not."

We make for the gate and stack on the wall beside it, readying for a sprint. We have to charge down exposed streets to our vehicle ramps.

Locke yells, "Suppressive fire when we round this corner."

The Boys slap in fresh magazines and change the drums on their machine guns, answering, "*Roger.*" I radio the Strykers, "We are about to move. On my call, drop hatches and suppressive fire."

Reese acknowledges, "Copy."

The squad leaders count heads, stepping on spent casings. Rounds ping. The Boys manning the courtyard wall jump down. Ready, set, and I radio, "Moving."

Locke calmly steps into the street, raises his M4 and sprays half a magazine. We run for the ramps. Guns atop the Stryker blaze. The enemy sees us moving. Once again, faraway windows light up with muzzle flashes. Doc runs to the aid vehicle with the boy in his arms, charges up the ramp, and sets the boy down on a litter. Twenty seconds later we are off.

The kid struggles as we race for the airfield. I rip off my fogged sunglasses. There is a tremor in my leg. I pop out the rear hatch and ride with torso in the wind. Baghdad wheels by: flat and tan, with jersey barriers for veins. These people, the Iraqis, I am here to fight them, but I have also inherited their problems and aspirations and bullet wounds. My own life is on hold while I sort out their shit. Where is Elizabeth?

This is military service.

17

THE OTHER SEALS

FORT LEWIS, WASHINGTON

SUMMER 2008

The boy makes it. The demolition of Baghdad goes on. We shoot our way to the end of the tour and lose no one. In our final hour on the ground, I give a hasty goodbye to the SEALs, mustering only the bare minimum courtesy, before exiting the command post. The SEAL chief, Diggs, follows me out the door, and once we are alone, quietly says, "I know this wasn't the best marriage. You have great guys. It was a privilege working with you. Good luck, sir."

He sticks out a hand, and we shake.

I reply, "I'm proud of what we did together. Always will be. You take care, Chief," then turn and leave, feeling outclassed by his farewell.

We make for the airfield. The same names that stepped off the plane are the same ones that step back on. We are the same, and we are different. I hate the men of Iraq and their tracksuits and progeny. Whatever they build for themselves, whatever we build for them, I will hate it.

We land in Washington, and I am supposed to stop acting like a savage, right . . . *now*. I drive home to the house on the hill overlooking the Sound. Douglas firs, some fifty feet tall, shade the house. There are apple trees in front. My first night home, Elizabeth and I don fleece sweaters and sit in Adirondack chairs to watch deer browse the apples. We sit in silence. Moths bump the front porch light.

I say to her, "Why so quiet?"

"I'm relaxed."

"C'mon."

She looks at me, and after a long pause, says, "You have to earn me back."

"Why?" I ask. "What did I do?"

"Nothing," she answers. "You just do."

She turns to watch the deer again.

"Okay," I say. "Let me take you somewhere. Where do you want to go?"

"Oh, I dunno. South America."

"No. It's gotta be in the States. Everything we ever wanted is here. No reason to leave."

She asks, "What if we go somewhere tropical?"

"Texas?"

"C'mon."

"Florida then. But you should know, Florida is a huge swamp."

We retire to our bedroom. Elizabeth brushes her teeth, while I position three guns: a pistol under the pillow, an assault rifle beside the bed, and a 12-gauge shotgun behind the door. Elizabeth strides out of the bathroom, still brushing, and mumbles with a mouth full of toothpaste, "I know where I want to go."

"Where?"

"Yellowstone."

"The park?"

"Yes."

"Okay."

Home less than a week, we go to the Fourth of July fireworks show in Steilacoom. A crowd gathers on a verdant hillside that slopes into Puget Sound. Kids with sparklers weave between families on blankets. There's a big sign lashed to a parked farm truck that says, HAPPY BIRTHDAY AMERICA. The smell of barbecue wafts over the crowd. At about eight thirty the fireworks boat launches from the town pier and anchors a quarter mile out. In back of the boat they ready the load. I pass the time thinking, *If I had a belt-fed machine gun and a shitload of tracers, I too could put on a show.* The sun burns down the sky over the Olympic Range, then winks out. From the boat, they touch off fireworks, peony shells, chrysanthemums, and diadems. The crowd oohs and aahs at the multicolor explosions; the spheres, glowing tendrils, and white-hot tails. All the time my body is in turbo. Each bang and rippling star jolts me. Elizabeth holds my arm. She feels me shudder.

She says, "Let's go, babe."

I jump up, saying, "Sorry. I just saw this show." On the walk back to the truck, I notice other young men with high-and-tights running for their cars. Many of the town residents are soldiers at Fort Lewis. If you want to see PTSD manifested, go to a fireworks show near an army base.

This time home I am prone to spells of melancholy. Sometimes I feel useless. I have to keep telling myself that no one can hurt me and that I have earned the right to relax. This condition is called hyperalert. Without warning, I spring into rage, which can only be quelled with physical destruction—my hand into a wall, smashing the Adirondack chairs, broken glass in the garage. I stand over my mess, chest heaving as I find baseline. I want to destroy things. I want to throw shit off a bridge. I want to crash a car. This condition is called crazy.

One act that feels good is burning money. Between my deployments, training, and Elizabeth's job, we have wealth for the first time in our lives. I have stored jump pay, hazard pay, combat pay, per diem, and time-in-grade. I am not going to buy the Dallas Cowboys, but shit. I have emptied my soul for this money, and it cannot buy happiness, but it can buy jewelry and that makes Elizabeth happy, so I'm blowing it.

I usher Elizabeth to Nordstrom in Tacoma and point at sparkling gems in the cases. Elizabeth paces in front of the glass, licking her lips, "Oh, look at it, just look at it." The lady behind the counter wears so much makeup, she looks like a clown.

Clown lady scowls, thinking we are street people wasting her time. I manage to communicate I am capable of premeditated murder. She lifts the pieces out and sets them on a black velvet pad. I pick out diamonds, emeralds, and rubies; all the precious gems, mounted in gold. In front of a mirror, Elizabeth swings, savoring the pieces on her neck. I think the pieces are beautiful and wondrous, and that Elizabeth's collarbones are better. She puckers her lips, turns her chin just so. The saleslady has come around and is now doing the spiel. "Oh, my goodness. That looks so great on you. Definitely goes with your eyes and your skin. Gosh, your skin is fantastic. Are you Mediterranean?"

The saleslady rings us up for nine grand. Elizabeth is still modeling in the mirror, saying, "Ohhh . . . this one is just too much. I have to wear it out." Then, Elizabeth tugs on my old T-shirt. "Look at you. We need to get you outfitted." She takes my arm and pulls me to the right, "This way." We click down marble tile toward the men's section, where I collect Italian suits and blue shirts with white collars like bankers wear. I buy a $400 tie that I don't know how to tie. Once, my dad showed me how to do a double Windsor on the tie that goes with army greens, my formal uniform. I don't remember how that works.

Material urges lead us to a car dealership, where I buy Elizabeth an Infiniti sedan, a red one with white leather seats. *Sign here, here, and here.* We screech off the lot. When I stomp the gas on Federal Boulevard, the engine purrs and pins us to the seats. We head north. I'm James fucking Bond driving down Interstate 5, doing eighty, ninety, a hundred. In Tacoma, the glass-domed art museum passes on the left flank. An Indian casino passes on the right. Elizabeth and I sing rap songs.

We drive into Seattle, to a wealthy neighborhood on a peninsula in Puget Sound. Beyond the land, white ferries churn the water, heading for wooded islands and the Olympics. At the bottom of a hill we see a sand beach pocked with picnic tables and beach towels. We drive down to it. On the beach there is a gathering of a hundred twentysomethings, many of whom are far too tan for the Pacific Northwest. They carry beer in neon cozies and wear loud bathing suits. Bikini-clad girls are playing volleyball. There is much prefucking. In the sand is a sign that says, YOUNG URBAN PROFESSIONALS OF SEATTLE.

Several years have passed since I've mixed with the citizenry and now I wonder what they talk like. With a lisp, probably. I say to Elizabeth, "Look at them. It's sad. This is the most alive they will ever be. And you know what—they'll never get it."

She asks, "What are they supposed to get?"

"Good and evil."

"You do what you do because you want to, not because others care. Right?"

"Spare me that shit."

"You won't get anywhere holding it against people. Anyway, we should steal their beer."

"We *should* steal their beer."

I park, pull my hat down, and stride into the gathering. I lift a cooler and lug it to the Infiniti. Two girls watch me, perhaps sensing I do not belong. My Levi jeans may have activated their sensors. I shove the cooler in the trunk and wave to them. We peel out.

* * *

At battalion I am promoted to executive officer of Alpha Company. I tell Locke I am out of the Seabass, onto bigger and better. I tell him, "Thanks for everything, Little Bear."

Locke laughs and pumps my hand. "No one has called me that for a long time. Brings back good memories. Remember your roots here."

"Of course."

"All right, sir," says Locke. "I'll see you around."

I say something I've been thinking for a while. "You were right about that boy."

"What? Oh, right." Locke shrugs. "Just so you know, they're a bunch of tools over in A Co."

I move my stuff across the quad. By *stuff*, I mean a photo of Elizabeth, some binders, and uniforms. It does not take long. I get a big office beside the commander, Major Meyer. When I report, Meyer asks where I am headed with my career. I say, "I want to stay in battalion as long as I can." I do not know after that.

The reality is I cannot stay in battalion forever. The standard trajectory is to attend the army's career course, then take command of a company unit in big army before returning to the Rangers at the next level of command. There are probably three cross-country moves in there, and another yearlong combat tour. This is the "career" trajectory, and with these wars on, I wonder about an endless mountain range; a place without grass where every summit is the same. What this means for Elizabeth, I'm not sure. The opposite path is to get out, as I'm well beyond my four-year commitment to the army. This decision amounts to heresy for a Ranger officer. I am not supposed to flame out. I am supposed to go to big army and inspire others into Rangerhood.

Orders arrive for the next trip. I will be a ground force commander this time, taking Second Platoon and attachments—meaning snipers, mortars, and some other small groups—to Afghanistan. Major Meyer will take the remaining Rangers to Iraq.

I will be the ranking man on the ground for an elite unit. It is an honor. Remembering those first images of the war in Afghanistan all those years ago, of hard men fighting in hard mountains, of supermen, I realize, *I'm that guy.* My area of operation will be Eastern Afghanistan: Kunar, Nangarhar, Laghman, Nuristan, to name a few. Of all these provinces, I shudder at the word *Kunar*, for its black heart is the Korengal Valley. I harbor secret thoughts of a collision with it and confess that in this interlude of life, the valley has grown into a phantom of gigantic proportions.

My company trains. We jump and shoot. We fly to faraway places to attack mock cities. Our ropes unfurl from helicopter doors before we slide onto rooftops. I understand the cycle now. No more riding the wave. I am making it; planning the exercises; securing all the ranges, vehicles, and land; developing targets for the Boys to hit; and critiquing the platoon leaders.

It is summer. One afternoon we have a water jump into American Lake. By platoons we board a Chinook that lifts us over the shining water. I fling myself off the ramp. My parachute pops and floating down, I see Puget Sound, the icy summit of Mount Rainier, and the snowy chaos that is the Olympic Range. Just above water, I activate a life vest and release from my chute and splash into the cold lake. A Zodiac assault boat zooms around picking us up. The crew pulls me over the tube, and I lie on the floor, organs chilled yet skin warmed in the sun. By the way, this exercise has no tactical application for the upcoming tour. It is just cool. Once out of the water, we change into tank tops and barbecue on the lakeshore. Elizabeth is beside me.

This is my best day in the army.

Not long after, my parents, Russ and Juliann, fly in from Texas. We take them up the Space Needle. Wind tosses our hair as we press eyes into looking glasses that cost a quarter. Back at the house, my folks insist on a family photo with me sporting Ranger decorum, which I protest out of habit, because Mom has been photo-chronicling the mundane since my birth. Dad gives me a look that convinces me it is a splendid idea. I don Class A's, jump boots, and tan beret. Dad helps with the tie, on account of me still not having that figured out. We set a camera on the Adirondack chair in the yard, and everyone squeezes in.

In the photo, our hair is still in disarray from the breeze up on the Space Needle. Mom and Dad's faces are shining. They are proud of me, and I am proud to be their son. I suppose this is the most a creature like me can hope for with his makers.

* * *

Bad days outnumber good ones. The upcoming trip has me thinking of the Korengal. I am still fused to it. I carry the black badge. When I feel confident and at ease, the panic comes. There is an exploding sense, crushing surprise. Barclay's disfigured face is with me, a burning husk that was once a Humvee, the muj with the gold machine gun.

One day Elizabeth and I rent a motorboat from the base. It is armed with four seats and a forty-five-horsepower outboard. I tow it to a gravel beach on Puget Sound and slide it in the water. I grab a pistol and a cooler of beer from the truck then help Elizabeth onto the boat. I pop a beer and take the wheel. Out we go, running north. My wake is a long V that rocks the buoys nearshore. The air smells of pine and salt.

Three beers later the Narrows Bridge soars overhead, momentarily blocking the sun from our necks. Bird droppings have whitened the trusses. We skip past the green prow of Point Defiance, then the docks of Tacoma, where a cargo ship is moored, red cranes lifting containers off the deck. We zoom past houseboats and pastel marinas. I pop a fourth beer. Elizabeth is sitting at the bow, sunning her legs. Seeing me, she asks, "How many is that?"

I raise my beer to her then swig.

She whips her hair and looks over the bow.

I drink so that I cannot feel the sun, the boat launching over swells and smacking back down. Green hills rise on the surrounding islands. Built into the hills are homes with glass-paneled balconies. A regatta of pleasure boats drifts past. I review the yacht in the lead. At the bow stands a handsome man wearing Ray-Bans and loafers. Looking down at us from his mighty vessel, he waves. I give him the finger. A fishing boat motors past, nets dripping water, the captain looking grizzled and tired. I salute him. Ahead is a beach. A rotten log lies just above waterline. A dozen gulls claw the log, waiting in a row. I reach under the seat for my pistol and chamber a round. Hearing this, Elizabeth yells, "There's people everywhere. What are you doing?"

With one hand, I aim at the gulls.

She springs up and grabs for the gun.

With my free hand I seize her wrist and attempt a sidestep. She throws herself into me. I teeter backward and trip over the cooler. She lands on top, determination etched in her face. I laugh. She hisses, "Sonuvabitch," and swings at my face. I twist away so that she only lands a glancing blow. I drop the gun, grab her shoulders, launch her sideways, and stagger to my feet, then lift her at the waist. In a rage she pumps her legs. One of her sandals flies off into the water. I slam her down in the copilot's seat and pin her to it. "Sit still, girl. I'm about to stop being nice."

She collects herself in the seat, takes a deep breath. Calmly, she says, "I hate you."

That stops me for a moment. "No you don't."

Gallantly, I mount the bow and level the pistol sight on a gull. It is a fifty-yard shot, and I've got nine to twelve beers in me. I slur, "Too easy," and pop off a round. A spout of water rises twenty-five yards short of the gulls. I shoot again and miss, then fire in quick succession. *Pow. Pow. Pow.* A puff of sand rises beside the log. The gulls are onto me now. They cry and take flight. Tongue to one side, I trace their flight with the pistol. *Pow. Pow. Pow.* Elizabeth has her head in her hands. *Pow. Pow. Pow.* I change mags and shoot the water off the bow again and again. I look into the water.

Emerald at the surface, it turns deep green near ten feet down. Down some more, the water turns dark blue then black. I think I can see bottom. I imagine starfish down there and an octopus wheeling across the shells and silt. Down there it is dark and there is never sound. It seems a wonderful place for an addled mind. I want to see bottom.

Elizabeth yells, "They are calling the cops on you, you fucking dick."

A fishing boat cruises fifty yards distant. The captain has a CB mike to his mouth. He is looking this way. I stagger back to the wheel and throw the accelerator forward. My head rolls back as we speed away. Soon I am doing forty, top speed on this rented piece of shit. I turn back and study the land beside the water, wanting to remember this spot, where the water turns black and there is never sound or light.

* * *

Alone the next day, I tow the boat down to the same launch and back it into the water. I have no beer, food, or music. I carry the pistol. My head is clear, as it must be for a vision quest. It takes an hour to reach my spot. Fully clothed, I dive into the water and swim down below the light. The weight of all the cold water above me is crushing. I try to touch bottom, though I cannot see it. Throat quivers, lungs scream. I am dazed and light. Fingers burn. Star-clusters burst. There are faces in the dark; the young medic who is dead because of me, dead before she even got to the war, and Robinson, Wilson, and Doc Vaccaro. *I miss you, Doc. You died while I was walking down the beach with my wife. It is on me.*

My dead are swimming in the dark with broken limbs and flower-shaped holes in their bodies.

At the surface, I cough water. How I arrived escapes me. A hundred yards away, my boat lolls on the swells. Suddenly, Pacific seals breach the surface in all directions, their eyes shining black, water beading on their whiskers. One slaps the surface with its tail. Another flips and twists, then honks at me. Another floats on his back, belly to the sun, passing so close I can touch him. They lap me. They live a hard life eluding killer whales, but they find *this* moment for joy. They lap some more.

I swim for the boat, climb in, and sit at the wheel, shivering violently.

I strip down to boxers, start the motor, and head south. Something is building on the way back. At first it is a clenched fist, a tapping foot. Then questions without answers, a scream into a canyon. By the time I've hit the Narrows Bridge, it demands acceleration, maximum speed, to an answer in the dark. Next thing I know I've missed the beach where I parked.

It's well into a moonless night when I get back to the launch, but I am cogent of mind. Too much of my life has been spent at war, practicing war. There is a day when the war will be over and I will never have to prove anything again. Everyone, I suppose, creates a mountain in the distance. Then one day you are on it, certain you will summit, and there is a terrifying sense of finality. Regardless, you must touch the top before you can sit in the grass.

It is summer in the Northwest. Elizabeth and I take on literal mountaineering pursuits, tramping routes that begin on trails blocked by a thousand cobwebs at face level, where blueberries can be had without breaking stride. The paths soon yield to scree and rock and pockets of amethyst for those who know where to look. Then come wrecked glaciers and buttresses of gleaming rock. Always on the approaches Elizabeth is slow, crusty-eyed, and prone to irritability. But on summit days she is fearless.

We bag Mount Baker, Mount Shuksan, and Mount Rainier.

Atop, the flaying wind breathes life into me.

At last we drive for Yellowstone National Park, the earn-back trip. On the way, Elizabeth devours books on the park's flora and wolves, so that by the time we arrive, she's my tour guide. We enter the park by way of the northeast corner, into the Lamar Valley, far from geysers, hot springs, and brigades of Chinese tourists. Wolves howl from the sagebrush bottoms along the river.

We pull off the road, fling open the truck doors, and stare. On a nearby hillside, a wolf devours a bison carcass. The crimson-snouted wolf thrashes inside the ribcage and soon breaks one off, paws its prize, then jaws it and trots away. Even from afar I can see this black wolf has yellow eyes. Just as the wolf crests the hill, it turns toward us, raises its head, and howls. Elizabeth and I giggle.

Elizabeth says, "All black wolves have yellow eyes." Then she strides away from the truck, to an overlook where she sits among sagebrush. Below is the Lamar River, meandering toward a canyon, the grape light of evening upon it.

For a time I wait on Elizabeth at the truck. She crosses her legs, keeps on looking at the Lamar. I walk to her and sit at her side, gathering that I should keep quiet. We both watch the river. It is an odd feeling to sit and watch for nothing in particular.

"Look at this," she says. "What if we could stay here?"

18

BACK IN THE STAN

AFGHANISTAN

SPRING 2009

A single C-17 ferries us toward Bagram Airfield, where I will land at war a ground force commander in the Rangers, a role I mythologized in my youth. Once, I had promised myself that if I could be this person, even for a moment, I would always be satisfied. Superman on a craggy summit. Right now, though, it is not satisfying in the least. It is responsibility and pressure. If I coast, Rangers will die.

Sitting beside me on the plane is the leader of Second Platoon, Lieutenant Kitrell. He is African American, which makes him unique in the battalion. For a long time growing up, Kitrell lived out of a car. He is quick to tell me about it, and for that matter, anyone. More notably, before becoming an officer, Kitrell was a grunt in the 82nd Airborne. He has the quiet confidence of a former enlisted man and is willing to lock up the Ranger noncoms and stick a finger in their faces. With Kitrell, I decide there is little I will need to do in the way of troop leadership.

Next to Kitrell is Shields, our lead sergeant. Shields is a classic Alpha Company type, an old-school Ranger. He sports a screaming high-and-tight and robotic mannerisms. Prior to this assignment, Shields had gotten out of the army for a time, and sadly, could find no meaningful work. After a few months, he landed a gig at Home Depot driving a forklift. I wince thinking about this: a decorated Ranger with multiple combat tours and all he can land on the outside is forklift operator. About three months in, Shields crashes the forklift when a customer steps in front of him. The damage is minimal but he is canned. He ejects from this civilian experiment and quickly returns to the Rangers, rising to squad leader and then platoon sergeant, in charge of more than forty men. Shields likes telling this story when young Rangers come up for reenlistment. His message to them is the army is our great mother, feeding her sons, housing them, and outfitting them with assault rifles and camo. Shields believes that the civilian world is cruel and confusing. "Think about it," he says. "What if every Ranger who crashed a vehicle got kicked out. I mean, there'd be like three guys left in regiment."

Everyone on the plane gets an Ambien to pass the time. When I wake, I read a few chapters of Bram Stoker's *Dracula,* which forces an underwear change, then walk to the bubble window to get my bearings. Snowy mountains pass beneath, sprawling to all horizons. Here is the Hindu Kush, a range I never wanted to see again. In the distance, Bagram Airfield takes form, a few long runways cut into a mountain plateau.

At Bagram we switch to a smaller plane. The flight to our staging airfield is short. Upon landing, we offload and board a waiting bus that brings us to a walled compound within the airfield perimeter. A bevy of Afghan soldiers spring to their feet and open the gate. We pass between Hesco walls until arriving at a second access guarded by US troops, who slide open the metal gate. We pull into a compound within a compound, within an airfield base. We shoulder our packs and get out.

Inside this compound is another wall topped with razor wire. Americans seeking entry must have the code for a metal gate. On the other side of the gate is the compound of a SEAL team of elite operators. We will work with them, sometimes *for them.* I am tepid about the arrangement, but the pecking order is beyond me. Their compound inside a compound, within a compound, on a base, says a lot about their attitude toward us, and for that matter, the rest of the military.

My entire Ranger force drops bags and kits in a stout one-story made of concrete. This is our house. We have two bathrooms, but the toilets are broken. Each squad has its own large bay with couches, recliners, and lockers for personal gear. The bays smell like blistered feet. Against the walls are bunk beds with Christmas lights dangling off the frames. A PlayStation and large TV adorn each squad bay.

Our quarters are symbolic of years of occupation. The life cycle of a war base begins with sandbags and foxholes. When first building a position, a unit thinks of survival and defensibility, and the occupants lead a grimy, lousy existence, like our effort to build the Korengal outpost in 2006.

The longer the war, the more comfortable unit quarters become. In the middle of a base life cycle, showers, bathrooms, and chow halls appear. At the mature stage, occupants turn their attention to leisure and aesthetics: couches, Christmas lights, big-screen TVs. Then come the fast-food stands, and in the climactic stage, base commanders promulgate rules that injure the warrior mindset. At Bagram, for instance, all soldiers must wear reflective belts when walking after dark, and the military police will ticket drivers—some returning from combat patrols—for rolling through stop signs.

Maybe this explains why the super SEALs live in a compound, inside a compound, within a compound, inside a military airfield.

I collect Kitrell and Shields, and we head for our first meeting with the super SEALs in the joint ops center. Inside we meet the SEAL officer who leads the strike force. His name is Tyler. In his midthirties, he is the youngest field grade officer I have seen. Tyler is six feet three and in superb shape. With his steel-blue eyes, he is a poster boy for the SEALs.

The Boys, of course, say, "I'd let him fuck me."

In the ops center, three plasma screens hang from the walls, showing feeds from intelligence, surveillance, and reconnaissance aircraft. Two attractive women, both analysts of some sort, are planted in nearby chairs. The SEALs have handpicked these women for the deployment. I think there is a reason for that.

The rest of the SEAL team enters, all wearing civvies: leather motorcycle vests with patches and jeans and vintage T-shirts. They are big men with long hair. Almost all are well into their thirties. They wear goatees and beards, but not huge ones like the Special Forces teams, the type that squirrels can nest in. They look every bit seasoned professionals. The SEALs are exceedingly polite to the two women.

They use first names with us, as in, "Call me Rob." "Call me Bill." "Call me

Jack." I spare them the bit about first names with my Rangers. The closest my Boys come to individualism is footwear. All have opted for the battalion-approved Asolo mountaineering boot. Beyond that our lives are issued.

We begin hitting targets. Joint missions. We plan in the evening, load aircraft and fly into the dark. Mostly, we land far away from our targets and hike in. Our sorties are everywhere, sometimes high in the mountains, some in the desert near Torkham Gate, some in the rolling hills near Mehtar Lam and the wastelands south of Jalalabad. The ops are easy gigs: Afghans gathered in a single compound. The aircraft overhead tell us everything. Don't get me wrong though, we are hunting tigers and crocodiles. It's just that one thing is true the world over: if you catch someone sleeping, he'll be docile, mostly.

One night at 0300, our lead element breaches a high-walled *qalat*. Once inside, four terrorists hiding in a barn begin spraying us with automatics. We lay suppressive fire, turning the barn to Swiss cheese and killing at least three terrorist goats that were surely in on it. One of the SEALs sneaks around the edge and throws a grenade that lands perfectly in the barn. The bad guys all die in one heap, human parts and animal parts mixed together. We gingerly comb the wreckage.

We come back from the op, drop kit in the ready room, and retreat to our house. I try sleeping while the Boys fire up the PlayStation, full volume. The sound of video game gunfire reverberates down the concrete hallways. I abandon plans for sleep and step into first squad's bay, finding two fire teams playing *Call of Duty*, a four-on-four arrangement, each team having their own screen. Another squad watches from the bunk beds, waiting for the winner. No one notices me.

Sergeant Willie, the squad leader, is ducking and leaning as he plays, as if this helps his video game maneuvers. He gives orders to his Rangers, "Go up the gut. Now left, left."

I say, "Willie, don't you get enough of this shit in real life?"

Willie kills one of his Rangers with a bazooka. The spectators go, "*Ooooh!*"

Willie tells the kid, "You're so fucking dead. I killed you so good."

Finally, Willie turns to me, "It's team building, sir."

* * *

After a few missions, we forge enough trust with the SEALs for them to reveal the code to their compound gate. It is an achievement of sorts. The SEAL chief, Rob, says we can use their gym. Much of the gym equipment in our house is broken. Rangers can't have nice things. And as a matter of principle, we won't go to the big army gym tent on the other side of the airfield. We are too cool for big army. The SEALs are too cool for us. We are cliques within cliques, all toting guns in a vile land.

Next morning I take one of our Boys, eager to learn boxing, to the SEAL lair. Three doors later we step into their gym, finding a million dollars in exercise equipment: dumbbells, free weights, squat racks, punching bags, kettlebells, treadmills, rowers, and stair-climbers. In one room is a sparring mat, boxing gloves, and padded shin guards. We get on the sparring mat, remove shoes, and try knocking each other out. The gym is not air-conditioned, and soon, our sweat flies with every punch. We leave moist footprints. A SEAL passing by stops to tell us, "Better wipe all that up when you're done."

I never see their living quarters but I'm pretty sure they have maids.

* * *

We are six weeks in. Sometimes we go three or four nights without launching, which does not seem to bother anyone in the SEAL chain of command. Boredom is our nemesis, and I cannot help thinking of the first tour in Afghanistan, which defined my sense of pace. We went everywhere all the time. If I let the Boys sit around, the captain would have crushed me. Then there was Iraq, when everything was burning down. We could hit two, three targets a night, and never answered questions when we left a pile of bodies. I suppose there is a sweet spot at the height of a war, when the chaos is so complete that you can kill a houseful of people every night and no one blinks. Part of me misses those days.

One morning I return from a jog around the airfield to find Kitrell and Shields standing at our compound gate, looking grave. They say one of our

Rangers is skimming opiates from the platoon medic. They want to know if I want to report this. I say no, definitely not to the chain of command, and not to our SEAL counterparts. It would destroy trust.

Kitrell and Shields nod. They are not asking me what to do. They are testing if I want to make a big deal of it. With my promise of silence, they spring into action, conducting a surprise search of the quarters and ready room. We find lots of weird shit, including the most gruesome porn imaginable—the stuff of nightmares, PTSD porn—but no pills and no drugs. By the pull-up bars, we gather the Rangers for an ass chewing. Shields and Kitrell let them have it, lowering their voices once or twice as SEALs stride by for their own compound.

I suspect one of the saltier Boys is self-medicating, but after the ass chewing, the skimming stops, and we move on.

The war has evolved along the Af-Pak border. We are only supposed to chase super legit terrorist targets. Some missions have to be cleared in Kabul, by three-star generals and diplomats who have chai with Afghan ministers. Our relationship with the Afghan government is tenuous. Afghan leaders are under pressure to expedite the withdrawal of the US military. Their own security forces, however, are weak, and without us, the Taliban would overrun large swaths of the country. These same government officials would face execution as American puppets.

Our uneasy alliance with the Afghan government means idleness. We have the very best in killing assets, but our gym equipment is getting the most use. And that's not to say there isn't combat in Afghanistan. Every evening the updates from the battlespace owners are plagued with the usual acronyms: SAF, GSW, IED, KIA, and WIA. In the daylight, the same rotten war that I saw in 2006 is going on. It rages under the sun, just beyond our compound walls. Big army is dying at the same pace, a guy here, two there. Some days a bomb in the road kills four. A helicopter crashes, and down go ten. Cavoli was right all those years ago. As a Ranger commander, I am spared this daylight war, the burdens of civil affairs. We march at midnight, wielding all the toys. This shit *is* easy.

The task force has a reputation as assassins, which does not help the idling. Our prisoner counts are low. The battlespace owners, big army, must deal with the smoking aftermath of our raids, and unfortunately for them, the native tribesmen often retaliate against the nearest base, launching attacks or planting IEDs, failing to distinguish one unit from another. Of course the platoon manning the nearest base can't say, *It wasn't us. It was these assholes from an airfield eighty miles away who are supposed to be chasing terrorists, and if you got on their radar, you probably are a terrorist, or at least kin to one.*

Maybe they can say that. I would. At any rate, big army deals with the aftermath, making payments and feigning sorrow, while we go to Pizza Hut and the SEALs change into motorcycle leather. A few years of this have made some battlespace owners reluctant to host raids from our task force. In fact, only one area in Afghanistan has units screaming for help: Kunar Province, the land of the Pech River and Korengal Valley.

Back at our airfield, we spin up for a mission, everyone giddy with the possibilities. In the ops center I learn there's one house on target. The SEALs, likewise, have gotten itchy and their guys are piling onto the mission. They ask for only one squad of Rangers. I send First and Kitrell. I remain at the airfield with Shields and the rest of the Rangers as the quick reaction force, or QRF.

As luck would have it, the ground element lifts off, infils, and gets into the shit. They begin demolition of the whole village. We run for the ready room, gear up, and make for a CH-47, where I plug into the intercom and confirm our landing zone with the pilots.

A SEAL charges up the ramp. He hangs around the ops center, but I don't know what his job is. He hurries down my row of seated Rangers, finding me by the Velcro patch on my armor, which glows with the lettering *LA-02,* my call sign. The SEAL leans into my face and yells over the rotors, "Are you McPadden?"

"Yeah," I yell back.

"I'm the QRF commander."

"Who are you?"

"I'm the QRF commander." He tells me his call sign. "Call Brad if you gotta problem."

"Where's *your* men?" I say.

"I'm the QRF commander."

There are a few squads of Rangers, fingering their guns, on both sides of me. I say, "Don't talk to my guys. You talk to me." Then he sits opposite. For twenty minutes we wait in the belly of the Chinook, the rotors thundering, our guts jingling, before command orders a stand down. Word is our men on the ground have captured the target. They are now moving for helicopter pick up.

* * *

Three more weeks drag by. I am sick of the SEALs, and more so, of our status as second-class commandos in this war of nothing to do. Luckily, task force command orders the SEAL commander, Brad, to take a harder look at Kunar Province. I seize this opportunity and volunteer for a reconnaissance mission, explaining that the battlespace owner is my old unit, 1-32 Infantry.

A helicopter ushers me to Camp Joyce, 1-32's headquarters west of the Kunar River, a mere rifle shot from Pakistan. On the camp perimeter is Carabello, my old sergeant major. He has snuck up on a gate-guard, who had his chin strap undone, and thereby undermined the war effort, national security on the whole, and for that matter, the sum of all American values. Putting the guard in the push-up position, Sergeant Major proceeds to verbally decapitate him. Then he massacres the onlookers, and before long, everyone in sight is cranking out push-ups and V-ups. A squad, wearing combat gear, rounds the corner to come upon the scene and, without hesitation, bounds backward.

I step into battalion and speak with Colonel O'Donnell, the new 1-32 commander, who has requested help with targets. As the former Ranger regiment operations officer, O'Donnell knows the right words to say to get the attention of my task force. I tell him I will come back with my Boys and take a swing at his list. Next, I fall in with a convoy heading for Camp Blessing, where another battalion is screaming for task-force help. To get there, we must follow the Pech River.

The five-truck convoy leaves Camp Joyce in the rain, me driving the third Humvee. We twist through the streets of Asadabad and veer left into the Pech River Valley. A few miles up we halt for a tire change. My eyes are riveted to the land. Everything is familiar, and I cannot help dismounting the Humvee and striding along the lane. There is a strange sense of home-coming. I spin in a circle, drinking in the land. The *bandeh* with the poppy field on the grassy hill is still there, and so is the yellow schoolhouse where I had my first firefight. Here is the land where I grew up.

We drive on. The positions we built in 2006 are still here, except patrol bases have become outposts, outposts have become camps, and camps have become bases. Our footprint is bigger, cleaner. Some things are the same, bomb craters in the road, bullet holes in the sandbags of passing outposts. Even the Humvee I drive, which has a hole in the rear panel from a rocket, is a reminder we have not come far.

The sky is abominable. It rains and rains. Our tires splash in puddles on the road. Clouds strike a wall of Himalayan peaks rising on the right flank. In the lead truck, the gunner pulls his hood over his helmet against the rain. He throws candy to children gathered along the roadside, a ploy to lure them near pooled water. As they fight over candy, the Humvee that follows accelerates and crashes into the pooled water, sending a muddy wave crashing over the children. Via intercom, the senior sergeant judges on a scale of one to ten.

The soaring ridge where I fell wounded appears, and in my turbid state, I ask, *Am I lucky or cursed?* Let me unpack that: Few warriors in Iraq and Afghanistan return to places they have already been. Many multitour veterans see the same country. Some manage to see the same region. A small percentage see the same provinces, like my old unit, 1-32. A fraction of them see the exact same bases, returning to Jalalabad Airfield, Salerno, Tikrit, Baghdad Airfield. They know which way to go at the roundabout. A miniscule number return to the same villages and valleys, remember-ing the boy by the bazaar, finding him still beneath the mulberry, a little older, his eyes harder.

It makes sense to send the same combat units back to the same zones, but it almost never happens. Too many other factors drive army and marine rotations. And I suspect many of my infantry brothers would rather not go back to the same village, because every unit and every tour has a trajectory. A unit nearing the end of a long bloody deployment has a way of nuking the bridges it built, whether that's getting loose with the rules of engagement or finally telling that one elder to get fucked. Picture the last day on a job you hate.

Speaking of shitty jobs, on my left flank are the rocky gates of the Korengal Valley.

I pore over the scene. Clouds drag across twin ridges. My hands shake. The valley has a terrible and irresistible pull. I am invited. We round a bend, and it fades from view. My hands still shake.

Four hours of driving brings us to Camp Blessing, where I meet Colonel Jakowski in his ops center. His troops call him Colonel J. His operations officer whacks a map with a pointer as the colonel fills me in on his best targets and intelligence sources. On the map we work east, following the Pech River downstream. Colonel J points to a village near the mouth of the Korengal, and I cannot take it anymore. I say, "Sir, I was first in the Korengal."

He says, "No shit," and pumps my hand. "Good man."

I say, "How is it out there, sir?"

"Hairy. Lots of casualties. We had to consolidate positions."

"Y'all killing bad guys, sir?"

"Ohhh, yeah. About a month on the ground, we knocked off the hearts-and-minds shit. Now we are just kinetic."

The radio squawks. It happens to be the fire-support officer in the Korengal, requesting 120 mm mortars.

Colonel J asks me, "Want to hang some shells?"

"Fuckin' A, sir."

We rush to the mortar pit, where two 120 mm tubes sit on bipods.

The mortar sergeant tells his crewman, "Hang it."

The crewman slides a shell half into the tube.

"Fire."

The mortarman lets go. A metallic bang sends the shell arcing east to the Korengal. The colonel urges me to, "Kill some of those fuckers." With both hands, I pick up a shell and heft it to tube. "Hang it." I lift the shell to where the tail sits in the mouth of the tube. "Fire." It is pretty easy from here. Let go. Gravity takes the shell down the tube, where the firing pin ignites the propellant. The mortar arcs into a moonless sky, climbs over the whale of a mountain before us, and sails for a minute before landing in the Korengal. We hang twenty rounds. I am killing every bad guy I ever fought. Colonel J is probably on the same plane as me when he says, "God, that feels good."

We return to his office and talk about his unit's operations in the Korengal. Colonel J is honest about his lack of tactical success. In this way he doesn't strike me as vainglorious, like many colonels I've met. The Korengal has claimed many of his men and he has little to show for it, two ingredients that breed guilt and impotence in field commanders. Been there, done that. I am not surprised when he tells me we can hit any target, any time in his area.

He wants me to kill his ghosts. His ghosts are my ghosts, and maybe he knows that but he does not say it. I say I will pitch some ops to the task force. Honestly though, there is not much meat on this bone. Top-tier terrorists are largely gone from this patch of Kunar. We have killed some. Many are hiding across the border in Pakistan or operating farther south. For the most part, Colonel J's men are dying against the locals, who are some of the best light infantry in the world, but tribesmen, not terrorists. We are not all that interested. The one terrorist still banging around is Objective Indian. I chased him in '06. His men killed my men, and I want him bad. He, alone, is worth a trip out here.

* * *

I return to home base and brief Brad on the results of the reconnaissance. We have two eager battlespace owners. The roads and valley mouths are navigable for Humvees, even for troop carriers. We can forward stage in Asadabad or Camp Joyce. Colonels O'Donnell and Jakowski will give us any support we ask for and have already provided valuable intelligence. Targets are not falling from the sky, but conditions are ideal and there is one big fish.

Brad says, "Excellent. To tell you the truth, I have too many men sitting here. It doesn't look good."

When I tell Kitrell and Shields where we are going, they high-five each other. Electricity runs in the Rangers. We have a target set. The SEALs are letting us off the leash. As we prepare to leave, Brad calls me to headquarters and notifies me that SEAL command has a mobility group sitting down south with nothing to do. They want to join us. They'll answer to me. If the SEALs drive, I can put more Rangers on the ground as assaulters. I say, "Bring 'em up."

The SEALs arrive within twenty-four hours, piloting light-armored vehicles called Pandurs. The vehicles are six-wheeled and weigh about fourteen tons, a lighter version of the army's Stryker. Each can carry a squad. We spread into the vehicles. The drive to Asadabad is long but uneventful.

The best move right now is to hit a target as soon as possible, for my own emotional well-being and to show command we are serious. One target is ripe, about twenty kilometers from Asadabad. We wait a couple nights, studying patterns at the house and in the surrounding village. It is midnight and the moon's gone down when we launch, speeding up the Kunar River Road. We stop and dismount and march over a bridge, while the Pandurs move to a high point on the road, where they can cover the house from the opposite riverbank. The foot march is two miles on rolling ground. At last we sneak into the village, breach the target *qalat*, and bag our man. No shots fired. No drama.

By noon next day, word has spread that the task force is hitting targets in Kunar. No one has done it for a while, and now, company commanders across the province are giving me the names of every Afghan who has ever given an American patrol the stink eye. Some of the company commanders know the secret phrase to get my task force to launch. I sift through the deck and pick a guy near the Shigal Valley, studying the roads and mountain trails leading to his compound. We gather reports on enemy contact in the vicinity. Kitrell and the Boys come up with a plan for ground infiltration.

Two days later, I am in the ops center preparing for the mission when frantic radio traffic bleeps on the net run by First Infantry in the Korengal. A squad patrol, about twelve Americans, was returning to the Korengal outpost from an incursion a few miles south. Reaching the river, they decided to use a footbridge where the enemy had rigged an artillery shell. As the patrol crossed, the enemy detonated their bomb and simultaneously fired belt-fed machine guns. The patrol fought out of the ambush and reached the nearest friendly position before realizing they were one man short.

A soldier is missing.

Everyone suspects that the enemy has hauled him away. Search and rescue of American forces is part of my mission. I rally my Rangers to launch, then speak with Brad, who tells me, "Do whatever you have to do."

If the enemy has our man, dead or alive, he is probably in a nearby village. They would not sit on a mountainside, exposed to aircraft. My Rangers will set overwatch positions and smash through houses until we find him. It will not be pretty, and it could take hours, even days. This op will escalate into a battle, and I am going to drop bombs all over the place. *Indiscriminate* is the word for it. I'll smoke the Korengal for old times' sake, for symmetry.

A drone arrives over the valley, circling the footbridge where the soldier disappeared. What has happened up until now has been abstract, little dots on a map. The drone makes it real. The southern reaches of the Korengal appear. Ant soldiers scurry through broken desolation. The real-time images dredge up nightmare memories. Fear avalanches over me. Sweat beads on my forehead. Droplets run down my back. My hands shake. My heel shakes, rattling the plywood floor so that others look at me.

I hustle for the bathroom to splash water on my face. My breath fogs a patch of the mirror over the sink as I review the Ranger before me. There is intensity in my eyes, a green flame. There are lines on my face from sleeplessness and stress.

It is time to die in the Korengal. I am supposed to. Life the last three years has been purgatory. This valley never lets go. Now it is time for the final sequence. It is not so bad. A blazing death is far better than a slow one by suburban poison. There is a missing American, and I am a commander of Rangers. *Lock and load.*

I march back to the ops room and call Brad, asking him, "When can the birds pick us up?"

"Birds?" he asks, sounding incredulous. "Take the Pandurs."

My heart thumps. I think he does not understand the geography of this mission, so I explain, "Brad, the last known location is seven miles deep in that valley. From Asadabad, it will take us two hours just to get to the valley mouth. First Infantry says there is a rock slide near the valley entrance, so the Pandurs won't make it far up the road. We'll have to march for hours just to get to the last known location. The climb is four thousand vertical. The longer we dick around, the more likely we are to lose that body." I cannot help but sound condescending. "Why is this not a priority?"

Brad says they have eyes on another target.

I argue, "If you give me a bird in the next half hour, it will be back before midnight chow. You can hit any target you want."

He says, "The crews don't want to fly in there. Too dangerous."

I am almost yelling now. "You see that imagery of the outpost? That's a goddamn helicopter landing zone in the middle. Chinooks keep these guys alive. All I want is a ride to the outpost. We'll take it from there."

Brad says, "Stand by." After a long pause, he says, "That's a negative on the birds. We've got other priorities. Take the Pandurs as far as you can."

I slam down the phone, pick up the receiver, and slam it down again. *You motherfuck.* I give the rally sign to Kitrell and Shields. Outside the Boys have serried. In the dark I issue the mission brief. The Boys have their faces set in the killer countenance, rifles resting in the crooks of their arms.

The Pandurs start, their diesel engines cutting the night. I load into my vehicle and plug into the intercom. "Hey Zero-two," says our vehicle commander. "Brad wants you on satcom."

"This is Zero-two."

"Stand down," says Brad. "They found him."

Tonight I have had a near-death experience without lifting a finger.

Kitrell, Shields, and I go to midnight chow for surf and turf. The food is magnificent. I lick butter and grease from my fingers, suck it off my thumbs, and scrape the plate clean. Classic rock plays on a boom box sitting on a far table, which ordinarily I find excruciating, but this music, in this moment, sounds wondrous. *Go Jimi.* Tonight I was supposed to die, and now I am alive and not entirely sure what to do with myself. I call Elizabeth but she does not answer.

At dawn I go to the gym and feel every fiber in my muscles. Across the gym Shields and Kitrell are doing bench presses near a wall of mirrors. I stride up to them, saying, "You should try the big-kid weights."

Kitrell finishes his set, racks the barbell, and stands. He asks me, "What was the deal with the birds last night?"

I say, "I don't know. But you guys rolled with it. It was a great job. You don't have to launch to do a great job."

Shields breaks in, "Don't you get it, sir. It's the Korengal. Remember Operation Red Wings? The boogeyman is in the Korengal. The navy don't want to be within fifty miles."

I have entirely forgotten about the single bloodiest day for American Special Ops in Afghanistan.

Shields goes on, "If they gave us the birds, but didn't come along, they'd be chickenshit. Other priorities. *Right.*"

In fairness to the navy, all units have off-limits places; the spot where the unit was ambushed, where something went terribly wrong, a graveyard of their own. Embedded in the units' collective memory is a sense of vulnerability and death. We are all superstitious about these places, no matter reputation or skill of the unit. My boogeyman also happens to live in the Korengal.

* * *

Two days after the aborted rescue mission, we track a target into a Taliban village near the Pech River, and—*oh, thank you*—it is Objective Indian, the enemy leader that has eluded the coalition for years. When I chased him in 2006, we had only shaky sources of intelligence and never got close. This dude is a big deal, and his presence on the Pech is brazen. He won't stay long.

In the ops center, I cannot sit still. About two hours after dark, our target settles into a house. I plan with the Pandur crew leads, Kitrell and Shields. We will drive to a rally point just south of target. Plenty of military traffic passes on the nearby road, so our approach will not rouse the Afghans.

The Pandurs will drop us simultaneously at two bridges, one upstream of the village, the other downstream, allowing us to approach from the east and west. Group Two, on the west, will be blocking. Group One, coming in from the east, will be assault. There are three houses in the target area. One squad will hit each house simultaneously, and it's shoot to kill. The Pandurs will cover us from a high point on the Pech River Road with clear fields of fire. My tactical plan feels perfect. Add in an AC-130 Gunship and I'm feeling like we're about to win the war.

About 2300 we are doing final prep when Brad calls for me on the net. I say, "This is Zero-two."

"Hey, Zero-two, stand down on the target."

"What happened? He move?"

"Negative. Weather's coming in. After midnight, visibility is going to shit. You'll have no air."

"I've got Pandurs. They can be our supporting fire." I read off the grid coordinates, explaining that the Pandurs will have an overwatch position there, and the target area will be well within range of their heavy weapons.

"That's a negative, Zero-two. Stand down."

I am pleading now, voice cracking, "Please, Brad. Hear me out. I've been after this dude since '06. He killed friends from my old unit. We'll get him. Fuck air cover. Fuck medevac."

"That's a negative. Sorry, Zero-two." He offers no further explanation.

I slam the radio hand mike against a wall until it breaks. Wiry guts splay out.

Shields says, "Sir, you surprised? That guy is too big a fish for the Rangers."

"Enough."

I stomp outside and continue my tantrum, smashing plastic chairs. With a mule kick, I crater the door on the Toyota Hilux we drive around camp. In the dark, with hands glowing red, I see old ghosts. They demand vengeance. And I want closure on this war. My friends and brothers died, and the bad guys keep going. They might go on forever. So will this war.

There must be an ending.

19

ONE LAST RAID

KUNAR PROVINCE

SUMMER 2009

The Objective Indian windup has all the satisfaction of dry humping with a sudden stop. Our replacements will land in one week, and I am desperate for a finale. No one wants to get killed at the end of a boring tour, but I can sense my Rangers are still hungry. One afternoon, a target comes up in the Korengal Valley. I have studied the target deck, but this one is unknown to me. He is bouncing between the Shuryak and Korengal Valleys, on a big mountain in deep forest.

Brad says, "He's yours if you want him."

Fuck. Not the Korengal again. I say, "I'll take him."

Brad tells me the target has been visiting Omar every few days. Omar! My old friends. I wonder if the people of Omar will remember me and my projects for the village: the school, the water system, a paved road. Back to the op, we can launch on our target up high or see if he descends to Omar. Better to wait. Another night passes, and sure enough, our guy descends from the forest and posts up in Omar. In the corner of the aerial feed appears the schoolhouse that I built for the chief. It has no roof. How can this be?

The target moves into a cluster of houses, one being the home of a man I remember too well: Abdul the policeman. I have stayed in his home, sheltered from snow and howling cold. I have eaten dinner with Abdul's family, overlooking the Pech River. Abdul has seen a photo of my wife. "She looks Afghan," he had said before making a fire to warm my men.

I say nothing to my Rangers. How would I put it? *This one might not be right. See, they are my friends, and we go way back.*

We sand table the mission, meaning we build a model of the village, trails, and surrounding terrain. We move army figurines around the model, talking through the op. The Pandurs will provide cover fire. My Ranger force will dismount, with the blocking group climbing the ridge overlooking the village to set up. I point out subtleties on the aerial imagery, saying, "Any runners will head uphill using this. The snipers can take the roof, here, and look for anyone trying to flee east. Chances are, runners from these houses will use this canal. It's got good cover. Assault should split at the fork, here, and enter the target houses from the west."

I trace the best alleyways for the assault squads.

Kitrell looks at me sidelong, asking, "This is your old area of operation, isn't it?"

I cringe. "Yeah."

"You been in this village?"

"Couple times."

"This your buddy or what?"

"Nah. Fuck these people."

The feeling that tonight may be the final mission of the trip, one last chance for the adrenaline boost, has our spirits up, yet I am unsure this is a legit target. The last thing I want to do, however, is throw doubt into their minds, then have someone get killed.

I must trust our intel and do nothing to hurt the instinct of my Rangers. To make this peculiar homecoming complete, we will stop at Firebase Michigan, a position built by my old platoon. There I will check in with the battlespace owner, a dismounted platoon from First Infantry, for final updates before the assault.

As I prepare my gear, my mind boils. This tour, these missions, were supposed to be the mountaintop, a defining experience; my flag-raising atop Iwo Jima, my D-Day landing. Yet here I am with the summit guarded by friends. And the only way up is to destroy what I've already built.

Game face.

In the mission brief, I address the Boys. "No need to dwell on the repu-tation of this area. Do your job tonight. I'm not asking anything else." We lie up until dark then load the Pandurs and roll. The valley mouths pass, spewing rivers. We pass police checkpoints and platoon firebases. Helmeted sentries stand in tapered watchtowers. Our aircraft reports no movement on target. About midnight we arrive at Firebase Michigan. I dismount and enter the perimeter through a metal gate, finding the place far more elabo-rate than the ring of bunkers built by my old platoon. There is a garage with Humvees parked inside. Beside the Humvees are two MRAPs, V-hulled trucks designed to deflect blasts from buried bombs.

The firebase command post is a plywood hut. Inside are tables and a matrix of TVs, each showing a feed from security cameras mounted on the perimeter and a blimp. In the next room are phones where two guys whis-per to their people back home. The platoon leader and sergeant from the First Infantry emerge and shake my hand. They are skinny from combat, their hair matted with dirt. The platoon leader looks right out of college. I see myself in him. He stands at attention.

I have forgotten I am a captain. Wanting to play it cool, I say, "Relax, dude."

He does. "Welcome to the Korengal, sir."

"I built this position in '06."

He cocks his head. "Yeah?"

"I love what you've done with the place."

"Thanks, sir. You guys need anything, water, bullets, AT4s? We got a shitload of chips if anyone is hungry."

"We are fine. You need it more than we do." We talk about tonight's target. I tell him everything because if this goes to shit, his platoon will mop up tomorrow. On a map, I point out the houses we are going to hit.

The platoon leader says, "We'll give you our radio freqs. You need anything, you call. We'll have a quick reaction force ready."

By foot we cross the Pech River, using a truss bridge, and once over, the Boys spread out. Our snipers walk point, searching for a footlog across the Korengal River. The trees overhead are full and thick and it's dark as a mine beneath. The river roars beside us, channeled by stone levies. The snipers pace in the river trees, eyes straining for the footlog. The column halts. The Boys fidget.

We practice the clusterfuck.

I stride to the front, link up with the snipers, laser the footlog, and say, "You got it?"

Our sniper says, "Roger. Uh . . . thanks, Zero-two."

"Step it out."

About 0230 I post up on a terrace with a view of the target. The assault squads fan out. The door on the target house is locked, so we blow it and storm in. The whole time I am coiled, muscles tight, as I wait for the shooting to start. A minute later the lead squad reports the first house clear. No target.

I order the assault squads to keep advancing. They take a second house. Women scream. Doors crack in half. Suddenly a man emerges from a doorway, sprinting right for my blocking position. He is ten yards and closing. The fire team with me opens up. The man twitches as bullets rip into him. He takes one last stride and falls facedown. His legs spasm. He rolls over so that he is faceup to the black sky. He moans, then lets out a long grunt and dies. The sound strikes me as funny, like a cheesy movie. I turn to Sergeant Tom and mimic the dying man's death groan.

Sergeant Tom gives me a feeble smile.

The lead squad hits a third house, and a fourth. As they do, it occurs to me that I may know the dead man. I toe out to his body. A tinge of anguish hits when I see he is the father of Abdul. "Fuck."

The radio bleeps with Shields's voice, "Zero-two, we've got him. Jackpot. Touchdown. Building Ninety-seven."

We collapse on the house, finding it smoky from flashbangs. Just inside the door, Willie's squad has guns on a row of detainees. Bulletproof vests and paratrooper AKs with collapsible buttstocks are stacked against the wall.

Abdul the policeman is on his knees, hands flex-cuffed behind his back. He'll be arrested with a handful of others.

His aquiline nose I will never forget. If this were a movie, at this point, we would lock eyes and one of us would say something with tremendous gravity. In reality I freeze, then spin away and duck out of the house, fearing Abdul has seen my face. I do not know what he would say to me, whether he'd insist this is a mistake and plea for release or maybe admit to being bad. Perhaps he will blame me for everything that afflicts his homeland: poverty, lack of social mobility, decades of civil war, scarce natural resources, corruption, economic instability, and religious fanaticism. I don't really know. I do know that when we shot Abdul's dad, I mimicked his death sound perhaps to convince myself that I don't care about these people. In any case, I decide the worst thing would be Abdul failing to remember me at all.

I retreat to a blocking position on the hillside and turn away from the village, examining the valley beyond. The Korengal Road looks the same. Washouts and sloughs have choked it back down to a tight jeep trail. There is no pavement. The skeleton of the school I started for the chief of Omar is there, a building never finished. It dawns on me that it's not failure I am seeing so much as the naive aspiration of a young officer.

* * *

Time to go home. My last act in Afghanistan is calling Elizabeth. It's during the workday in the US, and she does not answer. I leave a message saying I will be home at 1:00 p.m. next day, finish packing, and then call her back. Again she does not answer. "Make sure you pick me up at one p.m." *Probably at school. Or she's burned the house down and gone back to Texas.*

It is dark and warm when we load the aircraft home. I spend the first hour of the flight thinking of where Elizabeth might have gone. I spend the next few hours reading *The Big Sky* and wondering where Elizabeth might have gone. My mind drifts to Omar village and the school, to projects unfinished, then my readings about the war in Afghanistan, the lectures of policy experts and professors.

I recall how in the wake of 9/11, the US hatched two missions. First, to kill terrorists and their friends, and second, deny them safe haven. The first mission went exceedingly well. After all, revenge killing is something we are all wired for. The hard part is, and always has been, denying US enemies safe haven, as this second mission inevitably morphs into nation

building. At the core of a national-building enterprise is the belief that we
can create a world where nothing bad ever happens, a belief that is at once
noble and completely unachievable. Anyway, my epiphany right now is
that I've killed enough terrorists.

As we reach the ocean, I look at the Rangers sleeping under their
woobies on the floor, comatose with Ambien. For me, this ride is different. I have no desire for drugged sleep. I want to be in this moment, on
the mountaintop.

I decide I am really coming home. Endings are something for the old,
something I have not practiced. Already I can feel I am not good at them.
Cliché tells me that the last time you do something, you should savor it,
even a plane ride. I rue the combat pictures I never took. The faces of the
Boys will fade, I think. My memory will be my memory.

We land at Fort Lewis in the rain and head to battalion and turn in
our weapons. At 1:00 p.m. Elizabeth is not waiting to pick me up. I stand
in the doorway by the armory, out of the rain, and watch the parking lot. I
tell myself she has gotten used to these homecomings. Now she does them
the way she does everything else, twenty minutes late. Or maybe she left
me, and I'll stand here for hours like a jerk, which would be awful timing
given what I want to tell her. Right now she is testing me. This is a psychological test, watching everyone drift into the rain, watching the big drops
spatter the parking lot puddles. At 1:30 p.m. the lot is near empty. I can
hear the single Boys upstairs in the barracks, pounding beers and liquor
and planning a gang bang.

At 2:15 p.m. Elizabeth races up in the Infiniti and stops.

I run to the passenger door and jump in.

She says, "Hey, babe. Sorry. There was a wreck on I-5."

"Must have been a big wreck."

"A truck transporting animal parts. You should have seen it."

"Animal parts?"

"Legs, ribcages, hooves scattered across the road. Don't be mad."

"I'm not," I say. "Listen. This is it. I'm getting out of the army."

She smiles. "Okay."

Next day I submit a separation request from the army. It is a huge stack of forms, enough to dampen any impulsiveness. The battalion commander, Colonel Olsen, makes me report to his office to deliver the request. Olsen orders me to sit down. The regimental scroll, with the motto RANGERS LEAD THE WAY, is bright on the wall behind him. He asks, "Are you sure about this?"

"Yessir."

Olsen says his predecessor would throw separation requests in the trash, forcing young officers into the awkward position of arguing with a full colonel in the regiment. He reminds me this is a request, not necessarily a right. I say, "I've done my time, sir. It is a right."

He asks, "What is your plan?"

In my mind, Elizabeth and I are lying in the grass. "I want a business job."

"You don't seem the corporate type."

He is right. I have been on this trajectory so long that I have no idea what I want. I am twenty-seven years old and want to retire. I cannot say that either.

Olsen says, "I hope this isn't something rash."

"Not at all, sir."

20

THE VETERAN

After getting out of the Rangers, I say crazy shit in job interviews. I have a penchant for letting my mouth get away. *Y'all fuckers wanna hear a war story?* My normal is not normal. Separated from the civilized by a chasm, I am an expert in planning and leading raids, attacks, ambushes. I can strip a machine gun blindfolded, take dozens of men into position in deep woods on a moonless night. I can direct howitzer fire from an AC-130 Spectre Gunship. I captured Ratfuck Ridge, climbed Monster Mountain six times, and got blown up going for the Mad Bomber of Baghdad.

I have no transferable skills.

More than one interview ends abruptly. It takes a couple years to plot a good course. I get into graduate school at the University of Oregon. We move to Eugene. Elizabeth takes a teaching job at a local middle school and is happier than ever. I carry a backpack and ride a bicycle down leafy streets with Velcro wrapped around one pant leg so that my bike chain won't snag it. I interview to be a teaching fellow for an undergrad class— *Green Cities*—about land use, sustainability, carbon footprints, and the like. The professor is a raging leftist with a military lineage. He likes my war stories, so he hires me.

One day he tells me to lead the class to a protest about police brutality, and I do. Eugene, Oregon, is a protest town and it is fashionable for old warriors to shit on war, or to treat it, at best, like an estranged ex. But I am not antiwar, antipolice, anticapitalism, or antianything, except for Korengali. I am not lost. I like nature and the outdoors, and in Eugene, all this is tangled up. One night Elizabeth and I join some of the anti crowd for wine and intellectual sparring. Some of my grad school peers are wearing man buns and snickering about people who drive trucks. The priggish conversation moves to the latest water quality report for the McKenzie River. I burst out screaming, "*I'm bored!*"

I try not to act military. This goes on for ten years.

I watch no war movies or shows. I read no war books. When Iraq and Afghanistan come on the news, I turn it off. I don't wear the colors or fly the flag. I have no mawkish rituals for Memorial or Veterans Day. In my mind I boycott the war and the residue of it. Elizabeth and I dive into the rest of the world. We camp and climb, taking on mountaineering routes across the Cascades and the Rockies. I grow a beard and lose track of everyone I served with.

Elizabeth and I hold season passes for Loveland Ski Area in Colorado. We subject ourselves to traffic on Interstate 70, clogged parking lots and lift lines brimming with yuppie scum. But every time I'm on the mountain, it feels good. One day we arrive early, just as the lifts are groaning to life. We get in line behind a couple of recreation heroes, the types with Sprinter Vans and skis costing three paychecks, the types who will tell you that powder days lead to self-actualization.

The lift swings round and scoops us up, past Engelmann spruce and ski runs slashing a steep hillside. Falling snow collects on my lap. Up we go, seeing alpenglow on the Divide, the very spine of the continent. Early morning in the mountains gives me counsel. I put an arm around Elizabeth. She wants to start on the Divide.

Close by there is a tremendous explosion. I jump into Elizabeth's lap. The explosion echoes, bounces in the bowl. Elizabeth looks into my eyes and sees them darting for enemy positions. Body is taut. Hands clutch for a rifle. Elizabeth points to a slope spilling off the Divide, saying, "It's just avalanche blasting."

The sound bowls away. *Boom.* Another one. Ski patrol is throwing bombs at the upper slopes to trigger slides. The sound of artillery in the mountains casts me to a hillside in the Korengal. Cigrand and I are running between stunted hollies. Just below, a Humvee burns with dead Americans. Taliban flash between trees. My rifle punches my shoulder.

I have spent ten years demilitarizing. Some events I still remember in great detail; sequence and fact are clear. It is the sensation that I have lost. Today though, I have the old feeling, and in the aftermath, decide to chase down the old days, beginning with a hunt for the men I served with.

It is not so hard to find them. First thing I learn is that Siercks, my old platoon sergeant, was killed in Afghanistan in 2011. I never forgave him for getting injured in 2006. Whether this is childish, or matters at all, is something I promise to give no further thought. Siercks was a good man, and I am proud to record my name beside his in the annals of war.

Locke, on the other hand, is very much alive and in the fight. He has risen to the rank of first sergeant and is serving a final assignment with the 173rd out of Vincenza, Italy, before retirement. I call Locke on his cell, unsure whether he will remember me. He does, and quickly jumps to, "Remember that time we were in Iraq and the SEALs brought scuba gear? Fucking tools." Locke has done like a hundred combat tours. I gather he has no idea what peace is like. I worry about him at rest. He does not need me to, but I do.

On Facebook I connect with Sergeant Goff, one of my old squad leaders in the Korengal. He is posting strange pictures from a property in the woods, of his blue van, of himself surrounded by deep snow. He posts selfies alone in a hot tub. I get to thinking that he needs a woman. He posts a photo of a plant he is growing. A single leaf has just sprung from dirt in a pot. Seeing that photo, I think he is being a loser. A few days later, he puts a shotgun into his face and kills himself. Only then did I realize he was going to do it all along.

I find another one of my Boys, or rather, a friend finds me for him. This friend says that my Boy has done a couple felonies. And one night my Boy had gotten drunk, taken the wheel, and killed someone. That's vehicular homicide. I write a letter to the judge in his case, saying he was a good soldier some years ago, fighting under the worst circumstances. I do not know what he has become since, but I suspect he is not well.

Several others, I find, have fared poorly. Lack of success among some of my comrades is vexing, for as a military leader, the aim is to return your soldiers to society as better humans than when you received them. In the modern era, this is an order of skyscraper height, for our wars are infinite, and those serving are subject to spine-twisting, hole-punching combat as lifestyle, on wages that will, at best, earn them a rung in the middle class. Meanwhile, society gravitates toward stories from veterans on the margins. On one side are the superheroes, Medal of Honor winners, and deadliest snipers. On the other side are those fighting monsters like amputation, substance abuse, and the slow burn of PTSD.

The after-action status of the silent majority, those not on the margins, sounds something like this: "I made it through, doing great," which is a terrible headline.

Time has blunted the worst of my memories. Now, if you want my war stories, you have to spur me. Only a little. There are bits of metal in my leg, pushing to get out, and I am still prone to rage, to the Ranger smash. Sometimes in my smashing, I make Elizabeth cry. She yells back. She throws the kitchen at me. She swings and kicks me right out of the house. In a maggot world, I still believe in her. Marriages crumble around us, many being our friends from the military. Elizabeth and I are not afraid. What we have is pure, forged in the fire of war and distance and longing.

She is the scaffolding while I make a new career in the national parks. My mantra during reinvention of self is, if you let your rite of passage break you, then what are you? I saw bottom and pulled up on the risers. Advanced education. Goals. Pull up. There are no giveaways.

Pull up.

I am sitting in the grass in the Lamar Valley inside Yellowstone National Park. This is my grass. I earned it. All mine. I have a nine-foot, five-weight fly rod and hoppers galore but I ain't caught shit today. Elizabeth is beside me. She bounces our children on her thighs, one boy and one girl, both specialists in total destruction. Elizabeth sings to them, and by objective standards she is a terrible singer but she gives it her best, and I think she sounds lovely. We are in the grass, and I am out-of-body.

These days will go on.

I have never been to Hawaii or the Caribbean. I've never seen the Eiffel Tower or the Coliseum or Great Pyramids. But I've been to war. I was born there and part of me died there. Now I am a husband and a father. I will always be an infantry officer.